THE PERFECT NAME
FOR
THE PERFECT BABY

By Joan Wilen and Lydia Wilen:

CHICKEN SOUP & OTHER FOLK REMEDIES*
MORE CHICKEN SOUP & OTHER FOLK REMEDIES*
LIVE AND BE WELL
FOLK REMEDIES THAT WORK
SHOES IN THE FREEZER, BEER
   IN THE FLOWER BED
THE PERFECT NAME FOR THE PERFECT BABY*

*Published by The Ballantine Publishing Group

THE
PERFECT NAME
FOR THE
PERFECT BABY

Joan Wilen
and Lydia Wilen

BALLANTINE BOOKS • NEW YORK

Copyright © 1993, 1997 by Joan Wilen and Lydia Wilen
Illustrations copyright © 1993 by Vicki Wehrman

All rights reserved under International and Pan-American Copyright Conventions. Published in the United States by Ballantine Books, a division of Random House, Inc., New York, and simultaneously in Canada by Random House of Canada Limited, Toronto. Originally published in somewhat different form by Ballantine Books in 1993.

http://www.randomhouse.com

Library of Congress Catalog Card Number: 96-95198

ISBN 0-345-41235-4

Manufactured in the United States of America

First Revised Edition: April 1997

OPM   16   15   14   13   12   11   10   9   8   7

"People have within themselves a level of prophecy, and they experience it at least once in their lives—when they name a child."

—Hassidic Rabbi

Contents

Acknowledgments

Big thanks to Joëlle Delbourgo for making this publishing house a home for our book.

To our wonderful and innovative editor, Elizabeth Rosalie Zack, who pushed us mercilessly and refused to settle for second best, our gratitude and our respect. (This is probably the only page on which we won't have to do more work!)

To Elise Marton, our copy editor and Oops!-preventer, we truly value the masterful job you've done.

Our great appreciation to the writers whose research is in the public domain.

And to all the women and men who choose to be parents, many blessings!

A Wilen Welcome

Aside from life itself, one of the first and most influential gifts parents give their newborn babe is a name. Think about it: You're making a major decision for another person, one that's quite a responsibility. We're not looking to scare you here, but we *are* looking to prepare you. That's the whole reason for this book.

The Perfect Name for the Perfect Baby is a practical, informative, and informal guide to aid parents in the traditional and pleasurable task of naming their child. As you will see soon enough, this book is not intended as a scholarly work on onomatology—the study of names. In fact, that's as scholarly as it gets!

Instead, we have lists to inspire you (saints' names, biblical names, names of angels), lists to take you down memory lane (names in songs), lists of winners (Olympic medalists), lists that will take you back to your roots (foreign names), lists that will remind you of your favorite people and things (names from literature, soap opera characters, flowers, gemstones, and celebrities), and much more. Somewhere among them all is *sure* to be the right name for your own child.

So, with our book as your collaborator, enjoy the search and trust in your decision; the name that you finally select will be *perfect*!

Ready to get started? Take a pen or pencil and get prepared to record your list of possibilities on the pages at the end of the book. (You may also want something to munch on. Baby-naming has been known to work up *quite* an appetite.) Now make yourself comfortable, and—let the names begin!

Considerations to Keep in Mind when Selecting the All-Important Name(s)

START BY THINKING ABOUT YOUR OWN FIRST NAME

Would you give yourself the same name you already have? Before you answer that, take the time to go down memory lane. As a child, were you ever teased because of your name? Did you always change your name when you played "pretend" games? Did you go through stages when you asked your family and friends to call you by another name? If your answer is yes to any of these, figure out why. Once you've analyzed your "whys," it would be wise to take them into consideration when naming your own child.

THEN THINK ABOUT YOUR LAST NAME

If it's short and simple—Smith, Chan, Gold—then you might want to pair the last name with a long, intriguing first name—Aurora, Granville, Evander.

On the other hand, if the last name is long—Whitticomb, Yamaguchi, Costellano—you might want to think in terms of a short and easy-to-remember first name—Dawn, Glenn, John.

If your last name is obviously ethnic, be sure to read about ETHNIC NAMES on page 4.

A MIDDLE NAME

We are definitely in favor of giving today's child a middle name. At a time when everything is computerized, a middle name can be a real plus for identification purposes. There may be several John Crains out there, but the number decreases dramatically by adding a distinctive middle name . . . such as John Schuyler Crain.

And keep in mind that during certain stages of your child's growing up, he or she might not be too crazy about his or her first name. This way the child has a choice; he or she can use that middle name you so thoughtfully chose for him or her years before.

It's important that your child not be an "NMI" (no middle initial). We've heard about people in the military who have filled out forms stating that they have no middle name; from that point on, the computers actually list "NMI" as their middle name on military records.

At dinner parties, bringing up the subject of middle names can be fun. You may want to start the conversation with such interesting observations as: Author Henry Miller and twentieth-century Renaissance man Steve Allen share the same middle name—Valentine. And that perhaps it was Lizzie Borden's middle name, Andrew, that got her so angry. Or that it's Garth Brooks's *middle* name that is really Garth; his first name is Troyal.

Almost every United States president, from John Quincy Adams to William Jefferson Blythe Clinton, has had a middle name. And four-fifths of the people in *Who's Who* have middle names. So by all means, give your child a middle name . . . or, at the least, a middle initial. Which brings us to another important consideration . . .

INITIALS

Ah, superstition! It is said that people whose initials spell out a word will be wealthy. If you believe the superstition, then rig it so that your child's name will spell out a word. But be kind. Make sure the word is one with which your child will want to be associated.

It's great when initials spell out words like TEN, FUN, or

WOW. But be sure to steer clear of initials with questionable associations like BAD, PIG, or DUD. Did the parents of our lovely young editor, Elizabeth Zack, consider initials when naming their baby girl? Yes! That's one reason Elizabeth has a middle name, so that she would not be saddled with the nickname EZ.

You might also want to consider initials that are an acronym for a nickname. For instance: Theodore Evan Dodd. The initials are TED, the nickname for Theodore.

Our eighteenth president was baptized Hiram Ulysses Grant. As the story goes, the young student anticipated with dread the teasing he would get from his West Point classmates when they realized his initials spelled out HUG. Fortunately, the congressman who nominated him to West Point thoughtfully changed Hiram Ulysses Grant to Ulysses Simpson Grant (Simpson being the maiden name of Ulysses' mother). That took care of one problem for Ulysses, but created another: his nickname became "Useless"!

NICKNAMES

A Hungarian proverb says, "A child that is loved has many names." And most nicknames *are* a sign of affection. Studies have shown that people with nicknames tend to be better adjusted. Plus, nicknames seem to promote a certain intimacy and indicate a readiness for friendship on the part of the owner.

It might be wise, then, to select a name for your child that lends itself to one or more nicknames—Elizabeth (Liz, Lizzie, Beth, Bess, Bets, Bette); or William (Willie, Will, Billy, Bill).

Then there are those non-name-related nicknames—The Boss, The Queen of Mean, and so on. These names are earned, and they either say something about your child's personality or physical appearance or an event associated with him/her. They arise from the creativity—and, unfortunately, occasional cruelty—of his or her peers. It's a shame, but these names are beyond a parent's control.

INFORMAL VS. FORMAL NAMES

Throughout the last quarter of this century in America, there continues to be a trend toward informality in name-calling. Just as very few employees now address their boss as "Mr. or Ms. So-and-so," so does this informal trend extend itself to baby-naming. Names once considered nicknames are showing up on birth certificates throughout the country.

While there's nothing wrong with naming your baby Vicki instead of Victoria, or Danny instead of Daniel, we think that a formal name serves the baby better when she or he is an adult and can choose to be known by either the formal or the informal version of the name.

ALL KIDDING ASIDE

A funny name can be hysterical, and it's guaranteed to make people laugh. But will its owner—your child—be happy to be the brunt of a joke?

We've spoken to—or heard about—Ilene Forward, Rusty Hammer, Herbert Sherbert, Flip Side, Otto Graph, Rita Sedita, Rose Bush, Candy Barr and Clark Barr, Marsha Mellow, Solomon Gemorrah, and the Boston stockbroker's daughters Cash, Gamble, and Chance. We've been told there's the Dwopp family with a son named Wayne (a song cue if ever there was one): "Wayne Dwopp keeps falling on his head. . . ."

Are these names funny? Yes. Is it fair to give one to a child? We've met people with names that provoke laughter who love their names for that very reason. But we've also met people who regard their names as bad jokes, and they've never forgiven their parents for it.

So let your conscience (and not your sense of humor) be your guide.

ETHNIC NAMES

It's wonderful to remember your roots when it comes to naming a child, but there are a couple of other things to remember: Mixing two different nationalities—Vito McDonald, Zeus Feinberg, Mustafa Swenson—can sound comical; also, if you have an extremely ethnic last name and want to keep with tra-dition by giving your child a matching ethnic first name, take into account how hard the name may be to spell.

On his first day of kindergarten in America, a little boy from Israel told the teacher his name: "Yitzhak Menachem Eisenstadt." The teacher asked, "How do you spell that?" Yitzhak replied, "My mother helps me."

Funny, sure, but more than to amuse you, we tell the story to spark an awareness of possible problems that can accompany complex names that have not been Americanized.

There's a bit more we have to say about spelling, so read on.

SPELLING

Our first inclination was to say, keep the spelling conventional so that your child doesn't have to go through life correcting everybody. But our attitude changed once television personality Sharron Lovejoy shared her story with us.

It all happened during World War II. Captain Lovejoy, a pilot in the Air Force, told his pregnant wife, "If we have a girl, name her Sharron and spell it with two r's. That way, if I don't make it home from the war, my little girl will think of her daddy every time she has to tell someone how to spell her name correctly." Unfortunately, Sharron's dad did not return. And yes, she thinks of him each time she has to correct the spelling of her name.

A TOUGH ACT TO FOLLOW

It might be traditional to give a boy his father's name, tacking on a "Junior" or "II" or "III," but we think you can do better than that. *Give your son his own name!*

It's downright confusing having two guys with the same name around. To avoid such confusion, the inevitable happens. The father becomes "Big Whomever" and the son becomes "Little Whomever," or, worse yet, the boy is called Junior or some cutesy nickname.

Also, one child's having the father's name may make other siblings a wee bit jealous. After all, it stands to reason that Dad might feel closer to his namesake. And maybe he even *expects* more from that namesake.

So we are not in favor of Juniors, IIs, IIIs, etc. (Come to think of it, you're probably not either. If you were, you wouldn't be reading a baby-name book!)

TRENDS

Jennifer! Jason! Jessica! Amanda! Need we say more? (Maybe not, but we haven't let that stop us before!)

It's no fun to be in a classroom with six other children who have the same first name as you. Do your child a favor: Steer clear of all those trendy names.

RHYTHM

You may be surprised to know that there's a general rule that comes into play here: Names that follow each other should not have the same number of syllables, such as Barbra Streisand (2 and 2), Glenn Close (1 and 1), and Warren Beatty (2 and 2). See how it held all of them back? (That only goes to show that there are many exceptions to the rule.)

In general, though, it *does* sound better to vary the number of syllables in each name. Start with the given—your last name. Count the number of syllables in it. Select a first name that has fewer or more syllables than the last name. Then select a middle name with a different number of syllables then either the middle or last names.

Our parents instinctively did right by us: Lydia (3) Hope (1) Wilen (2), and Joan (1) Wilen (2). (They do lose points, however, for not giving Joan a middle name.)

If you have a very short last name, you can make up for it with a long first name or a long middle name. A good example is Alexander (4) Graham (2) Bell (1). Doesn't it have a nice *ring* to it?

RELIGION AND TRADITION

It's a wonderful idea to let religion and tradition influence you in baby-naming.

The Catholic religion, for instance, requires its followers to have the name of a saint as a first or middle name. (For a listing of saints' names and feast days, turn to pages 32 through 79.)

Frequently Jewish children are named for someone special who has passed on. Thus the child becomes a living memorial to that deceased relative or friend.

In parts of Africa, a naming-day ceremony takes place about

a week after the birth of a baby. The oldest member of the tribe whispers the name to the very newest member; once the baby has heard his or her own name for the first time, the name is then announced to the rest of the celebrants.

Today, many African-Americans are both changing their own names and giving their children African or Moslem names in recognition of their heritage before slavery.

One of the Chinese naming traditions is changing names. About a month after the baby is born, s(he) is given a "milk" name. For a girl it usually represents something of beauty; for a boy, the name is usually plain so that he will go unnoticed by the Devil. After the milk name, there may be a going-to-school name, then a marriage name, also an occupational name, and a casual name used just between friends.

It's a tradition of Hispanic-Americans to give a child the names of several male and female saints.

In a typical Russian family, children are given formal names known as "passport names." When each child is sixteen, s(he) is given the father's first name as his or her middle name, at which time s(he) adds on the appropriate feminine (-evna or -ovna) or masculine (-evich or -ovich) ending.

Greek tradition holds that the firstborn child be named after the paternal grandparent of the same sex.

By speaking to your particular religious leader you can learn about special religious and traditional guidelines associated with naming a child.

IS IT A BOY, OR IS IT A GIRL?

Robin, Terry, Carson, Jan, Corey, Lindsay, and Jamie make up the troop. But are they Boy Scouts or Girl Scouts? Judging solely by the names, it's anyone's guess.

If you're thinking about a unisex name for your child, talk to youngsters who have them. When we did, we found that while the girls *liked* having unisex names, the boys would have preferred names that didn't leave anyone guessing.

THE "MEANING" OF IT ALL

The meanings of names go way back to the beginning of recorded history, and it all depends on which historical record you go by. In other words, one name, because of different derivations, can have different meanings. For example, in Old High German "Alice" means "of noble birth" while in Greek it means "the truth." Our A-to-Z listing of names in the back of the book includes each name's most popular meaning(s). But if you attach special importance to the original meanings of names and have narrowed your choice down to several names, you may want to do additional research at the library. Start with the Subject catalogue, under "Names, Personal."

For more on the meanings of names, see the Introduction to the Main Name List (page 187).

SOUND IT OUT

When you find a name you like, link it with a middle name and with your last name. Say it out loud again and again. Does it sound good? Our cousin thought she came up with the perfect combination of first and middle names: Amanda and Lynn. Then she said them out loud, "Amanda Lynn," and realized it was a swell name for a musical instrument, but not for her beautiful little girl. "Amanda Leigh" sounded a lot better.

Check and make sure that your name choices have different last syllables. The same ending syllables for first and middle names sound funny when said together (Arthur Luther, Norma Sondra, Norman Simon), and the same holds true for first and last names said together (Madeline Bailin, Robert Talbert).

Keep in mind that when the first name ends with the same sound with which the last name begins (Phillip Pratt, Jane North, Michael Lear), it's hard to tell where the first name ends and the last one begins.

TEST MARKET THE NAME

In a notebook or on index cards, write down each name you're interested in like this:

> Full name—Benjamin Jay Chandler
> Initials—BJC
> First and last names—Benjamin Chandler
> Nicknames—Ben, Benny, Benjie, BJ, BC

Once the name works for you on paper, repeat the name out loud to others and ask them to tell you the picture that the name brings to mind. (That is, if you're not concerned about keeping your name choice a secret.) It's a good way to get insight on the reaction your own child will eventually get from his or her name.

CREATING THAT SPECIAL NAME

Here's your chance to be the mother or father of invention! And why not? Since your baby is a unique, special someone, create a name to reflect that uniqueness. Here are some ways to do just that:

Combining Syllables or Names

Use syllables from two names to create a new name. But don't do what our neighbor was going to do. She wanted to name her child after her father, Ferdinand, and her mother, Eliza. The child would then have been called Ferdiliza! But seriously . . .

Albert and Victoria = Altoria
Andrew and Claudine = Andine
Marla and Donald = Mardon

Or combine any two names that flow together: Lauralynn, Rosellen, Leeanna. (This doesn't seem to work well for boys—except maybe for those in Texas, like Billybob.)

Acronyms

Find a phrase, a line of poetry, or a grouping of words that's meaningful to you, and use the first letter of each word to form an acronym that can be used as a name. We know a couple named Charles and Lillian who named their baby Cally. It's an acronym for Charles And Lillian Love You.

One couple named their baby girl Camise. It's an acronym for Conceived At Maple Inn, South Evanston.

The Yagers—Ann Victoria and Earl Russell—had a little boy. They used their initials to create a name for the baby and it worked out great. In fact, each time that their son, Avery, who is now a young adult, has to spell out his name for someone, he says, "A as in Ann, V as in Victoria, E as in Earl, R as in Russell, and Y as in Yager."

A young man introduced himself as Boothe. When we asked about the name, he explained that it stands for *B*orn *O*ut *O*f *T*wo *H*earts *E*mbracing.

Ain't love grand? Well, so are acronyms!

Anagrams

Take a word you love and juggle the letters around to form a pleasing name for your little angel. Hey, there's an idea:

Angel = Elgan, Engal, Galen,
Glane, Glena, Lange, Nagel

Or select an anagram based on a word that has special significance for you and your partner. For instance, if you got married in April, or if the baby was conceived or born in April, then you may want to use an anagram of the name of the month:

April = Alpir, Piral, Prila, Pirla,
Parli, Prali, Plair, Lipra

Ananyms

When you spell a word or a name backward to form another word or name, that's an ananym. Try it with a word or name you love, or one with significance, and see if the result is pleasing. Here are some examples:

Adam = Mada
Asset = Tessa
Lyric = Ciryl
Six A.M. = Maxis
Nomad = Damon
Iron = Nori

How about your own name spelled backward? Would it make a good name for baby?

Name Dropping

Take a word or name that has some special meaning to you, and drop letters from it to form a new name:

Computerized = Cotie, Merie, Perie, Terie
Sagittarius = Sari, Sita, Gia, Tari, Taris

ALL IN THE FAMILY

Consider a family name for a first (or middle) name. Hume Cronyn and Jessica Tandy did so when they named their daughter Tandy. Please bear in mind, however, that some family names may be a little sophisticated for a tiny tot. Ask yourself if there's a shortened version (a nickname) of that name that would be appropriate until the child is old enough to carry the weight of an "important" name.

While you're at it, when you come up with a name that's fine for a baby, make sure it will suit an adult as well.

A SPECIAL NOTE FOR PARENTS: Despite all we've mentioned in the previous pages, there are countless numbers of people with names that defy every consideration. Among those people are the rich and the famous, the happy and the healthy. For instance, Arnold Schwarzenegger. "Arnold" is generally thought of as a nerdy, wimpish name. Schwarzenegger is hard to pronounce, difficult to remember, and impossible to spell. For all we know, his middle name starts with an S, making his initials . . . Well, as of this writing, Arnold Schwarzenegger, the former Mr. Universe, has married into the Kennedy family, headed the President's Fitness Program, and is one of the world's top movie stars. Did he become a bodybuilder to compensate for his name? Would he be such a big box-office success today if his name were as simple and common as Jim Larson? It's something to think about . . . but not for *too* long! You have more important things to do, like find the perfect name for your own baby.

Those Little Angels!
Angelic Names for Your Child

The Hebrew term *mal'akh*, which originally meant "the shadow side of God," was translated by the Greeks to *angelos* and came to mean "messenger." Thus angels are often thought of as messengers of light, reflecting God's radiance. Wouldn't those words also be the perfect description of a baby—a reflection of God's radiance? That's reason enough to consider giving your baby the name of an angel!

Initially we thought that compiling a list of angel names would be easy. All we'd have to do is look through the Old and New Testaments and gather together all the names. But while angels appear in just about every book of the Bible, and in many cases their appearances are crucial to the situations, they often don't get any billing at all. With the exception of Michael and Gabriel, the Bible reveals very little information on the personalities, natures, or names of angels.

However, the Bible tells us, "Seek and ye shall find." We did, and in so doing, came up with a stellar collection of angel names.

Before you read on, however, there are a few things you should know. We've omitted the angel names that are extremely long and unusual, difficult to spell, or hard to pronounce. We've also left in names that can be pronounced a variety of ways. We figure that if you love the name, you should be the one who says how it's pronounced. We know three women named Andrea. Each pronounces the name differently: *An´-dree-a*, *Ahn´-dree-a*, and *Ahn-dray´-a*. Remember, when it comes to names, there's no right or wrong pronunciation; *there's only your choice*.

Based on interpretations of scriptural passages in several foundational texts, including the *Summa Theologica* by Thomas Aquinas, there are three orders of angels, with three choirs in each, that surround the Divine Core. (The Divine Core is also called the Throne of Glory, or His Presence, or the Divine Source of Light and Love, and yes, it's God.) The first order of angels is seraphim, cherubim, and thrones; the second order is dominions, virtues, and powers; and the third order is principalities, archangels, and angels. (Please note, however, that no two sources seem to agree on the order of importance.)

While we were able to collect names of angels, we couldn't always find out which choir they belong to, or which culture or religion they're from. In most cases, we don't even know whether they're male or female! We're counting on your good judgment to determine whether a name is more suitable for a girl or for a boy.

Enough said. Here's the list of angel names. They're *heavenly* and certainly worth considering.

ANGELS

Arael—Angel of Birds.

Arel—Angel of Fire. According to *The Sword of Moses* by Moses Gaster, Arel is an angel who's summoned when ritual magic is practiced.

Dabria—According to *Revelation of Esdras IV*, Dabria is one of five angels who transcribed the books that the Hebrew prophet Ezra dictated. Also see ETHAN and SAREA or SARGA.

Dara—Angel of Rains and Rivers (according to Persian mythology).

Dina—Guardian Angel of Wisdom and of the Law, as is written in the Torah. Dina is also the angel said to have taught a total of seventy languages to new souls at the time of Creation.

Elijah—When he lived on earth, this Hebrew prophet was known as "the grandest and the most romantic character that

Israel ever produced." Many legends about Elijah exist. One is that he ascended to Heaven in a chariot of fire; another is that he was transformed into the angel Sandalphon; and still another is that he was an angel from the start. All *we* know is that Elijah is a strong and interesting name. Cher thought so too, and gave her son that name.

Ethan—One of five angels who transcribed the books the Hebrew prophet Ezra dictated. Also see DABRIA and SAREA or SARGA.

Farris—Angel who governs the second hour of the night.

Gabriel—One of what we call the two "superstar" angels among the Jewish, Christian, and Islamic religions. (Michael is the other.) Thought to sit on the left-hand side of God, Gabriel presides over Paradise, and—as if that weren't enough!—he is the Angel of Joy, Judgment, Mercy, the Holy Spirit, Annunciation, Resurrection, Truth, Vengeance, Death, Revelation, Prayer, Mysteries, Dreams, and more.

Geron—The angel who's called upon in magic-based prayer.

Hamal—Angel of Water. Hamal is invoked in Arabic ritual prayers.

Hariel—Angel of Tame Animals. This cherub is also the ruler of science and the arts.

Irin—Along with his twin Qaddis, he is among the most exalted of angels serving God.

Javan—Guardian angel whose territory is Greece.

Joel—According to *The History of the Life of Adam and Eve* by Frederick G. Conybeare, Joel is the archangel who gave Adam and Eve one-seventh of our earthly paradise. Joel is also recognized for his suggestion that Adam name all things.

Kadi—An angel who presides over Friday. He is summoned from the West and serves in the Third Heaven, according to Francis Barrett's *The Magus II*.

Laila, Lailah, or Layla—According to Exodus, "an angel appointed to guard the spirits at their birth."

Manuel—Angel whose dominion is the Zodiac sign Cancer.

Michael—One of the two "superstar" angels among the Jewish, Christian, and Islamic religions. (Gabriel is the other.) Michael is the Chief of Archangels, Prince of the Presence, Ruler of the Fourth Heaven, Angelic Prince of Israel, Purifier of People and Places Plagued with Disharmony and Evil, and Angel of Repentance, Righteousness, Sanctification, Mercy, and more. According to Maldwyn H. Hughes in *The Greek Apocalypse of Baruch*, Michael "holds the keys of the kingdom of Heaven." As recently as 1950, Pope Pius XII named Michael the Patron of Policemen. This angelic name has been on the list of the most popular boys' names in the Northeast since 1948, and number one in popularity for boys since 1980. Since the early seventies, when actress Michael Learned starred in the TV series *The Waltons*, it's no longer rare to meet a girl named Michael.

Miri—An angel from "Sagesse," a poem by Hilda Doolittle in her book *Tribute to the Angels*.

Neria—The name means "lamp of God" and is thought to be the same as *Neriel* who, in The Sixth and Seventh Books of Moses, is one of the angels governing the mansions of the moon.

Nitika—Angel of precious stones.

Oriel—Angel of Destiny and one of the rulers of the tenth daylight hour.

Paniel or Pariel—These angel names, according to *Hebrew Amulets* by T. Schrire, are inscribed on charms to ward off evil.

Raphael—One of the seven holy angels who attend the throne of God. Raphael is Ruling Prince of the Second Heaven, Guardian of the Tree of Life in the Garden of Eden, Governor of the South, Guardian of the West, and Overseer of the Evening Winds. Raphael, whose name means "God has healed," is, appropriately, the Angel of Healing. He is also the Angel of Science, Knowledge, Repentance, Prayer, Joy, Light, Love, and more.

Sarea or Sarga—One of five angels who transcribed the books the Hebrew prophet Ezra dictated. Also see DABRIA and ETHAN.

Sofiel—Angel of Fruit and Vegetables.

Suria—An angel-warden of the First Hall of the First Heaven. According to *The Zohar* by Harry Sperling and Maurice Simon, Suria is the "high angelic being who takes up all the holy words that are uttered at a table and sets the form of them before the Holy One."

Tabris—Angel of Free Will, according to occult lore.

Talia—One of ten angels who escort the sun on its daily course, according to an ancient Gnostic sect of Mesopotamia.

Tariel—Angel of Summer.

Uriel—The name means "fire of God," and, as evinced by his credits, there's a lot of firepower here. Uriel is said to be the "spirit who stood at the gate of the lost Eden with the fiery sword" and the angel who brought alchemy down to earth, and is supposedly the inspiration of writers and teachers. He's also the Angel of Prophecy and the Angel of September, and is described in Milton's *Paradise Lost* as the "sharpest sighted spirit of all in Heaven."

Yael, Yale, or Yehel—An angel who attends the throne of God and is summoned at the conclusion of the Sabbath for magic rituals.

Yahriel—Angel of the Moon.

Zachriel—The angel with dominion over memory.

Zaniel—An angel who presides over Monday. He is summoned from the West and has dominion over the Zodiac sign Libra.

Zazel—The angel summoned for love invocations when King Solomon practiced magic arts. According to *The Magus* by Francis Barrett, Zazel is the spirit of Saturn and has the cabalistic number 45.

And if these aren't enough angel names for you, read on!

ANGELS WHO GOVERN THE WINDS

Uriel—South Wind
Michael—East Wind
Raphael—West Wind
Gabriel—North Wind
Nariel—Noonday Winds

ANGELS ASSIGNED TO THE DAYS OF THE WEEK

Michael—Sunday: Angel of Earth
Gabriel—Monday: Angel of Life
Zamael—Tuesday: Angel of Joy
Raphael—Wednesday: Angel of Sun

Sachiel—Thursday: Angel of Water
Anael—Friday: Angel of Air
Cassiel—Saturday: The Earthly Mother

ANGELS WHO GOVERN THE MONTHS OF THE YEAR

Gabriel—January
Barchiel—February
Malchidiel—March
Asmodel—April
Ambriel or Amriel—May
Muriel—June
Murdad—July
Hamaliel—August
Uriel—September
Aban—October
Azar—November
Anael or Dai—December

THE ANGELS OF THE HOURS OF THE DAY AND NIGHT

Hours Day.	SUNDAY. Angels and Planets Ruling	MONDAY. Angels and Planets Ruling	TUESDAY. Angels and Planets Ruling	WEDNESDAY. Angels and Planets Ruling	THURSDAY. Angels and Planets Ruling	FRIDAY. Angels and Planets Ruling	SATURDAY. Angels and Planets Ruling
	Day.	*Day.*	*Day.*	*Day.*	*Day.*	*Day.*	*Day.*
1	Michael	Gabriel	Samael	Raphael	Sachiel	Anael	Cassiel
2	Anael	Cassiel	Michael	Gabriel	Samael	Raphael	Sachiel
3	Raphael	Sachiel	Anael	Cassiel	Michael	Gabriel	Samael
4	Gabriel	Samael	Raphael	Sachiel	Anael	Cassiel	Michael
5	Cassiel	Michael	Gabriel	Samael	Raphael	Sachiel	Anael
6	Sachiel	Anael	Cassiel	Michael	Gabriel	Samael	Raphael
7	Samael	Raphael	Sachiel	Anael	Cassiel	Michael	Gabriel
8	Michael	Gabriel	Samael	Raphael	Sachiel	Anael	Cassiel
9	Anael	Cassiel	Michael	Gabriel	Samael	Raphael	Sachiel
10	Raphael	Sachiel	Anael	Cassiel	Michael	Gabriel	Samael
11	Gabriel	Samael	Raphael	Sachael	Anael	Cassiel	Michael
12	Cassiel	Michael	Gabriel	Samael	Raphael	Sachiel	Anael

Hours Night.	SUNDAY. Angels and Planets Ruling	MONDAY. Angels and Planets Ruling	TUESDAY. Angels and Planets Ruling	WEDNESDAY. Angels and Planets Ruling	THURSDAY. Angels and Planets Ruling	FRIDAY. Angels and Planets Ruling	SATURDAY. Angels and Planets Ruling
	Night.	*Night.*	*Night.*	*Night.*	*Night.*	*Night.*	*Night.*
1	Sachiel	Anael	Cassiel	Michael	Gabriel	Samael	Raphael
2	Samael	Raphael	Sachiel	Anael	Cassiel	Michael	Gabriel
3	Michael	Gabriel	Samael	Raphael	Sachiel	Anael	Cassiel
4	Anael	Cassiel	Michael	Gabriel	Samael	Raphael	Sachiel
5	Raphael	Sachiel	Anael	Cassiel	Michael	Gabriel	Samael
6	Gabriel	Samael	Raphael	Sachiel	Anael	Cassiel	Michael
7	Cassiel	Michael	Gabriel	Samael	Raphael	Sachiel	Anae
8	Sachiel	Anael	Cassiel	Michael	Gabriel	Samael	Raphael
9	Samael	Raphael	Sachiel	Anael	Cassiel	Michael	Gabrel
10	Michael	Gabriel	Samael	Raphael	Sachiel	Anael	Cass el
11	Anael	Cassiel	Michael	Gabriel	Samael	Raphael	Sachael
12	Raphael	Sachiel	Anael	Cassiel	Michael	Gabriel	Samael

A table showing the hours of the day and night during which certain angels rule, along with the related zodiacal signs. From Barrett, *The Magus*.

Names from the Bible

The Bible is known as the Good Book. And it *is* a good book in which to find beautiful names.

"God formed man of the dust of the ground" (Gen. 2:7, 19). That refers to God naming the first man Adam, which means "of the earth." Adam named the cattle, birds, and wild animals, then *finally* got around to naming the first woman: "And the man called his wife's name Eve [meaning 'life']; because she was the mother of all living" (Gen. 3:20).

The tradition of choosing biblical names for newborns in America started way back, when the Puritans attempted to establish the Kingdom of God in the New World—in other words, at the time of America's colonization. In keeping with that divine tradition, we've compiled a list of names selected from both the Old and New Testaments. (Please note that our list does not differentiate between the two, simply because both books do belong to everyone . . . and with so many crossovers, it's too complicated to say who belongs where.)

Our research indicates that many children in the Bible had names that were apropos of their destiny in life, while others were named for their time of birth, circumstance at the time of birth, or place of birth. Children were also given names from nature, names that expressed how much like a treasure a baby is, and names that reflected the pain of childbirth.

Since there are *over* three thousand Biblical names, we've naturally chosen only a small number to list here, veering away from the names that reflect pain and steering more toward the precious names that sound good. We've also included names you already know, just to make sure you're aware they're from the Bible.

Many names represent more than one person in the Bible, so

we've confined our brief profile to the most prominent name-sake. The meaning of each name is given in parentheses.

One more thing: We found some wonderful men's names that we thought, in this day and age, would work better as women's names, and so we've *deliberately* included them in the *women's* list. (We're telling you this ahead of time because we don't want you to think we misplaced some names!)

Now, "Seek and ye shall find."

WOMEN OF THE BIBLE

Abigail (father's source of joy)—Beautiful wife of Nabal; later, wife of King David.

Ada, Adah (ornament, beauty)—Wife of Lamech.

Adria—Place name: a town near the River Po.

Ahava (pronounced Uh-hah´va; water)—Place name: a river, on the banks of which Ezra collected the second expedition that returned with him from Babylon to Jerusalem.

Anna (grace)—A prophetess in Jerusalem of the tribe of Asher.

Apollonia (belonging to Apollo)—Place name: a city of Macedonia through which Paul and Silas passed.

Ariel (lioness of God)—In the Book of Isaiah, it is used as another name for Jerusalem.

Atarah (pronounced Uh-ta´-ra; crown)—Wife of Jerahmeel; mother of Onam.

Bathsheba (daughter of the oath)—Beautiful wife of Uriah; later, wife of King David; mother of Solomon, Shimea, Shobab, and Nathan.

Bernice (bringing victory)—Daughter of Herod Agrippa I.

Beth—A general word for a house or habitation; specifically, a house of worship, usually used as the first word of a compound name, i.e. Temple Beth-Sholem.

Bethany—Place name: an obscure village near Bethabara where John baptized Jesus.

Beulah (pronounced Bew´-lah or Byou´-lah; married)—The name Israel will have when "the land shall be married."

Candace, Candice (prince of servants)—A dynasty of Ethiopian queens.

Carmel (fruitful place or park)—Place name: Mount

Carmel is a mountain ridge that extends about fifteen miles across northwestern Israel to the Mediterranean.

Cassia, Kazia, Kezia (plant or shrub that produces cinnamon)—One of Job's three beautiful daughters, born to him after the restoration of his prosperity.

Chloe (green herb)—A woman mentioned in 1 Corinthians.

Claudia (lame)—A Christian woman mentioned in 2 Timothy as saluting Timotheus.

Damaris (heifer)—An Athenian woman whom St. Paul converted.

Deborah (bee)—One biblical Deborah was Rebecca's nurse; another, a Hebrew prophetess who helped the Israelites conquer the Canaanites.

Delila, Delilah (delicate)—Mistress and betrayer of Samson.

Diana (the divine)—The representative of the Greek Artemis, the tutelary goddess of the Ephesians.

Dinah (judgment)—Beautiful daughter of Jacob and Leah.

Eden (pleasure)—The residence of the first couple, Adam and Eve, before they were cast out.

Edna (pleasure, delight)—Mother of Abraham.

Elisheba, Elisabeth, Elizabeth (God is her oath)—Old Testament: Wife of Aaron. New Testament: Wife of Zacharias; mother of John the Baptist; cousin of the Virgin Mary.

Esther (star)—Wife of Ahasuerus who saved the Jews from Haman's plotting.

Eunice (good victory)—Mother of Paul's disciple, Timothy.

Eve (life)—The name given in Scripture to the first woman.

Hali (necklace)—Place name: a town on the boundary of Asher.

Hannah (grace)—Wife of Elkanah; mother of the prophet Samuel.

Hava (life)—The Hebrew name for Eve.

Jael (pronounced Yah-ale´; to ascend)—A courageous Kenite woman who slew Sisera with a tent stake.

Janna (flourishing)—Son of Joseph; father of Melchi.

Japhia (pronounced Ja-fee´-yah or Ya-fee´-yah; splendid)—King of Lachish at the time of Canaan's conquest by the Israelites.

Jarah (honey)—A descendant of Saul; son of Micah; great-grandson of Mephibosheth.

Jemima (dove)—One the three beautiful daughters born to Job after the restoration of his prosperity.

Joanna (grace or gift of God)—Wife of Chuza.

Judith (praised)—Wife of Esau; slayer of Holofernes during the siege of Bethulia.

Julia (feminine of Julius: soft-haired)—Wife of Philologus who was saluted by St. Paul.

Leah (wearied)—Daughter of Laban; first wife of Jacob; mother of Reuben, Simeon, Levi, Judah, Issachar, Zebulun, and Dinah.

Lois (agreeable)—Mother of Eunice; grandmother of the Apostle Timothy.

Lydia (voluptuous beauty)—Place name: an ancient country in Asia Minor. Seller of purple-dyed cloth; the first European convert of St. Paul.

Magdalene (high tower)—With the first name of Mary, a disciple and friend of Jesus, who inspired her to go from sinner to saint.

Marsena (worthy)—One of the seven princes—"wise men which knew the times"—of Persia.

Martha (lady)—Sister of Mary and Lazarus; friend of Jesus.

Mary (rebellion, bitter, tear)—There are several women named Mary in the Bible. The most noteworthy is the Mary who was the Virgin Mother of Jesus.

Michal (who is like God?)—Daughter of Saul; wife of King David.

Miriam (rebellion)—Prophetess; daughter of Amram; sister of Moses and Aaron.

Moriah (chosen by Jehovah)—Place name: the mountain where Abraham was to sacrifice his son Isaac to God.

Myra—Place name: an important town in ancient Lycia.

Naomi (my delight, sweetness)—Wife of Elimelech; mother of Obed; mother-in-law of Ruth. After the death of her husband and sons, she wished to be known as Mara (bitterness).

Ophrah (fawn)—Place name: a town probably in Manasseh, five miles east of Bethel.

Orpah (pronounced Or´-pah; gazelle)—Wife of Naomi's son Chilion.

Peninnah (pronounced Pa-neen´-ah; coral, pearl)—Wife of Elkanah.

Phoebe (radiant)—One of the most important Christian

women, she strove to have deaconesses admitted to the apostolic Church.

Priscilla (ancient)—Energetic wife of Aquila who is used as an example of all that the married woman can do to serve the Church.

Rachel (female sheep)—Beautiful wife of Jacob; mother of Joseph and Benjamin.

Rainbow—The token of the convenant that God made with Noah when Noah emerged from the ark. It assured that flood waters would no longer destroy all that lived. And so the rainbow became a symbol of hope and an emblem of God's faithfulness and mercy.

Rebecca, Rebekah (trapper)—Beautiful daughter of Bethuel; sister of Laban; wife of Isaac; mother of Jacob and Esau.

Rhoda (rosy)—A maid who announced Simon Peter's arrival at Mary's house after his miraculous release from prison.

Ruth (female friend)—Wife of Mahlon. After her husband's death, Ruth devoted herself to her mother-in-law Naomi, telling her, "Whither thou goest, I will go. . . ."

Salome (peace)—Daughter of Herodias and stepdaughter of Herod Antipas. Before she would please her stepfather's guests with her famous dance, she asked for the head of John the Baptist on a silver platter.

Samaria (watch mountain)—Place name: a city thirty miles north of Jerusalem, one rich in Old Testament history.

Sara, Sarah (princess); Sarai (my princess)—Mother of Isaac, she changed her name from Sarah to Sarai when her husband changed his name from Abram to Abraham.

Sharon (flat plain)—Place name: a plain in western Palestine noted for its fertility, especially the growing of roses.

Shobi (pronounced Show´-bee; glorious)—Son of Nahash and one of the first to meet David at Mahanaim.

Susanna (lily)—The heroine of the story of the judgment of Daniel.

Tabitha (gazelle)—Known as Dorcas by St. Luke, she is noted most for her good works.

Tamar (palm tree)—Daughter of King David and Maachah; mother of twins Pharez and Zarah.

Tirza, Tirzah (pronounced Teer´-zah; delight)—Place name: ancient capital north of Jerusalem. The youngest of Zelophehad's five daughters.

Veronica (true image)—The woman who wiped Jesus' brow when he was carrying the cross to Calvary.

Zipporah (pronounced Zeh-poor´-ah; bird)—Daughter of Jethro; wife of Moses; mother of Gershom and Eliezer.

Zoe (life)—Egyptian translations of the name Eve.

MEN OF THE BIBLE

Aaron (to sing, to teach, messenger, mountain)—Brother of Moses and Miriam; son of Amram and Jochebed; first High Priest of the Israelites.

Abel (breath, vapor)—The son of Adam and Eve who was slain by his brother, Cain.

Abner (father of light)—Saul's first cousin and commander-in-chief of Saul's army; slain by Joab.

Abraham (father of many)—Forefather of the Jews; husband of Sarah; father of Isaac and Ishmael. Originally named Abram (God is exalted), he was renamed Abraham by God after he journeyed to Canaan.

Adam (of the earth)—According to the Book of Genesis, the first man created by God.

Adlai (refuge of God)—Father of Shaphat; overseer of David's herds.

Alexander (helper of men, brave)—The son of Philip and Olympias, Alexander III, as the king of Macedon, was given the epithet "the Great."

Alva, Alvah (injustice or height)—Member of Esau's family.

Amal (work, labor)—A member of Asher, one of the twelve tribes of Israel.

Amon (builder)—One of Ahab's governors.

Amos (to be burdened)—A shepherd and dresser of sycamore trees who was called by God's Spirit to be a prophet.

Amram (an exalted people)—Husband of Jochebed; father of Aaron, Miriam, and Moses.

Andrew (manly)—Disciple of John the Baptist; brother of Simon Peter; one of Jesus' apostles.

Ara (the altar)—Son of Jether and descendant of the tribe of Asher.

Aram or Arni (high, heights)—Place name: the country lying northeast of Palestine. Noah's grandson.

Ariel (lion of God)—Under Ezra, one of the chief men who led the caravan back from Babylon to Jerusalem.

Asa (physician, healer)—Son of Abijam; grandson of David. A king of Judah who reigned for forty-one years.

Asher in the Old Testament, Aser in the New Testament (blessed)—Eighth son of Jacob by Zilpah, Leah's handmaid. One of the twelve tribes of Israel.

Barnabas, Barnabus (son of exhortation)—Disciple of Paul; one of the first Christian missionaries.

Bartholomew (hill)—In the Gospel of Mark, he is listed as one of Jesus' twelve apostles.

Baruch (blessed)—Secretary and friend of Jeremiah.

Ben (son)—This Levite was one of the porters appointed by David to tend the Ark of the Covenant.

Benjamin (son of my right hand—denoting the favorite)—Youngest of Jacob's twelve sons. Originally named Benoni (son of my sorrow) for the pain his dying mother, Rachel, suffered during his birth, he was renamed Benjamin by his father.

Caesar (to cut, the hairy one)—The Roman emperor; the sovereign of Judea.

Caleb (faithful like a dog, brave)—One of Moses' spies sent to Canaan.

Cyrus (sun)—The founder of the Persian empire. Legend has it that his courage and genius led to numerous conquests.

Dan (judge)—The fifth son of Jacob and the first of Bilhah, Rachel's maid. Leader of one of the twelve tribes of Israel.

Daniel (judgment of God)—A great prophet whom God saved from the lions.

Darius (upholder of good)—The name of several kings of Media and Persia. One Persian king with this name was responsible for throwing Daniel to the lions.

David (beloved)—Slayer of the giant warrior, Goliath; great and wise king of Israel; father of Solomon, who was his successor.

Demetrius (lover of the earth)—The silversmith of Ephesus.

Elam (eternity)—Place name: a country south of Assyria and east of Persia. Son of Shem.

Elazar, Eleazar (God has helped)—The son of Aaron, he succeeded his father as high priest.

Eli (ascension)—Israel's high priest and last judge.

Elihu (pronounced El´-eh-hue; he is my God)—David's brother; chief of the tribe of Judah.

Elijah, or the Greek form, Elias (the Lord is my God)—Prophet who went to Heaven in a chariot of fire, traveling there in a whirlwind. He is said to be "the grandest and most romantic character that Israel ever produced."

Emanuel, Emmanuel, Immanuel (God is with us)—A name given to Jesus Christ by the apostle Matthew, because Jesus was God united with man and was God living among men.

Enoch (dedicated)—The eldest son of Cain, the son of Adam and Eve who slew his brother Abel.

Enos (mortal man)—Grandson of Adam and Eve; son of Seth.

Ephraim (double fruitfulness)—Son of Joseph and Asenath. Also a place name: a portion of Canaan named after Ephraim.

Esau (pronounced Ee´-saw; hairy)—Son of Isaac and Rebecca who sold his birthright to his twin brother, Jacob.

Ethan, Etan (strong, substantial, enduring)—One of the four sons of Mahol, whose wisdom was excelled by Solomon.

Ezekiel (the strength of God)—Son of a priest named Buzi, he was one of the greatest prophets and a member of a community of Jewish exiles who settled on the banks of the Chebar in Babylonia.

Ezra, Esdras (help, salvation)—A prophet and a great leader who was responsible for religious reforms among the Palestine Jews.

Felix (happy)—Husband of Drusilla; brother of Pallas. A Roman procurator of Judea appointed by the emperor Claudius.

Gabriel (God's strength)—One of the four angels who stood around the throne of God. Michael, Raphael, and Uriel are the other three. Also, the angel who announced to Zacharias the birth of John the Baptist, and to Mary the birth of Christ.

Garrison (to place erect)—A column erected in an enemy's country as a token of conquest; a fortified post.

Gideon (he that cuts down, mighty warrior)—One of the Judges of Israel; warrior-hero who defeated the Midianites.

Haran (mountaineer)—Third son of Terah; youngest brother of Abram.

Herod (herolike)—Herod the Great was the King of Judea.

Hillel (praise)—One of the Judges of Israel; father of Abdon.

Hiram (noble)—King of Tyre who helped Solomon build his temple and David his palace.

Hosea (salvation)—First of the minor prophets; son of Beeri.

Ira (the watchful of a city)—One of the heroes of David's guard.

Isaac, Isaak (laughter)—Son of Abraham and Sarah; half-brother of Ishmael; husband of Rebecca; father of Esau and Jacob.

Isaiah (salvation of the Lord)—Son of Amoz; one of the greatest prophets who also fought civil corruption in Judah.

Israel (prince that prevails with God, wrestling with God)—The name given to Jacob after he wrestled with one of God's angels. It became the national name of the twelve tribes collectively (see next entry).

Jacob (supplanter, to take the place of)—Son of Isaac and Rebecca; brother of Esau; husband of Leah and Rachel. The twelve tribes of Israel evolved from Jacob's twelve sons: Asher, Benjamin, Dan, Gad, Issachar, Joseph, Judah, Levi, Naphtali, Reuben, Simeon, and Zebulun.

James (Greek form of Jacob: supplanter, to take the place of)—There are two apostles named James in the New Testament: James the Greater, and James the Less. The latter, however, was not *less* important than the former, but was given that name because he came *after*. It was simply a way of distinguishing between the two.

Japhet, Japheth (pronounced Jay´-fit or Jay´-fith; enlargement)—Son of Noah.

Jared, Jered (to descend)—Place name: the original name of the River Jordan. Son of Mahalaleel; father of Enoch.

Jason (the healer)—Entertainer of Paul and Silas.

Jeremiah, Jeremy (exalted of the Lord)—A major prophet.

Jesse (wealthy)—Son of Obed; father of David.

Jethro (his excellence)—Father of Zipporah, who married Moses; Midianite priest or prince. He is also called Reuel, which is thought to be his proper name; Jethro is his official title.

Joel (to whom the Lord is God)—Eldest son of Samuel the prophet; father of Heman the singer.

John (God is gracious)—There are eighty-four saints named

John. The most notable may be John the Apostle, brother of the Apostle James, who is mentioned in five books of the Bible and who wrote his own book, the Gospel of John.

Jonah, Jonas (the dove)—Prophet who was thrown into the sea, swallowed by a whale, and yet survived.

Jonathan (God has given)—Son of Saul; friend of David; famous warrior.

Joram, Yoram (the Lord is exalted)—Son of Ahab, king of Israel.

Jordan (the descender)—Place name: the one river in Palestine, with a course of over two hundred miles.

Jose, Joses (exalted)—Son of Eliazer in the genealogy of Christ.

Joseph (increase)—In the Old Testament, he was the son of Jacob and Rachel, and was known for his prophetic dreams. In the New Testament, Joseph, the man of Nazareth, was the husband of Mary, the mother of Christ.

Joshua and its various forms: Hoshea, Oshea, Jehoshua, Jeshua, and Jesus (savior)—The successor of Moses who led the Israelites to the Promised Land.

Josiah (whom Jehovah heals)—The son of Amon and Jedidah, he succeeded his father as king of Judah when he was only eight years old.

Judah (praised, celebrated)—Fourth son of Jacob and Leah; founder of one of the twelve tribes of Israel.

Julius (soft-haired)—The Roman centurion to whose charge St. Paul was delivered as a prisoner.

Kenan, Cainan (possession)—Son of Enos. He begat a son at age seventy and died 840 years later at age 910.

Lazarus (Greek form of the Hebrew Elazar: whom God helps)—The brother of Mary and Martha whom Jesus raised from the dead.

Lemuel (dedicated to God)—Thought to be the king or chief of an Arab tribe that dwelt on the borders of Palestine.

Levi (joined)—Son of Jacob and Leah; father of Gershon, Kohath, and Merari.

Linus (net)—After the apostles, the first bishop of Rome.

Lucas, Luke (an abbreviated form of Lucanus: giving light)—A companion of the Apostle Paul; one of the four evangelists; the "beloved physician" credited with the Gospel of Luke.

Malachi, Malachy (pronounced Mal´-a-ky´ or Mal-ah´-ky; messenger of the Lord)—The last of the Hebrew prophets.

Marc, Mark (of Mars; warlike)—One of the four evangelists; credited with the Gospel bearing his name.

Matthew (a contraction of Mattathias: the Lord's gift)—Named Levi at birth, this apostle is credited with the Gospel of Matthew.

Matthias (gift of God)—The apostle elected to fill the place of the traitor Judas.

Michael (who is like God?)—One of the four angels who stood around the throne of God. Gabriel, Raphael, and Uriel are the other three.

Mordecai (pronounced Mor´-deh-kigh; little man, worshiper of Mars)—Uncle of Esther; with her aid, he saved the Jews from Haman's plotting.

Moses (drawn—i.e., from the water)—Son of Amram; brother of Aaron and Miriam; husband of Zipporah. This legislator led the Israelites out of Egyptian bondage to the Promised Land.

Nathan, Nathaniel (gift of God)—A prophet who reproved King David for causing Uriah's death.

Nehemiah (the Lord's comfort)—A Jewish leader who was empowered by Artaxerxes to rebuild Jerusalem.

Noah (rest, comfort)—The son of Lamech, he escaped the Great Deluge by building an ark. Father of Ham, Japheth, and Shem.

Omar (eloquent, talkative)—Son of Eliphaz, the firstborn of Esau.

Oren (pine tree)—One of the sons of Jerahmeel; the firstborn of Hezron.

Paul (small, little)—Named Saul at birth by his Jewish parents, this tentmaker became the best known and most revered of the apostles.

Peter (rock, stone)—One of the twelve apostles, he was born Simon bar Jonah and nicknamed the Arabic version—Peter—by Jesus.

Phares, Pharez, Perez (burst forth)—Twin brother of Zarah or Zerah; son of Judah.

Philip (lover of horses)—One of the twelve apostles.

Raphael (God's healer)—One of the four angels who stood

around the throne of God. Gabriel, Michael, and Uriel are the other three.

Reuben (behold a son)—Jacob's firstborn child with Leah; founder of one of the tribes of Israel.

Rufus (red)—Son of Simon the Cyrenian; he was saluted by the Apostle Paul as "elect in the Lord."

Samson (like the sun)—The son of Manoah who, it was said, was endowed with supernatural power and undaunted bravery; he was betrayed by Delilah.

Samuel (asked of the Lord)—Hebrew judge and prophet; son of Elkanah.

Saul (desired)—Of the tribe of Benjamin; son of Kish; the first king of Israel.

Seth (compensation)—Son of Adam; father of Enos.

Shiloh (pronounced Shy´-lo; place of rest)—Place name: the city of Ephraim, one of the earliest and most sacred of the Hebrew sanctuaries.

Silas (contracted form of Silvanis: woody)—One of the leaders of the Church at Jerusalem.

Simeon (heard)—The second of Jacob's sons by Leah.

Simon (contracted form of Simeon: heard)—A Canaanite; one of the twelve apostles (see Peter).

Solomon (peaceful)—Lastborn son of David; the king of Israel who reigned for forty years and was noted for his extreme wisdom.

Stephen (crowned)—The first Christian martyr, he was chief of the seven appointed to assist the apostles.

Thaddeus (wise)—Another name for Jude the Apostle.

Thomas (twin)—One of the apostles. According to Eusebius, his real name was Judas.

Timothy (God-fearing)—Child of a mixed marriage whose father's name is unknown; his mother is Eunice and his grandmother Lois.

Tobias (Greek form of Tobiah: goodness of God)—Father of Johanan; an Ammonite who opposed King Nehemiah.

Uri (fiery)—Father of Bezaleel; one of the architects of the Tabernacle.

Uriah—Devoted husband of Bathsheba; sent to death in battle by David, who wanted Uriah's wife for himself.

Zachariah, Zechariah (remembered by God)—The fourteenth king of Israel, who reigned for only six months; son of Jeroboam II.

Zacharias (Greek form of Zachariah)—Husband of Elizabeth; father of John the Baptist.

Zalmon (shady)—Place name: Mount Zalmon, near Shechem. An Ahohite; one of David's guard.

Zared (brook)—Place name: a brook or valley running into the Dead Sea near its southeast corner.

Names of Saints

A saint is a person who has lived a life of exceptional holiness, filled with good deeds and often the working of miracles. The Roman Catholic Church formally recognizes saints through the process of canonization and believes saints possess the ability to intercede for humans on earth.

At a baptism, the Catholic custom is to give the baby the name of a saint from the Roman Martyrology, or Calendar of Saints. The saint then becomes the guardian and inspiration for his or her young namesake. Down the road a bit, at confirmation, the child may select the name of another saint as a protector and role model.

Many Catholics observe their saint's "feast day" as their "name day"—in other words, by celebrating the same way you celebrate a birthday. In most cases, the saint's feast day is the day the saint died. Instead of it being a time of mourning, it is regarded as the saint's "heavenly birthday" and a time for celebration.

There is a feast day for every day of the year. In fact, since there are thousands of saints, most days belong to more than one saint. Also, there are many saints with the same name. For instance, there is St. Elizabeth of Hungary, whose feast day is November 17; St. Elizabeth of Portugal, whose feast day is July 4; and St. Elizabeth Ann Seton, whose feast day is January 4. For this book we've selected one saint for each day of the year and when appropriate, have noted what (s)he is the patron saint of, or why (s)he has been honored by the Church.

There aren't many saints from America, and, of those that are, most were born before modern times. That means that many of their names are foreign and very old-world, like Wulfric, Theodosius, and Maximus. The Church allows us to take the liberty of turning these names into modern-day derivatives. Wulfric might become Wilfred; Theodosius might become Theo or Theodore; and Maximus might become Maxwell, Maxie, or Max. (The main A-to-Z name list, found at the back of the book, can help you with derivatives.)

Also, bear in mind that you can use the feminine version of a male saint's name. For example, the feminine version of St. Brendan could be Brenda; the feminine version of St. Charles could be Charlene, Charlotte, Cheryl, Carla, Carol, Caroline, even Arlene and Arlette. While the male version of a female saint's name can be used, chances are, though, that the female name is *already* a derivative of a male name. For example, St. Louise could be Louis, Lewis, even Aloysius— and probably was!

To learn even more about the choice of saintly names available to you, check the reference section of your local library; *Butler's Lives of the Saints* is indispensable.

Meanwhile, to help preserve this truly beautiful and meaningful custom, let's let the saints go marching in!

NOTE: What follows first is an alphabetical listing of the saints we've profiled, so that you can quickly see what names appeal to you and/or find out if your favorite saint appears here. They are all cross-referenced by date, so that if a particular saint appeals to you, you can then look him/her up in the list that follows, which profiles each saint according to his or her feast day.

NAMES OF THE SAINTS WE'VE PROFILED AND THEIR FEAST DAYS

Aaron—7/3
Abraham—10/27
Abraham Kidunaia—3/16
Abraham of Smolensk—8/21
Adalbert of Egmond—6/25
Adamnan—9/23
Adela—12/24
Adelaide—12/16
Adele (See: Adela)—12/24

Adrian of Canterbury—1/9
Adrian of Nicomedia—9/8
Acdan (See: Aidan of Lindisfarne)—8/31
Aedh (See: Macartan)—3/26
Agape—4/3
Agatha—2/5
Agnes—1/21
Aidan of Ferns—1/31
Aidan of Lindisfarne—8/31
Albert the Great—11/15
Alexander Akimetes—2/23
Alexander of Lyons—4/22
Alexis—7/17
Aleydis (See: Alice)—6/15
Alice—6/15
Aloysius Gonzaga—6/21
Alphonsus Mary Liguori—8/2
Alphonsus Rodriguez—10/30
Amator—5/1
Amatre (See: Amator)—5/1
Amatus—9/13
Ambrose—12/7
Ambrose Barlow—9/10
Amé (See: Amatus)—9/13
Anastasia—12/25; 4/15
Anastasia Patricia—3/10
Anatolia—12/23
Andrew—11/30
Andrew of Fiesole—8/22
Andrew Hubert Fournet—5/13
Andrew Kim Taegon—9/20
Angadrisma—10/14
Angela Merici—5/31
Angelina of Marsciano, Blessed—7/21
Angelo—5/5
Anne (Also see: Susanna)—7/23; 7/26
Anselm—4/21
Anthelm—6/26
Anthony of Padua—6/13
Antonia of Florence—2/28
Antony the Abbot—1/17

Antony Mary Zaccaria—7/5
Anysia—12/30
Apollo—1/25
Arsenius the Great—7/19
Athanasius—5/2
Audrey—6/23
Augustine of Canterbury (See: Austin)—5/27
Augustine of Hippo (See: Austin)—8/28
Aurea—3/11
Aurelius—7/27
Austin of Canterbury—5/27
Austin of Hippo—8/28
Bairre (See: Barry)—9/25
Barbara—12/4
Barnabas—6/11
Barry—9/25
Bartholomew—8/24
Basil the Great—1/2
Basilissa (See: Basilla)—4/15; 5/20
Basilla—5/20
Beatrice of Ornacieu—2/13
Benedict—7/11
Benedict Biscop—1/12
Benen—11/9
Benet (See: Benedict Biscop)—1/12
Benignus (See: Benen)—11/9
Benjamin—3/31
Bernadette—4/16
Bernard—1/23
Bernard of Clairvaux—8/20
Bertilla Boscardin—10/20
Bertinus—9/5
Bertrand—6/30
Bibiana (See: Viviana)—12/2
Blaan (See: Blane)—8/11
Blaise—2/3
Blane—8/11
Boris—7/24
Brendan—5/16
Brigid—2/1
Bruno—10/6

Caedmon—2/11
Cajetan (See: Gaetano)—8/7
Camillus de Lellis—7/14
Canice (See: Kenneth)—10/11
Casimir—3/4
Cassian of Imola—8/13
Castor—9/2
Catherine of Alexandria—11/25
Catherine of Genoa—9/15
Catherine of Siena—4/29
Catherine of Sweden—3/24
Ceadda (See: Chad)—3/2
Cecilia—11/22
Cecily (See: Cecilia)—11/22
Chad—3/2
Chaermon—12/22
Charity—8/1
Charles Borromeo—11/4
Chionia—4/3
Christina of Aquila—1/18
Chrysanthus—10/25
Ciaran (See: Kieran)—3/5
Clare of Assisi—8/12
Clement I—11/23
Colette—3/6
Colm (See: Colum)—6/9
Colman of Lindisfarne—2/18
Colum—6/9
Columba—6/9
Conrad of Piacenza—2/19
Cormac—9/14
Cosmas—9/26
Cyprian—9/16
Cyran—12/5
Cyril of Alexandria—6/27
Cyril of Jerusalem—3/18
Damasus I—12/11
Damian—9/26
Daniel—10/10
Daria—10/25
David—3/1

David I of Scotland—5/24
Deirdre (See: Ita)—1/15
Demetrius—10/8
Denis—10/9
Dewi (See: David)—3/1
Dominic—8/8
Dominic of the Causeway—5/12
Dominic of Silos—12/20
Dominic Savio—3/9
Donald—7/15
Donatus—10/22
Dorotheus of Tyre—6/5
Dunstan—5/19
Dymphna (See: Dympna)—5/15
Dympna—5/15
Eadbert (See: Edbert)—5/6
Edan (See: Aidan of Ferns)—1/31
Edbert—5/6
Edmund the Martyr—11/20
Edward the Confessor—10/13
Elizabeth—11/5
Elizabeth Ann Bayley Seton—1/4
Elizabeth of Hungary—11/19
Elizabeth of Portugal—7/4
Elmo—6/2
Eric IX of Sweden—5/18
Ernest—11/7
Etheldreda (See: Audrey)—6/23
Eucherius—2/20
Eulalia of Mérida—12/10
Eve—9/6
Fabian—1/20
Faith—8/1
Felicity—3/7
Felix of Nantes—7/7
Fergus—11/27
Fidelis of Signaringen—4/24
Fina (See: Seraphina)—3/12
Finbar (See: Barry)—9/25
Flavian—2/24
Flora—11/24

Flora of Beaulieu—10/5
Florence—12/1
Florian—5/4
Frances Xavier Cabrini—11/13
Francis of Assisi—10/4
Francis Caracciolo—6/4
Francis de Sales—1/24
Francis of Paola—4/2
Francis Xavier—12/3
Frederick of Utrecht—7/18
Fulbert—4/10
Gabriel—9/29
Gabriel Possenti—2/27
Gaetano—8/7
Gatian—12/18
Gelasius I—11/21
Gemma Galgani—4/11
Genevieve—1/3; 5/8
George the Great—4/23
Gerald—4/5
Gerard of Brogne—10/3
Gerard Majella—10/16
Gerlac—1/5
Germain—5/28
Germanus (See: Germain)—5/28
Gertrude of Helfta—11/16
Gilbert of Sempringham—2/16
Gildas the Wise—1/29
Giles—9/1
Gleb (See: Boris)—7/24
Godfrey—11/8
Godric—5/21
Gregory Barbarigo—6/18
Gregory the Great—9/3
Gregory Nazianzen—5/9
Guido (See: Guy of Cortona)—6/16
Guy of Anderlecht—9/12
Guy of Cortona—6/16
Hannah (See: Anne)—7/26
Harvey—6/17
Helena—8/18

Henry of Cocket—1/16
Herbert—3/20
Hervé (See: Harvey)—6/17
Hilary of Poitiers—1/13
Hilda—11/17
Hope—8/1
Hugh of Rouen—4/9
Hyacinth—8/15
Hyacintha Mariscotti—1/30
Ida (See: Ita)—1/15
Ida of Herzfeld—9/4
Irenaeus of Lyons—6/28
Irene—4/3
Irmina—12/24
Isaac the Great—9/9
Isabella (See: Elizabeth of Portugal)—7/4
Isidore of Seville—4/4
Ita—1/15
Ivo of Chartres—5/23
James—4/30
James the Greater—7/25
James the Less—5/3
Jane Frances Fremiot de Chantal—12/12
Januarius—9/19
Jason—7/12
Jerome—9/30
Jerome Emiliani—2/8
Joachim—7/26
Joan of Arc—5/30
Joan Delanoue, Blessed—8/17
Joan de Lestonnac—2/2
John the Baptist—6/24
John Baptist de la Salle—4/7
John of the Cross—12/14
John of Egypt—3/27
John the Evangelist—12/27
John of God—3/8
Jordan of Saxony—2/15
Josaphat—11/12
Joseph—3/19
Joseph of Cupertino—9/18

Jude—10/28
Julia Billiart—4/8
Julian—2/24
Julian the Hospitaller—2/12
Juliana Falconieri—6/19
Julitta of Caesara—7/30
Julius—7/3
Julius I—4/12
Justin de Jacobis—7/31
Justin Martyr—6/1
Justus—8/6
Kateri Tekákwitha, Blessed—4/17
Kenneth—10/11
Kevin—6/3
Kieran—3/5
Laisren (See: Laserian)—4/18
Lambert of Lyons—4/14
Landericus (See: Landry)—6/10
Landry—6/10
Laserian—4/18
Laurence O'Toole—11/4
Laurence of Rome—8/10
Leger—10/2
Leo I the Great—11/10
Leo IX—4/19
Leodegarius (See: Leger)—10/2
Leonard Casonova—11/26
Leonard Murialdo—3/30
Leonard of Noblac—11/6
Lilian—12/8
Lillian (See: Lilian)—12/8
Lily (See: Lilian)—12/8
Louis of Anjou—8/19
Louis Mary of Montfort—4/28
Louise de Marillac—3/15
Lucian—10/26
Lucian of Beauvais—1/8
Lucius—2/24
Lucy of Syracuse—12/13
Lughaidh (See: Molua)—8/4
Luke—10/18

Macarius the Wonder-Worker—4/1
Macartan—3/26
Madeleine Sophie Barat—5/25
Maedoc (See: Aidan of Ferns)—1/31
Marcellus—11/1
Marcian—4/20
Margaret—7/20
Margaret Clitherow—3/25
Margaret of Cortona—2/22
Maria Goretti—7/6
Marian (See: Marcian)—4/20; 4/30
Marina (See: Margaret)—7/20
Marius—1/27
Mark—4/25; 10/24
Martha—7/29
Martin (See: Mark)—10/24
Martin I—4/13
Martin de Porres—11/3
Martin of Tours—11/11
Mary—1/1
Mary Magdalen Postel—7/16
Matilda—3/14
Matthias—5/14
Maura of Troyes—9/21
Maximilian Mary Kolbe —8/14
May (See: Marius)—1/27
Meda (See: Ita)—1/15
Medard—6/8
Melania the Younger—12/31
Mercedes—9/24
Michael—9/29
Mildred of Thanet—7/13
Modan—2/4
Molaisse (See: Laserian)—4/18
Molua—8/4
Monica—8/27
Montanus—2/24
Narcissus—10/29
Natalia—7/27
Nestor—2/26
Nicholas—12/6

Nicholas von Flüe—3/22
Nino—12/15
Non (See: Nonnita)—3/3
Nonna (See: Nonnita)—3/3; 8/5
Nonnita—3/3
Norbert—6/6
Odo of Cluny—11/18
Oliver Plunket—7/1
Olympias—12/17
Otto—7/2
Owen—8/23
Paschal Baylon—5/17
Pastor—8/6
Patricia—8/25
Patrick—3/17
Paul—6/29
Paul of the Cross—10/19
Paul Miki—2/6
Perpetua—3/7
Peter Canisius—12/21
Peter Damian—2/21
Peter Fourier—12/9
Peter Julian Eymard—8/3
Philip Evans—7/22
Philip Neri—5/26
Quentin—10/31
Quintinus (See: Quentin)—10/31
Radbod—11/29
Raphael—9/29
Raphaela Mary Porras—1/6
Raymond of Peñafort—1/7
Raymund—5/29
Regina—9/7
Reine (See: Regina)—9/7
Richard Gwyn—10/17
Richard of Lucca—2/7
Rita of Cascia—5/22
Robert Francis—9/17
Robert of Newminster—6/7
Roderic—3/13
Romanus—8/9; 10/23

Rosaria—10/7
Rose of Lima—8/30
Rudericus (See: Roderic)—3/13
Rufina—7/10
Rufinus—6/14
Rupert of Salzburg—3/29
Sabina—8/29
Samson—7/28
Sava—1/14
Scholastica—2/10
Secunda (See: Rufina)—7/10
Senericus (See: Serenus)—5/7
Seraphina—3/12
Serapion—3/21
Serenus—5/7
Silverius—6/20
Silvin—2/17
Simeon Metaphrastes—11/28
Solangia—5/10
Stephen the Deacon—12/26
Stephen of Hungary—8/16
Stephen of Perm—4/26
Sunniva—7/8
Susanna—7/23
Tarasius—2/25
Teilo—2/9
Teresa of Avila—10/15
Teresa of the Child—10/1
Teresa of Jesus—8/26
Ternan—6/12
Theodora of Alexandria—9/11
Theodore—12/28
Theodosius the Cenobiarch—1/11
Thomas Aquinas—1/28
Thomas Becket—12/29
Thomas More—6/22
Thomas of Villanova—9/22
Thrasius (See: Tarasius)—2/25
Timothy—1/26
Tobias—11/2
Tutilo—3/28

Urban V—12/19
Ursula—10/21
Valerius—6/14
Valentine—2/14
Veronica Giuliana—7/9
Victor Maurus—5/8
Victoria—12/23
Victorian—3/23
Victorinus (See: Montanus)—2/24
Vincent de Paul—9/27
Vincent Pallotti—1/22
Viviana—12/2
Walter of L'Esterp—5/11
Wenceslaus—9/28
Wilfrid—10/12
William of Bourges—1/10
William of Eskill—4/6
Wolstan (See: Wulfstan)—1/19
Wulfstan—1/19
Wulstan (See: Wulfstan)—1/19
Zachary—11/5
Zita—4/27

PROFILES OF THE SAINTS, ORGANIZED BY FEAST DAYS

January

1 **Mary,** the Blessed Virgin, has many feast days. The Solemnity of Mary, Mother of God—which is celebrated on the first day of the year—is one of them.

2 **Basil the Great,** one of the Four Doctors of the Greek Orthodox Church, is the patriarch of Eastern monks and the patron of Russia.

3 **Genevieve** is credited with saving Paris from the ravages of Attila the Hun through her prayers and fasting. She is patron of Paris and its disasters, including drought and torrential rains.

4 **Elizabeth Ann Bayley Seton** founded the Sisters of Charity, the first religious society in America. Elizabeth was the first American-born saint and was canonized in 1975 by Pope Paul VI.

5 **Gerlac,** to atone for the sins of his youth, spent seven years in Rome nursing the sick and doing penance. He then returned to his native Holland, gave all his possessions to the poor, and lived as a hermit in the hollow of a tree.

6 **Raphaela Mary Porras** overcame great opposition to start the congregation of the Handmaids of the Sacred Heart, which was devoted to educating children. She was canonized in 1977 by Pope Paul VI.

7 **Raymond of Peñafort** was famous for his preaching and was the confessor of Pope Gregory IX. He opposed heresy and is the patron of lawyers.

8 **Lucian of Beauvais,** a missionary in Gaul, was said to be the companion of St. Dionysius of Paris.

9 **Adrian of Canterbury,** a great scholar and abbot, is revered for his miracles, which helped students in need.

10 **William of Bourges** was named archbishop of Bourges by order of Pope Innocent III. He lived an extremely austere life, was known for helping the poor and the penitent, and defended the rights of the Church—even against the king.

11 **Theodosius the Cenobiarch** built a monastery for hermits and hospices for the sick, the aged, and the mentally disturbed. He was buried in a cell called the Cave of the Magi; the wise men who came to find Christ after his birth were said to have lodged in it.

12 **Benedict** or **Benet Biscop,** abbot, built many monasteries and is the patron of the English Benedictines.

13 **Hilary of Poitiers,** bishop and Doctor of the Church, was one of the most esteemed theologians of his time and a staunch defender of Christ's divinity. He is the patron against snakebites.

14 **Sava,** a trainer of young monks, was respected for his gentleness and leniency. He was also credited with teaching his people effective ways to farm the land and use windows—instead of doors—to let in air and light. He is the patron of the Serbian people.

15 **Ita,** also known as **Deirdre, Ida,** and **Meda,** was a virgin credited with creating an Irish lullaby for the Infant Jesus. In Ireland, she is second in popularity to St. Brigid.

16 Henry of Cocket was a Dane who had a religious calling very early in life. He became a hermit on the island of Cocket, off England's coast of Northumberland. He had only one meal a day—bread and water—which he ate after sunset.

17 Antony the Abbot, the founder of Christian monasticism, is the patron of those with skin diseases, of domestic animals, of basketmakers, and of gravediggers.

18 Christina of Aquila, baptized Matthia, became an Augustinian hermit at Aquila. She was known for her devotion to the poor and for her gifts of prophesy, ecstasy, and miracles.

19 Wulfstan or **Wolstan,** bishop, washed the feet of twelve poor men daily and was highly regarded for his humility. He was also an ardent advocate of clerical celibacy.

20 Fabian, a martyr for his faith, supposedly was elected pope because a dove landed on his head during the election.

21 Agnes, at age thirteen, refused to compromise her purity and so was tortured and murdered. It is said that when her clothes were torn off, her hair spontaneously grew long to cloak her body, and that a man who assaulted her went blind, until she asked that his sight be restored. One of the most famous Roman martyrs, she is, appropriately, the patron of virginal innocence.

22 Vincent Pallotti founded the Society of Catholic Apostolate, performed exorcisms, and is considered the forerunner of Catholic Action.

23 Bernard, archbishop of Vienne, was known for his insistence on strict ecclesiastical discipline.

24 Francis de Sales, bishop and Doctor of the Church, was known as "the Gentle Christ of Geneva." He is the patron of writers, editors, and the Catholic press.

25 Apollo, abbot, founded a community of monks at Hermopolis when he was close to eighty. The most astonishing miracle accorded to him is the continual multiplication of bread during a time of famine.

26 Timothy, bishop, was a missionary companion of Paul the Apostle and was called "the Almsgiver" because of his care for the poor. He is the patron against stomach disorders.

27 **Marius** or **May** was a monk who was cured of a serious illness at the tomb of St. Denis in Paris. Every year he spent the forty days of Lent alone in a forest. During one such period, he had a vision of the barbarians invading Italy and the subsequent destruction of his monastery. Unfortunately, both visions came true.

28 **Thomas Aquinas,** priest and Doctor of the Church, was one of the Church's most prolific writers and theologians. He is the patron of all universities, scholars, philosophers, theologians, and booksellers.

29 **Gildas the Wise,** abbot, is a celebrated teacher and thought of as the first English historian.

30 **Hyacintha Mariscotti,** named Clarice at birth, was forced by her family to enter a Franciscan convent. For more than ten years she was rebellious. Then, after surviving her second serious illness, she changed her ways and adopted the strictest of religious life-styles. She helped found two congregations that ministered to the sick, the aged, and the poor.

31 **Aidan, Edan,** or **Maedoc of Ferns** was a Bishop of Ireland known to be extremely kind, especially to animals. He is said to have performed many miracles.

February

1 **Brigid (Bride) of Ireland** is the second patron of Ireland and "the Mary of the Gael." She is the patron of poets, dairy workers, blacksmiths, and healers.

2 **Joan de Lestonnac** got married, had four children, and was widowed. As soon as the children were on their own, Joan entered the religious life and founded a community of nuns dedicated to educating young girls. She was canonized in 1949.

3 **Blaise** or **Blase,** bishop, healed sick and wounded animals. He is the patron of wild animals, wool combers, and those who suffer from throat problems. He is also invoked to help heal sick cattle.

4 **Modan** was an extremely austere monk who, against his will, became the abbot of his Scottish monastery. He then lived as a hermit.

5 **Agatha** was tortured and killed because she promised her virginity to God. She is the patron of nurses, wet nurses, and fire fighters.

6 **Paul Miki** was a Japanese Jesuit preacher who was martyred. His canonization, along with that of his martyred companions, led him to become one of the protomartyrs of the Far East.

7 **Richard of Lucca** was respectfully given the name "Richard the King" by the people of his town. His real name is unknown. Three of his children—Willibald, Winebald, and Walburga—also became saints.

8 **Jerome Emiliani** is the founder of the Somaschi, which saw to the education of youth in colleges, academies, and seminaries. He is the patron of both orphans and abandoned children.

9 **Teilo,** known as Eliud in his native Wales, was a successful preacher who founded several monasteries.

10 **Scholastica,** the twin sister of St. Benedict, is the patron of Benedictine nuns and is called upon for help against storms. Upon her death, her brother had a vision in which he saw her soul ascending to Heaven.

11 **Caedmon,** a laborer or herdsman at an English monastery, is said to have had a vision that taught him how to compose verses in praise of God. He became the first Anglo-Saxon writer of religious poetry and is called "the Father of English Sacred Poetry." His sole surviving hymn is said to have been composed during a dream.

12 **Julian the Hospitaller** is the patron of innkeepers, travelers, and boatmen.

13 **Beatrice of Ornacieu** lived an austere life and was gifted with visions of Christ. She was so moved by the sight of him that it was thought she would injure her vision by her abundant shedding of tears.

14 **Valentine,** a physician and priest from Rome, is a martyr and the patron of lovers and greetings. The medieval belief that birds begin to pair together on this date is thought to have inspired the sending of Valentine cards.

15 **Jordan of Saxony,** whose real name was Gordanus or Giordanus, was a powerful preacher who directed his

charismatic energies toward young students. He has been called "the first university chaplain." His writings about St. Dominic are the prime source of information about the founder of the Dominicans.

16 **Gilbert of Sempringham,** along with seven young women and the approval of Pope Eugene III, established the Gilbertine Order, the only religious order to originate in England during the medieval period. It eventually grew to twenty-six monasteries.

17 **Silvin** canceled his marriage plans to embark on a religious life of devotion to the needy. He used his wealth to build churches and to ransom slaves from the barbarians. He died a Benedictine monk.

18 **Colman of Lindisfarne,** bishop, was a staunch defender of Celtic, but not Roman, ecclesiastical practices. When King Oswy ruled in favor of the Roman way, Colman gave up his bishopric and moved from Lindisfarne to the Isle of Inishbofin to found a monastery in which he could practice Celtic rites.

19 **Conrad of Piacenza** was a Franciscan hermit who lived a life of extraordinary piety. He is invoked to heal hernias.

20 **Eucherius,** bishop, took an unpopular stand in France against using Church revenues for war expenses. He spent much of his life in prayer and contemplation.

21 **Peter Damian,** bishop, cardinal, and Doctor of the Church, worked zealously for the internal reform of the Church and fought against practices such as simony. He wrote some of the most beautiful poetry of medieval times.

22 **Margaret of Cortona** had an illegitimate son, but when her lover was killed, she saw it as a sign of God's disfavor and thereafter strove to resist "temptation." She then spent most of her life helping the sick and the poor.

23 **Alexander Akimetes,** a native of Asia Minor, was a convert to Christianity who retired to Syria to practice asceticism.

24 **Montanus** and his companions **Lucius, Flavian, Julian,** and **Victorinus** were all slain for upholding their faith. They share this feast day.

25 **Tarasius** or **Thrasius,** bishop and secretary to ten-

year-old Emperor Constantine VI, was patriarch of Constantinople and revered for his acts of charity.

26 **Nestor,** bishop, was tortured and crucified when he
refused to recant his obedience to God and submit to the
Emperor Decius.

27 **Gabriel Possenti** promised that if he recovered from an
illness, he would serve God. He did so—but it took until
the second time around. The patron of youth, students,
and the clergy, he was canonized in 1920.

28 **Antonia of Florence** ruled the monastery of Corpus
Christi under the strict rule of St. Clare. She had visions
and at times was seen to be in ecstasy and rise from the
ground.

March

1 **David** or **Dewi,** bishop, is the patron of Wales and perhaps the most celebrated of British saints.

2 **Chad** or **Ceadda** was one of four brothers, all of whom
became priests and of whom two—including Chad—
became bishops. Once a bishop, Chad traveled not by
horseback but on foot, in the manner of the apostles.

3 **Nonnita, Non,** or **Nonna,** born of noble birth, lived in a
convent and was seduced by Sant, a local chieftain. The
child of that union was St. David.

4 **Casimir,** a son of King Casimir III of Poland, is the
patron of Poland, Russia, Lithuania, and the ill.

5 **Kieran** or **Ciaran of Saighir** is known as Ireland's firstborn saint. Legend has it that when St. Kieran returned
to Ireland from Italy, St. Patrick recruited him as one of
twelve bishops to help him in evangelizing the country.

6 **Colette,** christened Nicolette in honor of St. Nicholas of
Myra, was known for restoring the original strict obser-
vance of St. Clare throughout France, Savoy, and Flanders. She had a great fondness for children and animals.

7 **Felicity,** along with **Perpetua,** was a victim of Christian
persecution in Carthage.

8 **John of God,** founder of the Brothers Hospitallers,
began his dedication to God by peddling sacred pictures
and books. He is the patron of printers and booksellers,
as well as of the sick.

9 **Dominic Savio** was the youngest nonmartyr to receive

canonization and is the patron of boys, juvenile delin-
quents, Pueri Cantors, and choirboys.

10 **Anastasia Patricia,** it is believed, was martyred under
Diocletian. Her popularity is due to the fact that her
memory is associated with the second Mass at Christmas.
She is the patron of weavers.

11 **Aurea,** a nun from Spain, lived her life as a solitary,
without material possessions, and was rewarded by the
vision of her patron saints, who assured her of God's
favor.

12 **Seraphina** or **Fina** lived her life in poverty and pain.
When illnesses left her paralyzed, she lay on a plank of
wood, in the same position, for six years. When she died
and her body was taken off the rotted wood, it is said that
the wood was covered in white violets. The white violets
that bloom during this feast day in St. Seraphina's town
of San Geminiano are called "Santa Fina's flowers."

13 **Roderic** or **Rudericus** was betrayed by his Moslem
brother, who falsely claimed Roderic had renounced
Christ. Imprisoned, Roderic still refused to deny his
Christianity and was eventually beheaded.

14 **Matilda,** also known as **Mechtildis** and **Maud,** was
queen of Germany and noted for her holiness and charitable works.

15 **Louise de Marillac** became a nun and, with St. Vincent
de Paul, founded the Sisters of Charity, which provides
education, hospitals for the poor, and homes for abandoned children. She is the patron of social workers.

16 **Abraham Kidunaia** is revered for converting an entire
town of pagans to Christianity.

17 **Patrick,** archbishop, was born in Scotland but was captured by pirates and taken to Ireland. After six years
he escaped, returned home, and vowed to go back and
organize the Irish Church. His success made him the
patron of Ireland and of Nigeria (whose people were
converted to Christianity primarily by Irish clergy).

18 **Cyril of Jerusalem,** archbishop and Doctor of the
Church, was erroneously charged with wrongful deeds
and spent years in exile. He was noted for his great
gentleness and reasonableness.

19 **Joseph,** husband of the Virgin Mary and foster father of

Jesus Christ, is the patron of the Universal Church, social justice, carpenters, doubters, travelers, Austria, Bohemia, Canada, Belgium, Mexico, Peru, Russia, and South Vietnam. St. Joseph is also a protector of working men and viewed as a good role model for fathers.

20   Herbert, a disciple and close friend of St. Cuthbert, asked that he not be abandoned but be "taken" at the same time as his friend, since they had both served God together in their earthly life. A year later both saints died—on the same day.

21   Serapion was called "the Scholastic" because of his great knowledge in matters both sacred and secular.

22   Nicholas von Flüe was a religious figure of major import in Swiss history; he helped prevent civil war. He is Switzerland's patron.

23   Victorian, one of Carthage's wealthiest citizens, was appointed proconsul by Huneric, Arian King of the Vandals. During Huneric's persecution of Catholics, Huneric urged Victorian to convert to Arianism. Victorian refused and was tortured to death.

24   Catherine of Sweden, the daughter of St. Bridget, is called upon for protection against abortion—perhaps because of her state of chastity despite her marriage.

25   Margaret Clitherow used her home as a refuge for England's fugitive priests and is one of the Forty Martyrs of England and Wales.

26   Marcartan or **Aedh MacCairthinn,** bishop, has little known about his life, although many outstanding miracles are attributed to him.

27   John of Egypt was one of the most famous of desert hermits because of his wisdom, his miracles, and his ability to read the minds of others, thus discovering their secret sins.

28   Tutilo was a monk of all trades: a master of poetry, painting, architecture, sculpture, and metalworking. He was also a musician, orator, and composer.

29   Rupert of Salzburg helped rebuild the old town Juvavum, which he renamed Salzburg. Considered the first bishop of Salzburg, he died on March 29—Easter Sunday.

30   Leonard Murialdo was devoted to educating poor boys and began Italy's first Catholic worker movement. He was canonized in 1970 by Pope Paul VI.

31 Benjamin, a deacon preaching Christianity in Persia, clung to his faith even while being tortured to death.

April

1 Macarius the Wonder-Worker, baptized Christopher, was known for his miracles of healing. He was imprisoned, tortured, and eventually exiled for his opposition to iconoclasm.

2 Francis of Paola is the patron of sailors, naval officers, and navigators.

3 Irene and her sisters **Agape** and **Chionia** were sentenced to death for owning and protecting copies of the Holy Scriptures.

4 Isidore of Seville, bishop, Doctor of the Church, and one of the most learned men of his time, is thought of as the last of the ancient Christian philosophers. He is the patron of Madrid and farmers.

5 Gerald, confessor, and founder of the abbey of Sauve-Majeure (Silver Major) near Bordeaux, was noted for his preaching.

6 William of Eskill, abbot, is known for the reforms he made at monasteries in Denmark.

7 John Baptist de la Salle, the patron of teachers, revolutionized the art of teaching with his many schools, which included a boys' reformatory and a school for adult prisoners.

8 Julia Billiart, devoted to helping the sick and the poor, helped found the Institute of the Sisters of Notre Dame. Paralyzed for twenty-two years, Julia was suddenly able to walk on the Feast of the Sacred Heart after a priest bade her to.

9 Hugh of Rouen is said to have used family connections to help him become bishop of Rouen, Paris, and Bayeux, and abbot of Fontenelle and Jumieges. He then used his family's money to benefit the churches, promoting both piety and learning.

10 Fulbert, bishop, was a poet and author of many hymns. An influential scholar for his day, he was regarded as another Socrates or Plato.

11 **Gemma Galgani,** plagued with physical pain and supernatural manifestations, underwent many extraordinary religious experiences, including the stigmata. She was canonized in 1940.

12 **Julius I,** the pope who succeeded Pope Mark, was involved with the controversy between the Catholics and the Arians. He was also responsible for building several basilicas and churches in Rome.

13 **Martin I,** unfairly tried for treason, was flogged, imprisoned, and then exiled. He was the last pope to die a martyr.

14 **Lambert of Lyons,** raised at the court of King Clotaire III, became a monk at Fontenelles and then the abbot. He founded the abbey of Donzère and then became archbishop of Lyons.

15 **Anastasia** and **Basilissa,** disciples of St. Peter and St. Paul, are said to have buried the bodies of two executed saints. Both women lost their lives for doing so.

16 **Bernadette,** baptized Marie Bernarde, had eighteen visions of the Virgin Mary beside the River Gave in Lourdes. As a result, a chapel, which is now the most-visited pilgrimage site in modern Europe, was built there. She is the patron of shepherds.

17 **Kateri Tekákwitha,** known as "the Lily of the Mohawks," was the first Native American proposed for sainthood. She is Blessed.

18 **Laserian, Laisren,** or **Molaisse,** named bishop and papal legate for Ireland by Pope Honorius I, was sent to Rome to settle the dispute between Roman liturgical usages and the Celtic practices. He decreed in favor of the Roman practices.

19 **Leo IX,** born Bruno, was quite a military man, both before he became a man of the cloth and while he was pope. He was responsible for proposing that popes be elected only by cardinals, a procedure still in effect to this day.

20 **Marcian** or **Marian** is famed for his great rapport with wild and domestic animals.

21 **Anselm,** archbishop of Canterbury and Doctor of the Church, was known for his patience and gentleness. He

was a superior theologian, called "the Father of Scholasticism."

22 **Alexander of Lyons** was persecuted by Marcus Aurelius; he was crucified when he stood fast by his faith.

23 **George the Great,** according to legend, slew the dragon and saved the princess. It's no wonder he's the patron of the Boy Scouts, as well as of England, Istanbul, Aragon, Portugal, Germany, Genoa, and Venice. He can be called on to defend against syphilis, leprosy, and the plague. His feast day is kept as a holy day of obligation.

24 **Fidelis of Sigmaringen,** born Mark Rey, championed the rights of the poor, earning him the nickname "the Poor Man's Lawyer."

25 **Mark,** evangelist, wrote the Second Gospel. He is patron of secretaries, notaries, Venice, and Egypt.

26 **Stephen of Perm,** a Russian bishop, translated the Liturgy and part of the Bible into a language for which he had invented the alphabet. He was a missionary as well as a champion of the downtrodden.

27 **Zita,** who often visited the sick, the poor, and prisoners, is the patron of housewives and servants.

28 **Louis Mary of Montfort,** in addition to being a hospital chaplain in Poitiers, was named missionary apostolic by Pope Clement XI. Through his emotional sermons and his writing of "The True Devotion to the Blessed Virgin," he fostered devotion to Mary and to the rosary.

29 **Catherine of Siena,** Doctor of the Church, was the youngest of twenty-five children and an extremely effective arbitrator who could end feuds. Referred to as "La beata popolaria," meaning "the blessed popular one," she experienced the stigmata and is the patron of Italy, Italian nurses, and fire prevention.

30 **James,** deacon, and **Marian,** lector, were imprisoned and tortured, along with hundreds of others, during Emperor Valerian's persecution of the Christians.

May

1 **Amator** or **Amatre** is thought to be the bishop who ordained St. Patrick.

2 **Athanasius,** bishop and Doctor of the Church, has been

named in history as "the Father of Orthodoxy," "Pillar of the Church," and "Champion of Christ's Divinity."

3   **James the Less,** a first cousin of Jesus and the first bishop of Jerusalem, was surnamed "the Just" for the great esteem in which he was held. He is the patron of the dying (because he forgave his murderers on his deathbed).

4   **Florian** surrendered during Diocletian's persecution of Christians and was tortured and thrown into the River Enns with a rock tied around his neck. He is the patron of Austria and Poland, and of those in danger from water, floods, and drowning.

5   **Angelo** is said to be the son of Jews from Jerusalem who converted to Christianity after a vision of the Virgin Mary. In Sicily, he successfully converted many Jews to Christianity, and it was there he suffered martyrdom.

6   **Edbert or Eadbert,** bishop, was a biblical scholar known for his generosity to the poor.

7   **Serenus** or **Senericus** was a renowned miracle worker credited with ending a plague and a horrendous drought through the power of prayer. Those nearby remarked that they heard celestial music while St. Serenus was on his deathbed.

8   **Victor Maurus** converted to Christianity at an early age and served as a Christian officer in the Roman army. Later on he was arrested under Emperor Maximilian and tortured to death. He is one of the patrons of Milan.

9   **Gregory Nazianzen,** a Doctor of the Church and archbishop of Constantinople, is often referred to as "the Theologian" for his eloquent sermons and masterful defense of the orthodoxy.

10 **Solangia,** sometimes called **St. Genevieve,** is the patron of the province of Berry in France. She had a way with animals and a great gift of healing. During her prayers and meditation a star was said to shine over her head.

11 **Walter of L'Esterp,** abbot, was noted for his ability to convert sinners and perform miracles.

12 **Dominic of the Causeway** was so named because he built a road, bridge, and hospice in the dangerous wilderness through which pilgrims had to pass to get to the shrine of St. James.

13 **Andrew Hubert Fournet** went from a frivolous life-style to a meaningful and pious one. It is said that prayers to St. Andrew bring an abundance of food to needy nuns and those under their care.

14 **Matthias,** apostle, was chosen by Christ to take the place of the traitor Judas Iscariot.

15 **Dympna** or **Dymphna** is the patron of the mentally ill and of nurses. She protects against possession by the Devil and sleepwalking (which was thought, in the Middle Ages, to be a form of possession).

16 **Brendan,** one of the most popular Irish saints, wrote the epic saga "Navigatio Sancti Brendani Abbatis," meaning "Abbot Brendan, Holy Navigator," about his seven-year journey to the promised land. Because of his many missionary voyages he is the patron of sailors.

17 **Paschal Baylon,** originally a poor shepherd, is the patron of shepherds, the Eucharist, and Italian women.

18 **Eric IX of Sweden** did a lot to establish Christianity as king of Sweden and was considered the principal patron of Sweden until the Protestant Reformation.

19 **Dunstan,** archbishop of Canterbury, is said to have been an excellent painter, embroiderer, harpist, and metal-worker. He is the patron of locksmiths, goldsmiths, and jewelers.

20 **Basilla** or **Basilissa** was promised in childhood to Pompeius, a Roman patrician. But when she converted to Christianity, she consecrated herself to the Lord and reneged on her commitment to marry. Emperor Gallienus gave her a choice of marriage or death by the sword; the virgin martyr was beheaded.

21 **Godric** was taught songs during visions of Virgin Mary; they remain today as the oldest surviving pieces of English verse with rhyme and meter. He also foresaw—and then prayed for—ships in danger of shipwreck.

22 **Rita of Cascia,** married at twelve to an abusive man, is the patron of those in desperate situations, of parenthood, and against infertility. In Spain she is the patron of matrimonial difficulties.

23 **Ivo of Chartres,** bishop, taught Scripture, theology, and canon law. He wrote abundantly, and many of his letters and sermons still survive.

24   David I of Scotland, son of King Malcolm Canmore and St. Margaret, succeeded his brother as king of Scotland. During his reign he founded many monasteries, established Norman law, and was known for his justice, charities, and religious devotion.

25   Madeleine Sophie Barat was one of the first members of the Society of the Sacred Heart of Jesus—the female counterpart of the Jesuits. Even though, at twenty-three, she was the youngest member of the group, she was named superior of the convent and school, and held that post for sixty-three years. By the time of her death, she had opened more than one hundred houses and schools in twelve countries.

26   Philip Neri was said to be a witty but gentle man who loved practical jokes. His ability to read consciences eased his conversion of many people. He is the patron of Rome and is called "the Second Apostle of Rome."

27   Austin or **Augustine of Canterbury,** the first archbishop of Canterbury, was a man of great patience. He was also known as "the Apostle of England."

28   Germain or **Germanus** was named bishop of Paris by King Childebert I, whom he miraculously cured of a fatal illness.

29   Raymund, along with eleven other members of Pope Gregory IX's Order of Preachers, was preaching the faith in Toulouse when they were driven out by the Albigensians. In good faith, they accepted an offer of lodging in a local castle, but during the night were massacred by soldiers.

30   Joan of Arc, also known as "the Maid of Orleans," was a young girl who heard the voices of Sts. Michael, Catherine, and Margaret encouraging her to help the king of France regain his kingdom. As a military leader she was captured, imprisoned, and trapped into making damaging statements. Condemned to death, she was burned at the stake. Thirty years later she was exonerated. She is the patron of France and French soldiers.

31   Angela Merici, a tertiary of St. Francis at thirteen years of age, established the first teaching order of women in the Church. She was possibly one of the first to grasp the changed role of women in a society transformed by the Renaissance.

June

1 **Justin Martyr** or **Justin the Philosopher,** the first great Christian philosopher, was beheaded when he refused to sacrifice to the pagan gods. He is the patron of philosophers and apologists.

2 **Elmo,** also known as **Erasmus,** is the patron of sailors. The bluish electrical charges seen around a ship's mast before or after a storm are thought to be a sign of his protection and are called St. Elmo's Fire. Because of his martyrdom (in which his intestines were drawn out), he is called upon for help with the pain of cramps, childbirth, and colic in children.

3 **Kevin,** also known in Ireland as **Coemgen** or **Caoimhghin,** had many sensational miracles attributed to him, such as feeding his community with the salmon brought to him by an otter. He is the patron of Dublin.

4 **Francis Caracciolo,** at age twenty-two, had a severe skin disease that was thought incurable. He vowed that if he recovered, he would devote his life to God and to serving others. He did recover and thereafter spent a life doing God's wishes.

5 **Dorotheus of Tyre,** scholar, author, priest, and bishop, was beaten to death when he was 107 for defending his faith against the persecution of Julian the Apostate.

6 **Norbert** was, at thirty-three, a handsome young man living a worldly life, when he was struck by lightning. While he was unconscious, a voice supposedly told him to reform his life. He did so and soon thereafter was ordained.

7 **Robert of Newminster,** abbot, is credited for his supernatural gifts, visions, and encounters with demons. It is said that his soul ascended to Heaven like a ball of fire.

8 **Medard**, bishop, is called upon to help cure toothaches and is the patron of corn and grape harvesting. It is said that if it rains on his feast day, the next forty days will be wet; if it's fair weather, the next forty days will also be good.

9 **Colum, Columba,** or **Colm** was later called **Columcille**, which seems to refer to the numerous *cells* or religious foundations he established. He is a patron of Ireland.

10   Landry or **Landericus of Paris,** bishop, was known for his kindness to the poor. During a famine, it is said, he sold church vessels and furniture to provide the poor with food. He erected his city's first real hospital.

11   Barnabas, born Joseph, was given the name Barnabas, meaning "man of encouragement" or "son of consolation," by the apostles. He is considered an apostle by the Church, although he is not one of the Twelve. He is the patron of Cyprus.

12   Ternan worked as a missionary among the Picts and founded the abbey of Culross, in Scotland.

13   Anthony of Padua, Doctor of the Church, is the patron of barren women, Flemish men, harvests, and Padua. He is called upon to help find lost articles. One of the greatest preachers of all time, Anthony was also called "the Living Ark of the Covenant" because of his marvelous memory for Scripture.

14   Rufinus and **Valerius** are thought to be part of a group of missionaries sent from Rome to evangelize Gaul. They were eventually tortured and beheaded for their faith.

15   Alice or **Aleydis** asked, at the tender age of seven, to live with the nuns in a convent. While still young, she contracted leprosy and had to be isolated. Although she suffered greatly, she also experienced visions and ecstasies and is credited with several miracles.

16   Guy or **Guido Vignotelli of Cortona** was known for his holiness and his miracles, which included resuscitating a little girl who had drowned.

17   Harvey or **Hervé** is a very popular saint in Brittany, and his name is very common for Breton boys. He was known for his exorcisms and is called upon for help with eye problems.

18   Gregory Barbarigo, bishop and cardinal, was compassionate and kind, although demanding when it came to himself. He worked to reconcile the Churches of the East and West.

19   Juliana Falconieri became a Servite tertiary when she was sixteen. Eventually, she headed and drew up a rule for a group of women dedicated to prayer and charity. The rule was approved 120 years later, and St. Juliana is now considered the founder of the Servite nuns.

20 **Silverius,** pope, incurred the wrath of Empress Theodora and the Byzantines when he stood steadfast by his principles; his stance eventually cost him his life.

21 **Aloysius Gonzaga** is the patron of Catholic youth and the protector of Jesuit college students.

22 **Thomas More,** a brilliant scholar, lawyer, and writer, was in favor of the education of women. He disagreed with Henry VIII's efforts to divorce Catherine of Aragon and later proclaimed, "I am the King's good servant but God's first." Eventually he was beheaded and his head exhibited on London Bridge. He is the patron of lawyers.

23 **Audrey** or **Etheldreda,** abbess, was married twice—for a total of fifteen years—but remained chaste, claiming she had consecrated herself to God.

24 **John the Baptist** is so called because he baptized many Jews. He was beheaded (without trial) and his head handed on a silver platter to Salome, simply because she requested it. He is the patron of monks because of his spartan and solitary life-style. His feast day is celebrated on his birthday, rather than on the day of his death, because he was born free of original sin.

25 **Adalbert of Egmond** successfully converted many nonbelievers because of his holiness, patience, and gentleness.

26 **Anthelm** or **Anthelmus,** bishop, set out to reform the noncelibate clergy and cared for lepers. Upon his death, a miracle occurred; when he was being lowered into his tomb, a lamp used only for important festivals lit spontaneously.

27 **Cyril of Alexandria,** bishop and "the Doctor of the Incarnation," is considered the most brilliant theologian of Alexandrian tradition.

28 **Irenaeus of Lyons,** bishop, was the first great ecclesiastical writer of the West. His writings stress the unity of the Gospels and the importance of both the Old and the New Testaments.

29 **Paul,** born Saul, originally persecuted Christians. But

when Jesus appeared to him, he converted and became one of the apostles. He is the patron of the lay apostolate, Catholic Action, Malta, and Greece.

30 Bertrand, bishop, founded a monastery, a hospice, and a church and was known for his interest in grape-growing, the development of land, and other forms of agriculture.

July

1 Oliver Plunket was the last Catholic to suffer martyrdom at Tyburn, a place of public execution in England. In 1975, he became the first Irish saint to be canonized since 1226.

2 Otto served as the mediator between Henry V and the pope. His most noted accomplishment was leading a group of missionaries to eastern Pomerania, to convert and baptize over twenty thousand people.

3 Aaron and **Julius** were two Britons executed for keeping the faith during Diocletian's persecution of Christians.

4 Elizabeth of Portugal, queen, was known in Portugal as **Isabella,** the Spanish version of the name. Because of her skills as an arbitrator, she prevented wars and was thus known as "the Peacemaker."

5 Antony Mary Zaccaria founded a congregation whose goal was to resurrect spirituality in the Church.

6 Maria Goretti, a twelve-year-old martyr, forgave her eighteen-year-old murderer right before her death. She is the patron of teenagers—especially girls—and the Children of Mary.

7 Felix of Nantes, bishop, was known for helping the poor and for building the cathedral at Nantes.

8 Sunniva, according to Norse legend, was the daughter of an Irish king. She fled to a cave on an island off Norway to escape her marriage. When she and her companions were entombed by a landslide, it is said that only her body remained intact and uncorrupt.

9 Veronica Giuliana, born Ursula, changed her name when she became a Capuchin nun in Umbria. She experienced visions of Christ as well as the stigmata.

10 Rufina and **Secunda,** daughters of a Roman senator, were each engaged to be married. During Emperor Valerian's persecution of Christians, their fiancés abandoned the faith. The sisters refused to do the same and fled from Rome but were captured, tortured, and beheaded for their Christianity.

11 **Benedict** is the patron of Europe, monks, farm workers, Italian speleologists (cave specialists), engineers, and architects. He is called upon for help against poison and death.

12 **Jason** welcomed St. Paul into his home on his second missionary journey. Greek legend says Jason was the bishop of Tarsus who evangelized Corfu, while Syrian legend says he evangelized the area around Apamea and was martyred there by being thrown to wild beasts.

13 **Mildred of Thanet,** abbess, was one of the most popular saints in medieval England. She was noted for her piety and for aiding the poor and the afflicted. Her sisters and her brother were also saints.

14 **Camillus de Lellis** contracted a painful disease in his leg. His horrible hospital experiences led him to revolutionize nursing and patient care.

15 **Donald,** on the death of his wife, formed a religious group with his nine daughters. Many hills, wells, and other natural features of Scotland are named Nine Maidens, in memory of St. Donald's daughters.

16 **Mary Magdalen Postel,** baptized Julia Frances Catherine, opened a school for girls when she was eighteen. When the school was closed during the French revolution, she and three other teachers founded the Sisters of the Christian Schools of Mercy. She was named superior, and it was then that she took the name Mary Magdalen.

17 **Alexis,** the son of a wealthy Roman senator, led a life of extreme poverty and virtue, and was known for a long time as "the Man of God."

18 **Frederick of Utrecht,** bishop, was noted for his holiness and sacred learning. When he helped mediate the emperor's family matters, he alienated Empress Judith. He was stabbed to death by assassins who, many speculated, were hired by the empress.

19 **Arsenius the Great** is said to have cried so much for his

shortcomings and those of others that he wore away his eyelashes.

20   **Margaret** or **Marina,** said to be one of the "voices" that Joan of Arc heard, is the patron of pregnant women, childbirth, and death. She is one of the most popular virgin martyr saints of the Middle Ages.

21   **Angelina of Marsciano,** Blessed, was married at fifteen, widowed at seventeen, and became a Franciscan tertiary. Accused of sorcery for preaching about celibacy to young women, she was exiled from her community. In Assisi, she founded an enclosed monastery. It was so successful that she established fifteen more in her lifetime.

22   **Philip Evans,** a Jesuit, was ministering to the Catholics of south Wales when he was arrested. When no evidence could be produced linking him or fellow prisoner John Lloyd with the Titus Oates plot, both were convicted of being priests illegally in England and executed. St. Philip was canonized in 1970 by Pope Paul VI.

23   **Susanna** or **Anne** fled to Leucadia, where she lived as a hermit, to escape the persecution of a rejected suitor. Since Leucadia is also known as Maura, this saint is also known as St. **Maura.**

24   **Boris** and **Gleb,** also known as **Romanus** and **David,** were the sons of the first Christian prince in Russia and were honored for being "passion bearers": blameless men who did not wish to die but who had refused to defend themselves. In this sense they had submitted to death just like Christ. St. Boris is the patron of Moscow.

25   **James the Greater,** the first martyr among the apostles, was beheaded by King Herod. He is the patron of pilgrims, Spain, Guatemala, and Nicaragua.

26   **Anne** or **Hannah** and her husband, **Joachim,** were childless. When an angel told Anne that she would have a child, Anne promised that the child would serve God for all its life. Her child was Mary, the mother of Jesus. St. Anne is patron of housewives, childless women, cabinetmakers, and miners.

27   **Natalia,** a convert, attended the churches of Cordova with her face unveiled, thus giving away her identity. She and husband **Aurelius** were beheaded.

28 **Samson,** after recovering from an attempt on his life by two nephews jealous of his ordination, lived as a hermit. Then he became a bishop, an abbot, a missionary, and the founder of many monasteries and churches.

29 **Martha,** the sister of Mary Magdalene, is the patron of housewives, servants, waiters, and cooks.

30 **Julitta of Caesarea,** a wealthy widow in the time of Emperor Diocletian, fell victim to his edicts against Christians. Unprotected by the law, she had to go to court to defend her estates from a neighbor's claims. When she would not offer sacrifice to the pagan gods, she was put to death and her estates given to her opponent.

31 **Justin de Jacobis,** bishop, overcame persecution, imprisonment, and extreme hardships. He managed to convert over twelve thousand Africans.

August

1 **Faith,** age twelve, **Hope,** ten, and **Charity,** nine, were the daughters of Divine Wisdom (known in the Roman Martyrology as Sophia). During Hadrian's persecution of Christians, the girls were beheaded. Three days later their mother died while praying at their graves.

2 **Alphonsus Mary Liquori,** bishop and Doctor of the Church, is the patron of confessors and moral theologians.

3 **Peter Julian Eymard** established the Servants of the Blessed Sacrament, founded the Priests' Eucharistic League, organized the Confraternity of the Blessed Sacrament, and wrote many books on the Eucharist. He was canonized by Pope John XXIII in 1962.

4 **Molua** or **Lughaidh,** a cowherd who became a monk, founded many monasteries. It is said that he never killed any living thing and that when he died, the birds wept.

5 **Nonna** converted her husband, Gregory Nazianzen (the Elder), to Christianity, and had three sons who became saints: St. Gregory Nazianzen the Divine, St. Caesarius, and St. Gorgonia.

6 **Justus,** age thirteen, and his brother **Pastor,** nine, were executed in Spain for proclaiming their faith as Christians. They are the patrons of Alcala and Madrid.

7 **Gaetano** or **Cajetan** helped institute pawnshops, which gave loans to the poor. He is thought of as one of the great Catholic reformers.

8 **Dominic,** the first domestic theologian for the pope, laid the foundation for the Dominican order.

9 **Romanus,** a Roman soldier, was baptized in prison by St. Laurence. When Romanus announced his conversion, he was beheaded.

10 **Laurence of Rome,** who met a fiery death, is the patron of cooks.

11 **Blane** or **Blaan,** bishop, is credited with several miracles, including striking fire from his fingernails to rekindle the church lights that had gone out.

12 **Clare of Assisi** helped found and lead the Poor Clares, the most austere of any female order. She is the patron of embroiderers and patron against sore eyes, and was made the patron of television in 1958 by Pope Pius XII.

13 **Cassian of Imola,** a teacher, refused to sacrifice to pagan gods during the persecution of the Catholics. His students were ordered to bring his life to an end—which they did.

14 **Maximilian Mary Kolbe,** baptized Raymond, harbored over fifteen hundred Jews and three thousand Polish refugees during the German occupation of Poland. After his arrest he voluntarily took the place of another man who was condemned to death in Auschwitz.

15 **Hyacinth,** born in Poland, joined the Dominicans in Rome and preached in Scandinavia, Prussia, and Lithuania. He is credited with many miracles and is revered as an apostle of Poland.

16 **Stephen of Hungary,** born Vaik, worked as the king of Hungary to establish sees and prohibit pagan customs in his land. He is the patron of Hungary.

17 **Joan Delanoue,** Blessed, received messages from God through a widow. They inspired her to turn to a religious, austere life of helping others and performing miracle healings.

18 **Helena** was kind to the poor, to soldiers, and to prisoners. St. Helena, an island in the Atlantic, was named after her because Spanish sailors had discovered it on her feast day.

19 **Louis of Anjou,** the son of the imprisoned King Charles II of Naples and Sicily, was traded for his father's release and only freed after seven years. When he refused to marry the sister of King James II, he gave up all rights to the throne. He chose to be ordained instead and thereafter lived a life of great austerity.

20 **Bernard of Clairvaux,** abbot and Doctor of the Church, was an eloquent and witty speaker, known as "the Honeysweet Doctor." He is considered one of the founders of the Cistercian Order, and his writings influenced medieval mysticism. He is the patron of Gibraltar.

21 **Abraham of Smolensk,** a biblical scholar and charismatic preacher, cared for the sick and the poor, but his preaching and his popularity offended the authorities. He was charged with heresy and deprived of his priestly duties. After five years he was completely exonerated and reinstated.

22 **Andrew of Fiesole** founded a monastery, rebuilt a church, and was known for his holiness.

23 **Owen,** whose name is the English translation of **Eoghan,** was kidnaped along with two other boys and sold into slavery in Britain. Legend has it that one day the slave master found the boys reading while angels ground their corn for them. The boys were released and returned to Ireland.

24 **Bartholomew,** apostle, is the patron of tanners, bookbinders, and plasterers.

25 **Patricia** fled from Constantinople to escape marriage and, while in Rome, took vows to consecrate her virginity to God. She is the patron of Naples.

26 **Teresa of Jesus Jornet E Ibars,** founder of the Little Sisters of the Aged Poor, is the patron of the elderly.

27 **Monica** prayed for the conversion of her dissolute son, Augustine, for nine years; finally he was converted, and eventually he became a saint. A model for Christian mothers because of her concern for her son, she is the patron of married women and mothers.

28 **Austin** or **Augustine of Hippo** was St. Monica's son. Called "the Doctor of Grace," he was known as one of the greatest intellects of the Catholic Church. He is the patron of theologians.

29 Sabina was converted to Christianity by Serapia, her Syrian servant. During Emperor Hadrian's persecution of Christians, Serapia suffered martyrdom for her faith; a month later, Sabina did, too.

30 Rose of Lima, baptized Isabel, was said to rub her face with pepper to disguise her beauty. It is thought that her prayers saved Lima from an earthquake. Known as "the Flower of Lima," she is the patron of florists and gardeners. She is also the patron of Peru, Central and South America, the Philippines, and India.

31 Aidan or **Aedan of Lindisfarne,** bishop, was a learned man, an eloquent preacher, and a miracle worker who was kind to the poor.

September

1 Giles or **Aegidius,** abbot, is one of the Fourteen Holy Helpers. His shrine attracted a great number of medieval pilgrimages. He is the patron of beggars, the lame, and blacksmiths.

2 Castor founded the Mananque monastery near Apt in Provence, France, and became its first abbot. He then became the bishop of Apt.

3 Gregory the Great, the last of the traditional Latin Doctors of the Church, nicknamed himself "Servant of the Servants of God." This pope made magnificent contributions to the Liturgy. He is the patron of music and is called upon for protection against the plague.

4 Ida of Herzfeld, granddaughter of Charlemagne, is said to have put food for the poor in a stone coffin made for her; she did this to remind herself, on a daily basis, of her own mortality and her responsibility to others.

5 Bertinus was a missionary who, with St. Mommolin and St. Bertrand, founded a monastery in Sithiu, France. They evangelized whole areas that were totally downtrodden.

6 Eve is the patron of Dreux, France, where she is honored as a martyr.

7 Regina or **Reine,** whose pagan mother died at her birth, was raised by her nurse as a Christian. Upon discovering this, her father disowned her. She lived as a shepherdess until a disgruntled suitor persecuted her to death.

8 **Adrian of Nicomedia** was condemned to die for his faith by burning, but a violent storm put out the flames. He was then beheaded. He is called upon for help against the plague and is the patron of prison guards and butchers.

9 **Isaac the Great,** bishop, was responsible for the launching of Armenian literature and is considered the founder of the Armenian Church.

10 **Ambrose Barlow,** bishop and Doctor of the Church, stressed the importance of the independence of church and state and was extremely influential in bringing St. Augustine back to the faith. He is the patron of bee-keepers and bishops.

11 **Theodora of Alexandria** reportedly left her husband to do penance for her sins and went to live, disguised as a man, as a monk in a monastery. Until her death no one knew she was a woman.

12 **Guy of Anderlecht,** born of poor parents, devoted his life to helping the poor, and invested what little he had in a business venture to earn more money to give to the poor. When he lost everything, he made a pilgrimage on foot to Rome, then to Jerusalem. After his death, miracles were reported at the grave of "the Poor Man of Anderlecht," as he was called.

13 **Amatus,** also known as **Amé,** was a Benedictine monk who converted Romaric, a nobleman who then founded a double monastery at Habendum. Amatus was its first abbot.

14 **Cormac,** King of Munster and the first bishop of Cashel in Ireland, was responsible for the creation of the book of psalms called the Cashel Psalter.

15 **Catherine of Genoa,** originally called **Caterinetta,** received communion daily for the rest of her life after she repented her sins. She wrote many impressive documents in the field of mysticism.

16 **Cyprian,** also known as **Thascius,** was a bishop, a pioneer of Latin Christian literature, and the patron of North Africa and Algeria.

17 **Robert Francis Romulus Bellarmine,** bishop, cardinal, and Doctor of the Church, is the patron of seminarians.

18 Joseph of Cupertino experienced ecstasies and was known for his supernatural abilities, especially his power of levitation, which earned him the nickname of "the Flying Friar." He is the patron of students, aviators, and astronauts.

19 Januarius, bishop, became most famous after his martyrdom; a solid red substance—supposedly his blood—that is still stored in a vial in the Naples cathedral suddenly liquefies and bubbles up several times a year—including on his feast day. He is the patron of Naples.

20 Andrew Kim Taegon was the first Korean priest and pastor to give up his life for his faith.

21 Maura of Troyes dedicated her life to prayer, fasting, and helping the poor. She was noted for her piety and the miracles credited to her intercession.

22 Thomas of Villanova, bishop, was called "the Almsgiver" because of all that he gave the poor. He was said to have the power not only to multiply food, but to heal. He is the patron of Valencia.

23 Adamnan or **Eunan,** abbot, was responsible for the principle that neither women nor children should be taken prisoner or slaughtered during times of war. This philosophy was thereafter called Adamnan's Law. He also wrote about the life of St. Columba. One of the most outstanding hagiographical documents in existence, it's also the most complete and important biography from the early Middle Ages.

24 Mercedes, from *merces*, meaning "mercy," is a name in honor of the Blessed Virgin Mary and her title "Our Lady of Mercy."

25 Barry, Bairre, or **Finbar,** bishop, was baptized Lochan, but the Irish monks called him Fionnbharr—or "white head"—because of his blond hair. He is the patron of Cork, Barra, and the Outer Hebrides.

26 Damian and **Cosmas** were brothers who practiced medicine without ever charging for their services. They are the patrons of doctors, surgeons, chemists, pharmacists, barbers, and the blind.

27 Vincent de Paul was one of the greats of the French

Church. He is the patron of charitable organizations,
Madagascar, hospitals, and prisoners.

28 **Wenceslaus** became king of Bohemia at age eighteen,
and in that capacity he ended his country's persecution
of Christians. He is patron of Bohemia.

29 **Michael, Gabriel,** and **Raphael** are three of the seven
archangels said to stand closest to God; all three share
the same feast day.

Michael, the chief of the archangels, is the patron of
battle, policemen, paratroops, Brussels, banking, radiolo-
gists, death, cemeteries, England, Germany, Papua New
Guinea, the Solomon Islands, the sick, and those pos-
sessed by the Devil.

Gabriel, as a deliverer of messages, is the patron of
telecommunications, television, radio, postal services,
and philatelists. And, because he was thought of as
"God's ambassador," he is patron of Argentinian
ambassadors and of Spain's and Argentina's diplomatic
services.

Raphael is the patron of travelers, safe journeys, young
people leaving home, pharmacists, health inspectors,
and the blind, and patron against eye diseases.

30 **Jerome,** Doctor of the Church, spent thirty years
preparing the Latin Vulgate translation of the Bible; it is
still in use today. He is patron of students and librarians.

October

1 **Teresa of the Child Jesus of Lisieux** was baptized
Marie-Françoise-Thérèse. She wrote *The Story of a
Soul*, one of the most popular modern spiritual autobi-
ographies. Nicknamed "the Little Flower," she is the
patron of florists and flower growers, foreign missions,
Russia, and France.

2 **Leger** or **Leodegarius,** bishop, was an effective mediator and reformer and was concerned for the poor.

3 **Gerard of Brogne,** abbot, renounced his military life
for a religious life and spent twenty years reforming the
abbeys in Flanders, Lorraine, and Champagne.

4 **Francis of Assisi,** baptized John, abandoned his affluent
lifestyle to embrace extreme poverty. He holds claim to
the first certain recorded incidence of stigmata, and

started the Franciscan movement. He is the patron of Italy, Italian merchants, and ecology.

5   **Flora of Beaulieu** was noted for her many mystical experiences, including levitation, prophecies, and visions.

6   **Bruno** chose the life of a hermit and began the Carthusian Order, referred to as "the angels of the earth." Due to the Carthusians' aversion to publicity, Bruno was never canonized, but Pope Leo X gave permission to keep his feast.

7   **Rosaria,** from "rosary," is a name in honor of the Blessed Virgin Mary and her title "Our Lady of the Rosary."

8   **Demetrius,** a soldier martyred for his faith, is, along with St. George, patron of the Crusaders and Christian fighting men.

9   **Denis** is thought of as the first bishop of Paris. He is the patron of Paris and France and is called upon for help against headaches.

10 **Daniel** accompanied six Franciscan friars as their superior to Africa. Before they could accomplish their mission and evangelize the Mohammedans, they were arrested in Morocco. Since they refused to renounce their faith, they were beheaded.

11 **Kenneth** or **Canice,** abbot, converted numerous pagans in Ireland and Scotland and founded the church at Kilkenny, Ireland. He is the patron of Kilkenny.

12 **Wilfrid,** bishop, championed the replacing of Celtic practices with Roman ways in northern England.

13 **Edward the Confessor,** king of England for twenty-three years, was known for his goodness and fairness and for solving problems with wisdom rather than warfare.

14 **Angadrisma** was promised in marriage but wanted to become a nun. She asked God to make her physically repulsive, so that her fiancé would no longer want her. Her wish was fulfilled when she got leprosy. Once she became a nun, her leprosy disappeared, and she became known for her holiness and beauty.

15 **Teresa of Avila** was the first female Doctor of the

Church. She is the patron of headache sufferers, Spanish
Catholic writers, and the Spanish army.

16 **Gerard Majella** earned his reputation as "the most
famous wonder-worker of the eighteenth century"; he
was supposedly able to read minds, exert power over
inanimate objects, and be in two places at one time. He
is the patron of expectant mothers and childbirth.

17 **Richard Gwyn,** born in Wales, was raised Protestant
and converted to Catholicism. When his presence at
Anglican services was missed, he was arrested, tortured,
and convicted on trumped-up charges of treason. He
was hanged, drawn, and quartered. He was canonized
by Pope Paul VI in 1970 and is the protomartyr of
Wales.

18 **Luke,** evangelist, is the patron of doctors, artists, sculp-
tors, painters, lacemakers, notaries (as a result of his
account of Christ's life), and butchers.

19 **Paul of the Cross,** one of the most esteemed preachers
of his time, brought faith back to the biggest of sinners
and the most hardened of criminals. He is said to have
had the gifts of prophecy and healing.

20 **Bertilla Boscardin,** christened Anne Frances, was
given the unkind nickname "Goose." When she was
accepted by the Sisters of St. Dorothy at Vicenza, she
said, "I'm a poor thing, a goose. Teach me. I want to
become a saint." She worked hard by caring for the sick,
and eventually reached her goal.

21 **Ursula,** believed to have been martyred at Cologne, is
the patron of schoolteachers.

22 **Donatus,** legend has it, was on his way from Rome to
Ireland when he stopped off at Fiesole. As he entered the
town's cathedral—where its congregants had gathered
to elect a new bishop—the church bells rang and the
candles spontaneously ignited. Donatus was immedi-
ately declared bishop.

23 **Romanus,** bishop, worked to root out idolatry and ministered to criminals sentenced to death.

24 **Mark** or **Martin,** as a hermit on Mount Marsicus in
Campagnia, is said to have performed many miracles.

25 **Daria** was a priestess of Minerva who married
Chrysanthus when she agreed to convert and have a

chaste marriage. The couple then converted many Romans, but when word of it reached the ears of Emperor Numerian, he ordered everyone's execution.

26 **Lucian** and **Marcian** practiced black magic but publicly burned their magic paraphernalia and converted to Christianity when they found their witchery had no effect on a Christian maiden.

27 **Abraham,** often called "the Poor" or "the Child," was a disciple of St. Pachomius. He chose the eremitic life and lived in a cave for seventeen years.

28 **Jude,** also called **Thaddeus** or **Lebbeus,** was an apostle and is the patron of those in hopeless situations.

29 **Narcissus,** a Greek who was a bishop in Jerusalem, wrought miracles and was said to have been 119 when he died.

30 **Alphonsus Rodriguez** went back to grade school in his forties, was then admitted to the Jesuits as a lay brother, and took his final vows at age fifty-four. He was consulted on many spiritual matters because of his wisdom.

31 **Quentin** or **Quintinus** was tortured and killed for his faith. He is called on for help against coughs.

November

1 **Marcellus,** as bishop of Paris, defended his city against barbarian attacks. He was noted for his holiness and miracles.

2 **Tobias,** a Christian soldier stationed in Armenia, was burned at the stake because he would not participate in a pagan sacrifice.

3 **Martin de Porres,** known as "the Father of Charity" by his Lima, Peru, community, nursed the sick, cared for animals, and founded both an orphanage and a foundling hospital. He is the patron of race relations; social justice; Peru's public education, TV, and health services; Spanish trade unionists; and people of mixed race.

4 **Charles Borromeo,** bishop and cardinal, was important in the Counter-Reformation and a great supporter of learning and the arts. He is the patron of seminarians.

5 **Elizabeth** and **Zachary,** also called **Zacharias,** had reached a childless middle age when an angelic vision

told Zachary that the couple would have a son, who should be named John. Zachary was skeptical and so lost his power of speech. At the baby's birth, Zachary regained his voice and named the baby John. Thus Zachary and Elizabeth became the parents of John the Baptist.

6 **Leonard of Noblac,** abbot, was a favorite saint of Western Europe in the late Middle Ages. He is patron of childbirth, prisoners, and those in danger from robbers and thieves.

7 **Ernest,** a Benedictine abbot of South Germany, participated in the Crusades, then stayed in Palestine to preach the Gospel. When he moved on through Arabia, he was put to death by the Moslems at Mecca.

8 **Godfrey,** bishop of Amiens, was unrelentingly strict, making him unpopular with the less diligent clergy.

9 **Benen** or **Benignus** became St. Patrick's disciple, companion, and confidant, and eventually succeeded him as chief bishop of Ireland.

10 **Leo I the Great,** pope and Doctor of the Church, created stability in a time of chaos and is historically known for convincing Attila the Hun not to attack Rome. His actions affected the concept of the papacy for centuries to come.

11 **Martin of Tours,** bishop, is the patron of soldiers, beggars, France, horses and their riders, and wine makers.

12 **Josaphat,** bishop, was born in Poland and was the first Eastern saint to be formally canonized (in 1867).

13 **Frances Xavier Cabrini,** born in Italy, founded the Missionary Sisters of the Sacred Heart. When she was thirty-nine, she went to New York to work with Italian immigrants. In less than three decades, her congregation spread across the U.S. and established more than fifty hospitals, schools, orphanages, and convents. She became an American citizen in 1909 and was the first U.S. citizen to be canonized (in 1946). She is the patron of emigrants and migrants.

14 **Laurence O'Toole,** archbishop of Dublin and a strict disciplinarian, was responsible for many clerical reforms.

15 **Albert the Great,** bishop and Doctor of the Church, is called "the Universal Doctor" and is ranked as one of the

first—and greatest—natural scientists. He is the patron of scientists.

16   **Gertrude of Helfta** experienced revelations and is one of the most outstanding of medieval mystics. She is the patron of the West Indies.

17   **Hilda,** as abbess of a double monastery in England, was noted for her great spiritual wisdom.

18   **Odo of Cluny** was known for his hymns, treatises on morality, and an epic poem on the Redemption.

19   **Elizabeth of Hungary,** daughter of the king of Hungary, founded a Franciscan convent and provided for helpless children. She is the patron of Catholic charities.

20   **Edmund the Martyr** became the king of East Anglia at the young age of fourteen. He ruled wisely for fifteen years, until the Danes invaded and beheaded him.

21   **Gelasius I** was a pope known for his holiness, justice, charity, and learning.

22   **Cecilia** or **Cecily** is the patron of music and musicians. Supposedly when the organ played she sang only to God.

23   **Clement I,** pope, is the patron of marble workers, lighthouses, and lightships.

24   **Flora,** whose father was a Mohammedan, was secretly raised Christian by her mother. She was then betrayed by her own brother.

25   **Catherine of Alexandria,** one of the "voices" heard by Joan of Arc and one of the Fourteen Holy Helpers, is the patron of philosophy, learning, students, young women, nurses, Christian apologists, librarians, and wheelwrights.

26   **Leonard Casonova of Port Maurice,** baptized Paul Jerome, set up nearly six hundred Stations of the Cross throughout Italy and is the patron of parish missions.

27   **Fergus,** an Irish bishop surnamed "the Pict," founded several churches in Scotland in honor of St. Patrick.

28   **Simeon Metaphrastes,** one of the most celebrated medieval Greek writers, recorded the legends and stories of the Byzantine saints for Emperor Constantine VII Porphyrogenitus. His feast day is observed by the Byzantine or Orthodox Church but is not recognized in Rome.

29 **Radbod,** bishop, wrote hymns and was known for helping the poor.

30 **Andrew,** apostle, was a fisherman and Christ's first disciple. He is the patron of fishermen, Scotland, Greece, and Russia.

December

1 **Florence** was a hermit who practiced much penance and fought against the temptations of the Devil.

2 **Viviana** or **Bibiana,** legend has it, suffered under Emperor Julian the Apostate and was a martyr.

3 **Francis Xavier,** called "the Apostle of the Indies and Japan," is credited with more than 700,000 conversions. He is the patron of foreign missions, India, Pakistan, and Outer Mongolia.

4 **Barbara** took secret instruction in Christianity and was baptized. Her conversion cost her her life at the hand— and ax—of her father. She is the patron of firemen, mathematicians, and carpenters.

5 **Cyran,** also known as **Sigiramnus,** broke his engagement to a nobleman's daughter to enter the religious life. When Cyran's father died, Cyran gave all his family's wealth to the poor. Authorities initially thought him insane and imprisoned him. When he was released, he made a pilgrimage to Rome, founded monasteries, and was known for helping criminals as well as the poor.

6 **Nicholas,** bishop, is one of the most popular saints of all time and the patron of children. The idea of "St. Nick" being representative of Santa Claus may have started when children were given gifts on St. Nick's feast day. He is also the patron of brides, unmarried women, bakers, pawnbrokers, perfumers, travelers, sailors, Russia, Greece, Sicily, Lorraine, Apulia, and of many cities, dioceses, and churches.

7 **Ambrose,** bishop and Doctor of the Church, is the patron of bishops, bees and their keepers, candlemakers, and domestic animals.

8 **Lilian, Lillian,** and **Lily** are names given in honor of the Blessed Virgin; her symbol is a white lily, for purity. This day is celebrated as the Immaculate Conception of the Blessed Virgin Mary.

9   **Peter Fourier** worked toward free education for the poor.

10 **Eulalia of Mérida** was burned at the stake; legend has it that a white dove flew out of her mouth as she died.

11 **Damasus I,** pope, poet, and biblical scholar, is the patron of archaeologists. In his lifetime he was the patron of St. Jerome who commissioned him to revise the Latin text of the Bible, resulting in the Vulgate version.

12 **Jane Frances Fremiot de Chantal,** under the spiritual tutelage of St. Francis de Sales, founded sixty-five convents. According to St. Vincent de Paul, she was "one of the holiest souls I have ever met."

13 **Lucy of Syracuse,** one of the most illustrious of the virgin martyrs, is the patron of sufferers of eye diseases, hemorrhages, and throat infections.

14 **John of the Cross,** Doctor of the Church and one of Spain's most celebrated poets, wrote masterpieces of Spanish literature and Catholic mysticism. He is the patron of mystics.

15 **Christiana** (so called in the Roman Martyrology) or **Nino** (so called by Georgians in Russia) performed miracles of healing, which she claimed were the work of Christ.

16 **Adelaide,** called "the Peacemaker of Europe," restored monasteries and strove to convert the Slavs.

17 **Olympias,** a deaconness of the Church, was extremely generous to the poor and gave shelter to expelled monks.

18 **Gatian** is thought to have been the first bishop of Tours.

19 **Urban V,** born William de Grimoard, was elected pope, succeeding Innocent VI. He is best known for working to move the papacy from Avignon to Rome, instituting more clerical discipline, and reviving religion.

20 **Dominic of Silos,** abbot, was known for his miraculous healings. It is believed that the invocation of his name helped rescue Christian slaves from the Moors.

21 **Peter Canisius,** Doctor of the Church and "the Second Apostle of Germany," is thought to have led the Catholic Counter-Reformation in southern Germany.

22 **Chaermon** was an Egyptian bishop who took to the

Arabian mountains to avoid persecution and was never seen again.

23   **Anatolia** and **Victoria** were responsible for many conversions and many miracles, respectively. Suitors whom they had rejected instigated their executions when the women refused to denounce their faith.

24   **Adela** or **Adele** and **Irmina,** daughters of the king of Germany, founded a convent in which they lived a holy and charitable life. Adele was a disciple of St. Boniface.

25   **Anastasia** is said to have ministered to persecuted Christians. She is the patron of weavers.

26   **Stephen the Deacon** was the first martyr and is the patron of stonemasons (as he was stoned to death) and deacons. He is called upon for help against headaches.

27   **John the Evangelist** was the only apostle present at the foot of Christ's cross and the only apostle not to suffer martyrdom. He is the patron of Asia Minor and of protection against poison.

28   **Theodore** and his brother Theophanes, tortured for opposing Emperor Theophilus's iconoclasm, had twelve lines of verse branded on their foreheads. After they were banished to Apamea, Theodore died.

29   **Thomas Becket** went from riches to rags when he was elected archbishop of Canterbury. After one of many major disagreements with the archbishop, King Henry II ordered the death of his longtime friend, and Thomas was murdered in his own church, at the foot of his altar.

30   **Anysia** used her inheritance to help the poor. She lost her life to a soldier while defending her faith.

31   **Melania the Younger** was one of the great religious philanthropists of all time, freeing over eight thousand slaves.

Names from Mythology

Myths are the creative imaginings of primitive people in a pre-scientific world. Their stories of how the world began, along with its early history and its evolvement, are studded with the deeds of heroes, knights, nymphs, magicians, maidens, muses, titans, warriors, royalty, gods, and goddesses.

Although we attempted to eliminate from the following list the names of those mythological characters—Phaedra, for example—who were responsible for extremely mean-spirited acts, some undoubtedly slipped by us. (In case you're wondering, Phaedra caused the death of her stepson Hippolytus by falsely accusing him of rape.)

And talk about Hippolytus ... We're not going to! We've also excluded complex names like his which would be "myth-pronounced" more often than not.

That leaves us with a variety of names, all possessing strength, beauty, and intrigue. The more we researched, the more we saw that no two mythographers agree on the details of the lives of these mythical characters. Therefore we decided that along with each name, we would give you only *one* very brief version of his or her identity.

Most of the names we've selected have their origins in Greek and Roman mythology simply because they are the ones most like our Anglicized names, and therefore the most usable.

We've adopted the spellings from familiar current usage, and, in some rare instances, we've included the pronunciation we think sounds best.

Without further ado or adon't, here is a compendium of these classical beauties.

FEMALE MYTHOLOGICAL NAMES

Anteia (An-tay´-uh)—Greek: Wife of the sea god Proteus, she tried to convince the Corinthian hero Bellerophon (who killed the fire-breathing Chimaera) to elope with her.

Ariadne—Greek: Daughter of Minos who gave Theseus the thread by which he escaped from the labyrinth. After being deserted by him on the island of Naxos, she married Dionysus, the god of fertility, wine, and drama.

Artemis—Greek: Goddess of the moon; virgin goddess of the hunt; twin sister of the sun god Apollo.

Astraea (As-tray´-uh)—Greek: Goddess of justice; daughter of Zeus and Themis, the Titaness. After witnessing too much of the world's wickedness, Astraea returned to heaven and became the constellation Virgo.

Athena—Greek: Goddess of wisdom, arts and crafts, fertility, and warfare.

Aurora—Roman: Goddess of the dawn.

Camilla—Roman: Loved and protected by Diana, the daughter of Metabus, king of the Volsci, was able to run through grain without trampling it beneath her and cross the sea without wetting her feet.

Cassandra—Greek: Daughter of Priam, king of Troy, twin sister of Helenus. She was endowed by Apollo with the gift of prophecy, but when she wouldn't return his love, he ensured that henceforth, nobody would believe her prophecies. She was sometimes called Alexandra. The Hellenistic poet Lycophron made her the star of his epic poem *Alexandra*.

Castalia (Kuh-stal´-yuh)—Greek: Wife of King Delphus (the hero who gave his name to Delphi); mother of Castalius, who ruled over Delphi after his father died.

Chloris—Greek: The only surviving daughter of Niobe and Amphion, a couple who had anywhere from two sons and three daughters to ten sons and ten daughters, depending on which mythographer you follow. When Niobe bragged about her brood to Leto, who had just one son and one daughter (they were, respectively, Apollo and Artemis),

Leto asked her children to get revenge. And so Apollo killed all but one of Niobe's sons, Artemis all but one of Niobe's daughters. The surviving daughter was pallid with terror and took the name Chloris, which means "green."

Clementia—Roman: Goddess of pity; depicted in statues with a goblet in one hand to refresh the weary and a lance in the other to defend the oppressed.

Clio—Greek: The muse of history.

Cybele—An Asiatic goddess who found acceptance in both Greece and Rome. She took responsibility for every phase of her worshipers' well-being, including extending to them a promise of immortality. Cybele was often identified by the Greek mythographers with Rhea.

Daphne—Greek: A nymph who, when pursued by an amorous Apollo, was saved by being changed into a laurel tree.

Diana—Roman name for Artemis.

Dione (Die-oh´-knee)—Greek: Titan goddess; believed to be the mother of Aphrodite.

Doris—Greek: Daughter of Oceanus and Tethys; sea goddess who married Nereus and then had fifty sea nymphs called the Nereids.

Echo—Greek: A nymph of the trees and springs whose love for Narcissus was unrequited. She faded away until all that remained was her voice . . . her voice . . . her voice. . . .

Elissa—Greek: As Dido she was the queen of Carthage. When she lived in Tyre, she was called Elissa. She killed herself when abandoned by Aeneas, hero of Virgil's *Aeneid*.

Eris—Greek: Goddess of discord.

Evadne—Greek: Daughter of Poseidon and Pitane, she was raised by Aepytus, ruler of Arcadia. She was loved by Apollo and they had a son.

Feronia—Roman: A goddess of springs and woods, she is said to be the mother of Erylus, a hero who had three bodies and three separate lives.

Flora—Roman: Goddess of flowers.

Freya (Fray´-ha)—Norse: Daughter of Njord, god of fertility; goddess of love, beauty, and reproduction, she is the second most important Norse goddess. (The first is Frigg, mother of the gods.)

Galatea (Gal´-uh-tee´-uh)—Greek: An ivory statue of a beautiful maiden that Aphrodite brought to life to answer the fervent prayers of its sculptur, Pygmalion, who had fallen in love with his creation.

Harmonia—Greek: Some say she was the daughter of Ares and Aphrodite, while others claim her parents were Zeus and Electra. All seem to agree, however, that she was the wife of the Phoenician prince Cadmus, who founded Thebes.

Helen (of Troy)—Greek: Daughter of Zeus and Leda; the incredibly beautiful wife of the Spartan king, Menelaus. Her abduction by Paris is said to have been the cause of the Trojan War.

Hera—Greek: Queen of Olympus; goddess of marriage and childbirth. She is both the sister and wife of Zeus, the supreme deity of the ancient Greeks.

Hestia—Greek: Goddess of the hearth; sister of Zeus.

Iris—Greek: Goddess of the rainbow; a messenger for Zeus and Hera who rode the rainbows between heaven and earth.

Juno—Roman name for Hera.

Lara—Roman: Daughter of the River Tiber, this nymph— whose real name is Lala, "the Gossip"—was loved by Mercury, a Roman god who was also messenger of the gods. Their union begot the Lares, the Roman guardian gods.

Larissa—Greek: No two sources agree on this heroine's story. Some say she was from Argos; others claim Thessaly as her birthplace. Some say she was the mother of Pelasgus by Zeus, others say by Poseidon; still others believe she was the *daughter* of Pelasgus. The only thing *not* arguable is that her name is pretty! It's also the name of a Greek city in the eastern part of Thessaly.

Lavinia—Greek: Second wife of Aeneas, the Trojan hero and star of Virgil's *Aeneid.*

Lucina—Roman: Goddess of childbirth.

Macaria (Ma-kair´-ee-uh)—Greek: Virgin daughter of Heracles (a.k.a. Hercules) and Deianira. When an oracle pronounced that for victory over Eurystheus (the ruler of Tiryns, Mycenae, and Midea) a human sacrifice was necessary, she ensured that victory by offering herself up as the sacrifice.

Maia (May´-uh or My´uh)—Greek: One of the seven daughters of Atlas. According to the Roman: Goddess of spring;

daughter of the ancient woodland deity Faunus (Pan); wife of Vulcan.

Marica (Ma-reek´-uh)—Roman: A nymph whom Virgil described as the mother of Latinus, king of the Aborigines, and wife of Faunus, protector of shepherds and their flocks. Marica is thought to be Circe deified.

Megara (Meg´-uh-ruh)—Greek: Daughter of Cron of Thebes, and wife of Heracles (Hercules).

Melia (Meh-lee´-ah)—Greek: The nymph daughter of Oceanus, the Titan god of the outer sea encircling the earth. After an affair with Apollo, she gave birth to two sons, one of whom was Tenerus, the famous soothsayer and king of Thebes.

Melissa—Greek: Nursemaid to the infant Zeus. She taught humankind the value of using honey.

Nanna—Norse: Wife of Baldur, who was the son of Odin and Frigg and the most gentle and best loved of the gods.

Nike (Nigh´-key)—Greek: Goddess of victory.

Penelope—Greek: The faithful wife of Odysseus, king of Ithaca and star of Homer's *Odyssey*, who turned away many suitors while awaiting Odysseus' return from ten years of wandering.

Phyllis—Greek: Daughter of King Phyleus of Thrace. Legend has it that Phyllis was metamorphosed into a leafless almond tree. When Demophon, her lover, embraced the tree, it grew leaves. At that moment, the Greek word for leaves changed from *petala* to *phylla*.

Rhea—Greek: A Titaness, she is the daughter of Uranus, the personification of Heaven and ruler of the world; and Gaea, goddess of the earth. Also wife of the Titan Cronus, who dethroned Uranus; and mother of Zeus, Poseidon, Hera, Hestia, Hades, and Demeter. (Also see: Cybele)

Selene—Greek: The Greek mythological sun and moon pair is Helios (god of the sun) and his sister, Selene (goddess of the moon). She loved Endymion, who is kept immortally beautiful and youthful through eternal sleep.

Sibyl—Greek and Roman: The name given to all prophetesses, probably thanks to a young girl named Sibyl who had the gift of prophecy and earned a great reputation as a soothsayer. She was the daughter of Dardanus, who was the son of Zeus and Electra.

Thalia (Thuh-lie´-uh, Thayl´-ya, or Thuh-lee´-yuh)—Greek: The muse of comedy and pastoral poetry.

Timandra—Greek: Daughter of Tyndareus, a hero at Sparta, and Leda. She married Echemus, defender of the Peloponnese, but allowed herself to be abducted by Phyleus, who gave up the throne of Elis to take part in the Calydonian boar hunt.

Vesta—Roman name for Hestia.

MALE MYTHOLOGICAL NAMES

Adonis—Greek: The beloved of Aphrodite, the goddess of beauty and love. His name has become synonymous with masculine beauty. According to Near East mythology, Adonis, known as Tammuz, embodies the spirit of the fruitful year.

Andreus—Greek: Son of the River Peneius, which flows through a region in ancient Greece.

Apollo—Greek: God of the sun, manly beauty, prophecy, music, healing, and poetry; twin brother of Artemis.

Arion—Greek: A musician who was thrown overboard by pirates and saved by a dolphin.

Auster—Roman: The south wind.

(The) Cabiri (Kuh-beer´-ee)—Greek: The gods of fertility. Said to be four in number, they were worshiped in Phrygia, an ancient country in west-central Asia Minor.

Cadmus—Greek: A Phoenician prince, married to Harmonia. He introduced writing and founded Thebes with the warriors who sprang from the dragon's teeth he had planted.

Dymas (Dee´-mahs)—Greek: King of Phrygia in ancient Greece and father of Hecate, a goddess of the earth.

Eryx (Ehr´-ix)—Greek: Son of Aphrodite and Poseidon. He gave his name to Mount Eryx in Sicily, where he built the Temple of Aphrodite Erycina.

Evander—There are several mythological Evanders: the son of Sarpedon; one of Priam's sons; and the one we favor, who is said to be the son of Hermes and an Arcadian nymph. As founder of Pallantium (which would later become Rome), he was a benevolent ruler who taught writing, music, and other then-unknown skills to his people.

Geb—Egyptian: Earth god; father of Osiris, the king and judge of the dead.

Hermes—Greek: Herald and messenger of the gods; god of roads, commerce, invention, cunning, and theft. The Romans called him Mercury.

Janus—Roman: God of gates, doorways, and beginnings. Usually depicted with two back-to-back bearded faces looking in opposite directions. His festival month is January.

Jason—Greek: Heroic leader of the Argonauts who, with the help of Medea, retrieved the Golden Fleece. He married Medea, the sorceress-daughter of the king of Colchis, but then deserted her for Creüsa. Medea sent her rival a gift: a wedding dress dipped in poison that would make the wearer's veins burn violently.

Linus—Greek: A musician and poet; the inventor of rhythm and melody.

Maron—Greek: According to Euripides, he was the son of Dionysus, god of the vine, of wine, and of mystic ecstasy.

Myles—Greek: Son of Lelex, king of Laconia, whom Myles later succeeded. Myles is said to have invented the corn mill.

Nestor—Greek: King of Pylos; noted most for his wise counsel in the Trojan War.

Orion (Oh-rye´-un)—Greek: Giant-size hunter; lover of Aurora. Slain by Artemis, he was then placed in the sky near Gemini and Taurus as a constellation.

Paris—Greek: Son of King Priam and Hecuba; prince of Troy whose abduction of Helen caused the Trojan War.

Priam (Pry´-em)—Greek: King of Troy; father of many children (some mythographers say he had as many as fifty sons). Three of his most acknowledged offspring are Paris (see above), Cassandra, and Hector, the much-loved leader of the Trojan army. Priam was killed when his city fell to the Achaeans.

Regin—Norse: In the *Volsunga Saga*: A blacksmith; brother of Fafnir who raised Sigurd and encouraged him to kill Fafnir.

Sigmund—Norse: In the *Volsunga Saga*: Son of Volsung, king of Hunland, and Liod; father of Sigurd, who performed heroic deeds.

Syrus—Greek: The Syrians got their name from him. He is credited with inventing arithmetic and introducing the doctrine of metempsychosis, the transmigration of souls.

Talos (Tay´-lohss)—Greek: A bronze, robotlike giant who

was created by the god Hephaestus to protect Minos' island of Crete. And protect it he did, until Medea's magic pierced his one vulnerable vein and destroyed him.

Thor—Norse: God of thunder, rain, and farming, and the son of Odin and Frigg. Thor, the hammer-hurler, is usually represented wielding his hammer Miölnir (or Mjollnir) as he rides a goat-drawn chariot.

Zeus—Greek: Last, but certainly not least, is the presiding and greatest god of the Greek pantheon, Zeus! He is ruler of the heavens; god of light, clear skies, and thunder; father of other gods and mortal heroes; and protector of strangers and guests.

Names Foreign Wide
Popular Names from
Foreign Countries

For those of you who have a special feeling about or a link to a particular country of the world, you might want to consider a name for your baby that will reflect that ethnic connection.

The following lists offer a sampling of popular, contemporary names from twenty-eight different cultures. There are many different ways to pronounce these names, but we've given you some help by including the standard pronunciations of those names hardest to figure out.

To get in the mood, sip a cup of Chinese tea and grab some Swiss cheese on Italian bread with Russian dressing and a side of French fries—and then pretend you're lunching at the United Nations as you thumb through the lists.

AFRICA

Swahili Names for Eastern and Central Africa, including Kenya

Girls' Names
Asha (Ah´-shah)—Life
Aziza (Ah-zee´-zah)—Precious

Dalila (Dah-lee´-lah)—Gentle
Hadiya (Hah-dee´-yah)—Gift
Jamila (Jah-mee´-lah)—Beautiful
Marjani (Mahr-jah´-knee)—Coral
Ramla (Rahm´-lah)—One who predicts the future
Rashida (Rah-shee´-dah)—Righteous
Safiya (Sa-fee´-yah)—Pure
Zalika (Zah-lee´-kah)—Well born

Boys' Names
Abasi (Ah-bah´-see)—Stern
Bakari (Bah-kah´-ree)—Of noble promise
Jabari (Jah-bah´-ree)—Brave
Khalfani (Khal-fah´-knee)—Destined to rule
Masud (Mah-sood´)—Fortunate
Nuru (Noo´-roo)—Born during the day
Sadiki (Sah-dee´-kee)—Loyal, true
Salim (Sah-leem´)—Peace
Shomari (Sho-mah´-ree)—Forceful
Sudi (Soo´-dee)—Luck

ARABIC NAMES

Girls' Names
Alima (Ah´-lee-mah)—Wise
Anan (A-nahn´)—Clouds
Basimah (Bah-see´-mah)—Smiling
Hayat (Ha-yaht´)—Life
Lateefah (Lah-tee´-fah)—Gentle
Malak (Mah´-lak)—Angel
Nawal (Na-wahl´)—Gift
Sabirah (Sah-bee´-rah)—Patient
Thana (Thah´-nah)—Gratitude
Yasmin (Yahs-meen´)—Jasmine

Boys' Names
Ahmad (Ah´-mahd)—Worthy
Ali (Ah-lee´)—Form of Allah, the supreme being of the
    Mohammedan religion
Faris (Fah´-rees)—Knight

Jabir (Zhah-beer´)—Comforter
Kadar (Kah´-dahr)—Powerful
Muhammad (Muh-hahm´-mud)—Praised one
Nadir (Nah-deer´)—Rare
Rashid (Rah-sheed´)—Divinely faithful
Tabari (Tah´-bah-ree)—Famous Muslim historian
Zaid (Zah´-eed)—To add to

ARMENIA

Girls' Names
Anoush (Ah-nush´)—Sweet
Astrid—Star
Elmas (El-mahss´)—Diamond
Gadar (Gah-dahr´)—Purity, perfection
Lucine (Loo-seen´)—Moon
Ohanna (Oh-hahn´-nah)—God's gracious gift
Perouze (Pair-ooze´)—Turquoise
Shoushan (Shoe-shahn´)—Lily
Siran (Seer-ahn´)—Alluring
Zagir (Zah-geer´)—Flower

Boys' Names
Ara—Heroic Armenian king
Armen—Armenian
Avedis (A-vee´-dis)—Good news
Bedros (Be-drohs´)—Rock
Dareh—Rich man
Haig—Famous Armenian forefather
Nishan (Nee´-shan)—Sign
Raffi—Noted nineteenth-century writer
Yervant (Yer-vahnt´)—An Armenian king
Zeroun (Zer-oon´)—Elderly sage

CHINA

Girls' Names
An (Ahn)—Peace
Chow—Summer
Chyou (Chee-oh)—Autumn

Eu-meh (You´-meh)—A great beauty
Guan-yin (Kwah-yin´)—Goddess of mercy
Hua (Hwah)—Flower
Jun (Joon)—Truth
Lian (Lee-ahn)—Graceful willow
Lien (Lee-en)—Lotus
Tao (Tau)—Peach (symbol of long life)

Boys' Names
Chen—Great, expansive
Chung—Intelligent
Gan (Gahn)—Bold, courageous
Li (Lee)—Strength
Manchu (Mahn´-choo)—Pure
Park—Cypress tree
Quon—Bright
Shen—Spiritual, deep-thinking
Wang (Wahng)—Hope
Wing –Glory

CZECHOSLOVAKIA

Girls' Names
Anezka (Ah´-nez-kah)— Gentle, pure
Dana (Dah´-nah)—God is my judge
Emilie (Em-meel´-lee)—Industrious
Jana (Yah´-nah) –God's gracious gift
Katrina, Katra—Pure
Ludmila (Lood´-mill-ah)—Beloved by the people
Marjeta (Mahr´-jee-tah)—Pearl
Nadia (Nahd´-ya)—Hope
Pavla (Pavh´-lah)—Little
Velika (Vel´-lee-kah)—Great one

Boys' Names
Evzen (Ev´-zen)—Of noble birth
Ivan (Ee´-vahn)—God's gracious gift
Jan (Yahn)—God's gracious gift
Jiri (Yir´-zee)—Farmer
Karel (Kahr´-el)—Strong, virile

Risa (Ree´-shah)—Strong and rich ruler
Stanislav (Stahn´-yih-slav)—Glory of the camp
Tomas (Toe´-mahs)—Twin
Vladimir (Vlad´-eh-meer)— World prince
Wenzel—To know

DENMARK

Girls' Names
Agneta (Ahg-neh´-tah)—The chaste
Dagmar—Glory of the Danes
Dagny—Dane's happiness
Dania—God is my judge
Grette (Gret´-tah)—Pearl
Hanne (Hahn´-uh)—Gracious
Inger—Daughter of a hero
Kirsten (Keer´-sten)—Christian
Laila (Lah´-ee-la)—Night
Saffi—Wisdom

Boys' Names
Bo—Commanding
Diederik (Dee´-dah-rick)—Ruler of the people
Henerik—Landlord
Jorgen (Your´-gehn)—Farmer
Klaus—Victory of the people
Lief (Life)—Descendant
Mikkel (Mee´-kel)—Who is like God?
Nils—Champion
Peder—Stone
Roeland—Fame of the land

FRANCE

Girls' Names
Félicité (Fay-liss-i-tay´)—Fortunate
Françoise (Fran-swahs´)—Free
Ghislaine (Zhees-layn´)—Sweet pledge
Joelle—God is willing
Lisette—Consecrated to God

Mignon (Me-nyown´)—Delicate, petite
Monique—Adviser
Odile (Oh-deal´)—Rich
Solange (So-lahnje´)—Rare jewel
Sylvie—From the forest

Boys' Names
Alain—Handsome
Bernard—Courage of a bear
Clément—Merciful
Donatien (Dough-nah-tyen´)—Gift
Grégoire (Greh-gwah´)—Vigilant
Jacques/Jaques—Supplanter
Luc (Lewk)—Light
Maxime (Max-eem´)—Greatest
Philippe—Lover of horses
Yves (Eve)—Little archer

GERMANY

Girls' Names
Antje (Ahnt´-yeh)—Grace
Berta—Glorious
Didrika (Did-ree´-kah)—People's rule
Franziska (Fran-sees´-kah)—Free
Heidi—Kind
Katherina—Pure
Katja (Cot´-yah)—Pure
Rebekka—Servant of God
Tamara—Palm tree
Ursula—Little bear

Boys' Names
Bernhard—Courage of a bear
Christian—Christian
Gunther—War
Hagan—Strong defense
Johann (Yo´-hahn)—God's gracious gift
Konrad—Honest counselor
Lothar—Famous warrior

Matz—Gift of God
Otto—Prosperous
Tobias—God is good

GREECE

Girls' Names
Aleka—Defender of humankind
Athena—Goddess of wisdom
Charis (Kahr´-iss)—Love
Euphemia (You-fem-ee´-yah)—Well known
Irene—Peace
Kalliope (Kahl-ee-oh´-pee)—Beautiful voice
Sofi—Wisdom
Stefania (Stef-an-ee´-ah)—Crown
Theodosia (Tay-oh-do-see´-ah)—Gift of God
Zoe—Life

Boys' Names
Apostolos—Apostle
Christos—Christ
Cosmo—Well ordered
Demetrios—For Demeter, goddess of the harvest
Nicholas—People's victory
Soterios—Savior
Stavros—Crowned with laurels
Stefanos—Crown
Thanos (Tahn´-os)—Noble
Vasilis (Vah-see´-lees)—Kingly

HAWAII

Girls' Names
Alani (Ah-lah´-knee)—Orange tree
Haunani (Ha-oo-nah´-knee)—Beautiful dew
Kalea (Kuh-lay´-uh)—Bright
Lahela (Lah-he´-lah)—Innocence of a lamb
Luana—Enjoyment
Malu (Ma´-loo)—Peace
Nani—Beautiful

Oliana (Oh-lee-ahn´-ah)—Oleander
Pualani (Poo-ah-lah´-knee)—Heavenly flower
Wanika (Wah-knee´-kah)—God's gracious gift

Boys' Names
Alika (Ah-lee´-kah)—Defender of humankind
Havika (Ha-vee´-kah)—Beloved
Kalani (Kah-lah´-knee)—The heavens
Kapono (Kah-pone´-oh)—Righteous one
Keoni (Kee-own´-ee)—God's gracious gift
Lani (Lah´-knee)—Sky
Makani (Ma-kah´-knee)—The wind
Manu (Man´-oo)—Bird
Nohea (No-he´-ah)—Handsome
Palani (Pah-lah´-knee)—Free man

INDIA

Girls' Names
Aruna (A-roo´-nah)—Radiance
Chandra—Moon
Guri—Goddess of abundance
Kalinda—Sun; place name Kalinda Mountains
Lalasa (Lah-lah´-sah)—Love
Latika (Lah-tea´-kah)—Name of a god
Ramya—Beautiful, elegant
Sarisha—Charming
Tulsi—Sacred tulasi plant
Vidya (Vee´-dyah)—Knowledge and education

Boys' Names
Anand—Happiness
Chander—Moon
Jafar (Jah-fahr)—Little stream
Kamal (Kah-mahl´)—Name of a god
Mohan—Delightful
Ravi—Sun god
Sahir—Friend
Taj—Crown

Vadin (Vah´-dean)—Speaker
Vishnu—Protector

IRELAND

Girls' Names
Briana—Strong
Caitlin (Cat´-leen)—Pure
Dierdre—Young girl; in Irish legend, she was a princess of Ulster who eloped to Scotland
Erlina—Girl from Ireland
Glynis—Valley
Keara—Name of a saint
Meara—Merry
Pegeen—Pearl
Sheena—God's gracious gift
Treasa—Strong

Boys' Names
Aidan—Fiery
Bevan—Youthful warrior
Cullan—Handsome
Darby—Free man
Éamon (Eh´-mon)—Happy warrior
Ferris—Rock
Keefe—Well-being
Nolan—Noble, famous
Shane—God's gracious gift
Torin—Chief

ISRAEL

Girls' Names
Aleeza—Joy
Davida (Dah-vee´-dah)—Beloved
Edrea (Ed´-ree-uh)—Mighty
Jaffa or Yaffa (Yah´-fah)—Beautiful
Malka (Mahl´-kah)—Queen
Nira—Of the loom
Ora, Orah—Light

Rena (Ree´-nah)—Joyous song
Shoshana—Rose
Ziva (Zee´-vah)—Aglow, splendor

Boys' Names
Akiva (Ah-kee´-vah)—Supplanter
Dov (Dove)—Bear
Elan (E-lahn´)—Tree
Gedalya (Geh-dahl´-yah)—God is great
Namir (Nah-meer´)—Leopard
Ravid (Rah-veed´)—Wander
Sasson (Sahs´-son)—Joy
Tovi (Toe-vee´)—Good
Uri (Oo´-ree)—My light
Zelig (Seh´-leeg)—Blessed

ITALY

Girls' Names
Benedetta—Blesses
Carmelina—Vineyard
Fiorenza—Flower
Giovanna—God's gracious gift
Grazia (Grah´-tsee-ah)— Grace
Lucia (Loo-chee´-ah)—Light
Oriana—Golden
Pia—Pious
Renata—Reborn
Serafina—Seraph (angel)

Boys' Names
Angelo—Messenger
Carmine—Vineyard
Donato (Dough-not´-oh)—Gift
Fabiano (Fah-bee-ah´-no)—Bean farmer
Georgio—Farmer
Guiseppe (Joe-sehp´-ah)—God will add
Guido (Gwee´-dough)—Life
Luciano (Loo-chee-ah´-no)—Light

Sergio (Sehr´-gee-oh)—Attendant
Vincenzo (Veen-chenz´-oh)—Conqueror

JAPAN

Girls' Names
Akina—Spring flower
Cho—Butterfly
Etsu (Et´-sue)—Delight
Hoshi (Ho´-she)—Star
Kohana—Little flower
Mika—New moon
Nami—Wave
Sachi—Bliss
Takara—Treasure
Yori—Trustworthy

Boys' Names
Akira—Intelligent
Hiroshi (Here-oh´-she)—Generous
Joji (Joe´-gee)—Farmer
Kiyoshi (Kee-oh´-she)—Quiet
Masao—Righteous
Naoko (Nay-oh´-ko)—Honest
Ringo—Peace be with you
Taro—First son
Tomi—Rich
Yukio (You-kee´-oh)—Gets his heart's desire

KOREA

Girls' Names
Cho—Beautiful
Dae—Greatness
Hea (Hay´-ah)—Grace
Jin—Jewel
Kyon—Brightness
Min—Cleverness
Soo—Long life
Sun—Goodness

Yon—Lotus blossom
Young—Flower

Boys' Names
Bae—Inspiration
Chin—Precious
Doh—Accomplishment
Gi (Gee)—Brave
Ho—Goodness
Ki (Key)—Vigor
Kwan—Strong
Sam—Achievement
Sook—Light
Yong—Bravery

NIGERIA

Girls' Names
Abeo (Ah-beh-o´)—Happy she was born
Akanke (Ah-kahn-keh´)—To know her is to love her
Ayo (Ah´-yo)—Joy
Bayo (Bah´-yo)—To find joy
Fayola (Fah-yo´-lah)—A healthy baby is joyous
Ifama (Ec-fah´-mah)—Everything is fine
Jumoke (Jew-mo´-keh)—Everyone loves the baby
Nayo (Nah´-yoh)—We are elated
Omolara (O-mo´-lah-rah)—Born at the right time
Urbi (Oor´-bee)—Princess

Boys' Names
Ajani (Ah-jah´-nee)—Winner
Akin (Ah-keen´)—Hero
Banjoko (Ban´-jo-ko)—Stay with me forever
Chi (Chee)—Personal guardian angel
Jaja (Jah´-jah)—Honored
Kayin (Kah-yeen´)—Celebration of long-awaited baby
Mongo (Mon´-go)—Famous
Ola (Aw´-lah)—Great wealth
Osaze (Oh-sah´-zeh)—Loved by God
Tor—King

NORTH AMERICAN INDIAN

Girls' Names
Alaqua (Ah-lah´-qwah)—Sweet-gum tree
Chumani (Chew-mahn´-ee)—Dewdrops
Eyota (Ee-yoh´-ta)—Greatest one
Halona (Ha-loan´-ah)—Fortunate
Koko—Night
Kwanita—God is gracious
Nita—Bear
Satinka—Magic dancer
Tehya (Tay´-yah)—Precious
Winona—Generous

Boys' Names
Anoke (Ah-no´-kee)—Actor
Delsin—Truthful one
Dyami (Die-ahm´-ee)—Eagle
Halian (Hah-lee-ahn´)—Youthful
Kuruk (Koo´-rook)—Bear
Kwam—God's gracious love
Makya (Mahk´-yah)—Eagle hunter
Motega (Mo-teh´-gah)—New arrow
Quanah (Kwan´-ah)—Fragrant
Takoda (Ta-kode´-ah)—Friend to all

NORWAY

Girls' Names
Andras (Ahn´-drahs)—Breath
Erika—Ever powerful
Kelsey—From the ship's island
Liv (Leev)—Life
Magna (Mahg´-nah)—Strength
Mathea (Mah-teh´-ay)—Gift of God
Nora—Light
Siv (Seev)—Kinship; wife of the Norse god Thor
Sonja (Son´-yah)—Wisdom
Trine (Tree´-neh)—Pure one

Boys' Names
Aksel (Ahk´-sel)—Father of peace
Anders—Masculine, virile
Bjarne or Bjorn (Byarn or Byuhrn)—Bear
Borg—From the castle
Canute—Knot
Dag (Dahg)—Day
Erik—Ever powerful
Ivar (Ee´-vahr)—A Norse god; archer
Lars (Larss)—Laurel
Vidar (Ve´-dahr)—Tree-warrior

PHILIPPINES

Girls' Names
Amalia—Industrious
Corazon—Heart
Imelda—Industrious
Julita—Youth
Malaya (Mah-lay´-ah)—Free
Milagros (Me-lah´-gross)—Miracles
Paz (Pahz)—Peace
Rosario—Rosary
Soledad (So-lee-dahd´)—Health
Victoria—Victory

Boys' Names
Arturo—Noble
Bayani (Bay-ahn´-ee)—Hero
Ferdinand—Courageous
Gregorio—Vigilant
Juan—God's gracious gift
Manuel—God is with us
Matalino—Bright
Pacifico—Peaceful
Renato—King
Salvador—Savior

POLAND

Girls' Names
Basha (Bosh´-ah)—Stranger
Felcia (Fehl´-shah)—Lucky
Gita (Gee´-tah)—Pearl
Helenka (Hel-ehnk´-ah)—Little Helen, light
Jolanta (Yo-lahn´-tah)—Violet blossoms
Lilka—Famous warrior-maiden
Lucyna (Loot´-sih-nah)—Bringer of light
Marya (Mar´-yah)—Bitter
Tola—Priceless
Zosia (Zo´-shah)—Wise

Boys' Names
Bazyli (Bah-zih´-lee)—Of royalty
Dobry (Do´-bree)—Good
Gerik (Gehr´-ik)—Prosperous spearman
Hilary—Cheerful
Karol—Strong, virile
Ludwik (Lood´-vik)—Famed warrior
Marek (Mah´-rek)—Warlike
Stasio (Stah´-shyo)—Stand of glory
Tymon (Tee´-mon)—Honoring God
Ziven (Zie´-ven)—Alive, energetic

PORTUGAL AND BRAZIL

Girls' Names
Antonia—Priceless
Bibiana—Lively
Carlota—Womanly
Elzira (Ehl-see´-rah)—Consecrated to God
Laurinda—Praise
Palmeira—Palm tree
Paula—Little
Rosa—Rose
Susana—Lily
Vidonia—Vine branch

Boys' Names
Alexio—Defender of humankind
Antonio—Priceless
Carlos—Strong, virile
Enrique (Ehn-ree´-keh)—Ruler of an estate
Fernando—Courageous, adventurous
Francisco—Free
Gilberto—The will to be bright
Julio (Zhool´-yo)—Youthful
Ramiro—Great judge
Silvino—Forest

RUSSIA

Girls' Names
Dasha (Dahsh´-ah)—Gift of God
Galina—God has redeemed
Kira—Light
Larisa—Cheerful
Marina (Mah-ree´-nah)—Sea maiden
Natasha—Born on Christmas
Olga—Holy
Sonya—Wisdom
Svetlana (Svet-lah´-nah)—Star
Tatyana (Taht-yah´-nah)—Fairy queen

Boys' Names
Alexei—Defender of humankind
Anatolii/Anatoly—From the East
Boris—Warrior
Fyodor—Divine gift
Gavril (Gav-reel´)—Man of God
Igor—Farmer
Nicolai—Victory of the people
Vanya—God's gracious gift
Vladimir—World prince
Youri/Yuri/Yurii/Yury—Farmer

SCOTLAND

Girls' Names
Coleen—Girl
Elspeth—Consecrated to God
Fiona—White, fair
Gillian (Jill´-ee-an)—Youth
Glynis—Valley
Lorna—Crowned with laurel
Moira—Great
Robina—Robin
Sibyl—Wise woman
Vanora—White wave

Boys' Names
Alister, Alaster—Defender of humankind
Blair—Child of the fields
Colin—Child
Fergus—Strong man
Gawain—Hawk of battle
Grant—Great
Lawren—Laurel
Murdoch—Sea protector
Nairn—Place name in Scotland; from the river narrows
Payton—Pastor or guardian

SPAIN

Girls' Names
Aldonza—Sweet
Carmen—Song
Esperanza (Ess-per-ahn´-zah)—Hope
Guadalupe (Gwah-dah-loo´-pay)—Virgin Mary
Ines (Ee-nehss´)—Gentle
Jacinta (Hah-seen´-tah)—Hyacinth
Monica—Adviser
Paloma—Dove
Rocío (Ro-see´-oh)—Dewdrops
Solana—Sunshine

Boys' Names
Alfredo—Wise counselor
Carlos—Manly
Emilio—Winning one
Esteban (Ehs-tay´-bahn)—Crown
Fernando—Brave
Gilberto—Noteworthy pledge
José—God will increase
Luis—Renowned warrior
Plácido—Serene
Tajo (Tah´-ho)—Day

SWEDEN

Girls' Names
Annika (Ah-knee´-kah)—Grace
Brigitta—Strength
Erika—Powerful
Gala—Singer
Inga—Hero's daughter
Kerstin (Care´-sten)—Christian
Lena—Light
Maj (My)—Pearl
Sigrid—Victorious counselor
Ulla (Oo´-lah)—Will

Boys' Names
Anders (Ahn´-dersh)—Strong, macho
Bjorn (Bee-orn´)—Bear
Gunnar—War
Hans—God's gracious gift
Ingmar—Famous son
Kalle (Kahl´-uh)—Powerful, manly
Lars—Laurel
Magnus—Strength
Nils—Champion
Ulf—Wolf

VIETNAM

Girls' Names
Am—Of the moon
Be (Bay)—Doll
Cam—Sweet
Cara—Precious gem
Hanh (Han)—Faithful, moral
Hoa (Hwah)—Peace
Kim—Needle, gold
Le (Le´-ah)—Pearl
Thanh (Tan)—Brilliant
Thuy (Two´-ee)—Gentle

Boys' Names
Antoan (An´-twan)—Safe, protected
Cadao (Ka-dah´-oh)—Folk song
Chim (Kim)—Bird
Gan—Close to
Hy (Hee)—Hope
Lap—Independent
Son—Mountain
Tai (Tah-ee)—Talent
Thang (Tahng)—Victory
Tuyen (Tuing)—Angel

ZIMBABWE

Girls' Names
Chipo (Chee´-poh)—Gift
Dorleta (Door-lay´-tah)—A name honoring the Virgin Mary
Jendayi (Jen-dah´-yee)—Show gratitude
Kambo (Kam´-boh)—Must work for everything
Maiba (Mah´-ee-bah)—Serious
Mudiwa (Moo-day´-wah)—Beloved
Rufaro (Roo-fah´-roh)—Happiness
Sibongile (See-bon-gee-leh´)—Thanks
Sitembile (See-tem-bee-leh´)—Trust
Sukutai (Soo-koo-tay´-ee)—Hug

Boys' Names

Banga (Bang´-gah)—Knife
Dakarai (Dah-kah´-rah-ee)—Happiness
Gamba (Gam´-bah)—Warrior
Hondo (Hoan´-doh)—War
Jabulani (Jah-boo-lah´-knee)—Be jubilant
Kokayi (Koh-kah´-yee)—Summon the people
Mashama (Mah-shah´-mah)—Surprised
Petiri (Peh´-tee-ree)—Where we are
Runako (Roo-nah´-koh)—Handsome
Zuka (Zoo-kah´)—Sixpence

A Bouquet of Names
Flowers and More

Dorothy Parker described flowers as "Heaven's masterpiece." How appropriate, then, to give your little masterpiece a floral name! We bet you'll be surprised to see how many lovely and usable floral names there are. We certainly were.

However, since most of the blooming names are feminine, we decided to include the names of herbs to make this a more "equal opportunity" list. We broke with style here and did not separate male and female names. We'll leave that up to you and your good judgment.

FLOWERS AND HERBS

Amaryllis	Clover	Lavender
Angelica	Daffodil	Lilac
Aster	Dahlia	Lily
Azalea	Daisy	Linden
Basil	Fern	Lotus
Bay	Geranium	Mace
Begonia	Ginger	Magnolia
Berony	Hazel	Marguerite
Blossom	Heather	Marigold
Bryony	Holly	Myrtle
Burnet	Hyacinth	Olivia, Olive
Camellia	Iris	Orchid
Cassia	Ivy	Pansy
Cicely	Jasmine	Petunia
Cinnamon	Lark	Poppy
Clove	Laurel	Rose

Rue	Tansy	Violet
Rosemary	Tulip	Willow
Saffron	Valerian	Zinnia
Sage		

The Family Jewel
A Gem of a Name

Good name in man and woman, dear my lord,
Is the immediate jewel of their souls.
　　　　　　　— WILLIAM SHAKESPEARE
　　　　　　　Othello, Act 3, Scene 3

Just as with babies, when we think of gems, the word "precious" comes to mind. Precious and semiprecious gemstones are more popular than ever, not only because of their great beauty but because these natural wonders of our earth are thought to have mystical powers. Today New Agers are practicing age-old methods of harnessing the stones' powers to supposedly attract, protect, and/or heal.

While you may not want to name your child Aquamarine, we do have a list of names from the mineral kingdom well worth considering. As in the chapter of flower and herb names, we are not dividing the list into male and female names. We're leaving gem-name-gender to your good judgment, so keep that in mind as you're mining for a name.

Also, keep in mind that when a child has a *gem* of a name, it's easy to buy him or her a gift—a piece of gemstone jewelry or, as they say in the insurance-company commercial, "a piece of the rock."

Gem	Family and/or Origin	Colors
Amber	Fossilized resin of the extinct conifer trees	Light yellow and gold to brown and red

When you rub amber against silk or wool, it becomes electrically charged. So, appropriately enough, its old Greek name was *elektron*, from which the modern word *electricity* is derived. Amber's energy is believed to lift one's spirits, replacing depression with joy. In other words, it's a real upper.

Amethyst	Quartz	Pale purple to deep violet

The Greek word *amethustos* means "without drunkenness," and the stone was used, in Greco-Roman times, to prevent intoxication and protect against the discomfort caused by overeating. Now known as the tranquilizer of the mineral kingdom, the amethyst's energy supposedly restores calm and brings peace to those who are stressed out. It's also thought to bring out one's psychic ability.

Anatase	Ore of titanium	Ranges from blue to blue-black to lavender, and from yellow to brown

Because of its eight-sided crystal structure, this rare mineral is also known as octahedrite . . . a great name for an octopus, but stick with Anatase for a child. The word *anatase* is derived from the Greek *anateinein*, meaning "stretch up," as is characteristic of the gem's long crystals.

Beryl	Beryllium aluminum silicate	Usually bluish green or light yellow, some of these stones are green, gold, pink, white, or colorless. Deep green beryls are called emeralds; pale, greenish blue and transparent beryls are aquamarine.

The beryl's energy is said to give a lazy person some needed get-up-and-go. Plus, it is believed that if you visualize a lost object while holding a beryl in your hand, you will suddenly see its whereabouts in your mind's eye.

Carnelian Quartz   Orange-red to orange-
                                     brown, salmon, sienna, rust,
                                     and various shades of gold

Carnelian comes from the Latin word for "flesh," probably because the stones are often salmon or flesh colored. It is thought that the carnelian's energy helps one look at the bright side of life, clears up problems with the reproductive organs, and stimulates one's appetite.

Cinnabar Mercuric sulfide   Chinese red, red, reddish
                                     brown, gray, black

This abundant ore is said to protect objects (rather than living creatures).

Coral   Calcified skeletons   Pale to deep red, white,
            of marine animals   black, all shades of pink
                                     and orange

White coral's energy is said to strengthen self-esteem and help with the handling of family frustrations, while reddish coral's energy is said to relieve the fear of decision-making. Coral is thought to be a good gemstone for small children, because of its powers to encourage growth.

Crystal Quartz   Clear; able to reflect every
                                     color of the rainbow

The word *crystal* comes from *krystallos*, a Greek word meaning "ice." The Greeks thought that crystal was water frozen forever by the gods. Supposedly the energy of the crystal puts one's body in harmony.

Diamond Carbon   Clear and colorless; blue-
                                     white; shades of blue,
                                     yellow, pink, green, red,
                                     gray, and black

The diamond's energy is thought to encourage one to follow the golden rule. It also promotes honesty with oneself, as well as with others. The diamond is supposedly of the greatest benefit when used in conjunction with other gems, as it enhances their properties.

Emerald   Beryl   Deep green

Emerald is derived from the Persian word for "green." The emerald's energy is believed to open one's heart to wisdom and love.

Flint   Quartz   Gray, brown, black

Prehistoric men used flint for making tools. Later on it was used to strike sparks from a piece of steel and start a fire. Those same sparks were used in early rifles to set off the powder charge. Today flint is used in Brazil for divining gold, water, gemstones, and other underground treasures.

Galena   Lead sulphide   Gray

The most common of all lead minerals, Galena is said to bring a sense of calm to one's system.

Garnet   Silicate minerals   Red, brown, black, green,
                                            yellow, white

The name comes from the Latin word *granatus*, meaning "seed," because of this stone's tiny, seedlike crystals. The garnet's energy is thought to help develop the patience and perseverance necessary to achieve one's goals.

Ivory   Dentine of   Off-white
               elephants' tusks

It is believed ivory provides both spiritual and physical protection.

Jacinth   Zirconium silicate   Red, orange, and brown
                                            Zircon

In ancient times, jacinth (or hyacinth) was known as "the protector stone from Heaven," and travelers wore it to assure safe passage and warm welcomes. The energy of the jacinth is believed to heal the spirit and bring inner peace.

Jade	Two different opaque minerals: jadeite and nephrite	Many shades of green; black, red, pink, brown, white, cream

Legend has it that the most powerful symbol for attracting true love is a jade butterfly. Jade's energy supposedly prevents illness, prolongs life, nurtures healthy plants, and attracts money to its wearer.

Jasper	Form of quartz/ opaque variety of chalcedony	Red, green, brown, mottled

When held in the hand of a woman during childbirth, jasper is thought to relieve pain as well as protect both the mother and the child. Jasper is also thought to attract rain, which is why Native Americans call it "rainbringer."

Jet	Fossilized wood millions of years old	Black (*jet* black)

Jet's energy is absorbent and is believed to rid one of negativity. It is said that when a small piece of jet is placed momentarily on a newborn baby's stomach, the stone safeguards the infant from the wickedness of the world.

Mica	Complex aluminum silicates	Muscovite mica is light yellow, red, green, brown, or white. Phlogopite mica is yellowish brown, green, or white. Lepidolite mica is light lavender or pink. Biotite mica is dark green, brown, or black.

The energy of mica is said to expand intuitive awareness, thus giving one insight into what the future holds.

Onyx	Chalcedony-type quartz	Black and white, gray and white, black and red, white and red

The onyx's energy supposedly helps one end—and/or recover from—a negative relationship. It is also thought to improve concentration and devotion—perhaps the reason why so many rosaries are made out of onyx.

Opal	Silica or quartz	White, milky, black; shades of blue or gray. There's a great variety in the play of colors or iridescence of opals.

In Greco-Roman times, the opal was used to treat eye problems, and in fact, its name is derived from the Greek word *opthalmos*, meaning "eye." These days, it is believed that the opal's energy enhances inner beauty and one's psychic powers.

Pearl	Aragonite/crystallized calcium carbonate	White, cream, pink, rose, yellow, gray, blue, black

Pearls come from sea creatures and are traditionally worn by deep-sea divers as protection against the dangers of the sea. The energy of the pearl supposedly stimulates one's sense of femininity.

Ruby	Corundum	Many shades of red, from rose to deep red to deep purplish red

From the Latin *rubeus*, meaning "red," the ruby was thought of as the king and queen of gems and was used by the ancients in wedding rings. Today it is still thought of as an expression of everlasting love. It is also believed that the strong, fiery stone energizes one's spirit and self-esteem.

Sapphire Corundum	All shades of blue; clear, white, pink, orange, green, purple, black. (When this corundum gemstone is red, it's a ruby.)

Believing that the world rested on a colossal blue sapphire, the ancient Persians credited the gemstone for giving the sky its color. *Sapphire* is derived from a Sanskrit word meaning "beloved of Saturn." Appropriately, the stone is the symbol for the natural sciences, astronomy, and astrology. It is believed that wearing a sapphire heightens the study of the sky, sun, moon, stars, planets, and planetary influences on human events.

Topaz Topaz	Yellow, colorless, white, gray, blue, pink, brown

Topaz in Sanskrit means "fire," but the gem may have gotten its name from the island Topazion in the Red Sea, off the coast of Egypt, where the stone was first found thousands of years ago. It is believed that you will bring light and warmth into your life with the energy of the sun-colored topaz, knowledge and wisdom with the energy of the clear topaz, and peace and understanding with the energy of the blue topaz.

Turquoise Turquoise	Shades range from greenish blue to sky blue to darker sky blue; yellowgreen to apple green to blue-green

This is one gem that all cultures—from the Far East to the Southwestern United States—have in common, and all consider it a lucky stone. Turquoise is said to emit protective energy, but (according to some beliefs) only if given by a friend.

And when it comes to names, don't forget: There's always Jewel or Gem or Gemma.

They Deserved a Medal!
Olympic Winners

In 1981, when a baby girl was born to a former tennis player, the new mom, inspired by the greatness of Martina Navratilova, named her infant Martina. In 1996, at age fifteen, that girl, Martina Hingis, became the youngest-ever Wimbledon champ by capturing the doubles title and the youngest player to reach the Australian Open quarterfinals. She also reached the semifinals in the U.S. Open.

If you dream of your child being part of the Dream Team or going for the gold in tennis, swimming, cycling, or softball, you may want to consider naming your child after a *real* winner.

Here are the names of the talented, courageous, disciplined athletes who medaled for the United States in the memorable 1996 Summer Olympics held in Atlanta, Georgia.

NOTE: The names of those atheletes who have won more than one medal will be indicated the second time and thereafter by their initials.

ARCHERY

Men's Individual:	Justin Huish (gold)
Men's Team:	J. H. (gold)
	Richard "Butch" Johnson (gold)
	Rod White (gold)

ATHLETICS

Decathlon:	Dan O'Brien (gold)

100m:	Gail Devers (gold)
200m:	Michael Johnson (gold)
400m:	M. J. (gold)
110m Hurdles:	Allen Johnson (gold)
	Mark Crear (bronze)
400m Hurdles:	Derrick Adkins (gold)
	Kimberly "Kim" Batten (silver)
	Calvin Davis (bronze)
	Tonya Buford-Bailey (bronze)
4x100m Relay:	G. D. (team gold)
	Chryste Gaines (team gold)
	Inger Miller (team gold)
	Carlette Guidry (team gold)
	Jon Drummond (team silver)
	Michael Marsh (team silver)
	Tim Harden (team silver)
	Dennis Mitchell (team silver)
	Timothy Montgomery (team silver)
4x400m Relay:	Alvin Harrison (team gold)
	Derek Mills (team gold)
	Lamont Smith (team gold)
	Jason Rouser (team gold)
	Kimberly "Kim" Graham (team gold)
	Rochelle Stevens (team gold)
	Gwendolyn "Gwen" Torrence (team gold)
	Linetta Wilson (team gold)
	Maicel Malone (team gold)
	Jearl Miles (team gold)
	Anthuan Maybank (team gold)
High Jump:	Charles Austin (gold)
Long Jump:	Frederick "Carl" Lewis (gold)
	Joe Greene (bronze)
	Jackie Joyner-Kersee (bronze)
Triple Jump:	Kerry "Kenny" Harrison (gold)
Shot Put:	Randy Barnes (gold)
	John Godina (silver)
Hammer Throw:	Lance Deal (silver)

BASEBALL

Chad Allen (team bronze)

Kris Benson (team bronze)
Robert Allen "R.A." Dickey (team bronze)
Troy Glaus (team bronze)
Chad Green (team bronze)
Seth Greisinger (team bronze)
Kip Harkrider (team bronze)
Andrew Jay "A.J." Hinch (team bronze)
Jacque Jones (team bronze)
Billy Koch (team bronze)
Mark Kotsay (team bronze)
Matt LeCroy (team bronze)
Travis Lee (team bronze)
Braden Looper (team bronze)
Brian Loyd (team bronze)
Warren Morris (team bronze)
Augie Ojeda (team bronze)
Jim Parque (team bronze)
Jeff Weaver (team bronze)
Jason Williams (team bronze)

BASKETBALL

Women's Basketball: Jennifer Azzi (team gold)
(Alice) Ruthie Bolton (team gold)
Teresa Edwards (team gold)
Venus Lacey (team gold)
Lisa Leslie (team gold)
Rebecca Lobo (team gold)
Katrina McClain (team gold)
Nikki McCray (team gold)
Carla McGhee (team gold)
Dawn Staley (team gold)
Kathryn "Katy" Steding (team gold)
Sheryl Swoopes (team gold)

Men's Basketball: Charles Barkley (team gold)
Anfernee "Penny" Hardaway (team gold)
Grant Hill (team gold)
Karl Malone (team gold)
Reggie Miller (team gold)

Hakeem Olajuwon (team gold)
Shaquille O'Neal (team gold)
Gary Payton (team gold)
Scottie Pippen (team gold)
Mitch Richmond (team gold)
David Robinson (team gold)
John Stockton (team gold)

BOXING

Featherweight:	Floyd Mayweather (bronze)
Lightweight:	Terrance Cauthen (bronze)
Light Middleweight:	David Reid (gold)
Middleweight:	Rhoshii Wells (bronze)
Light Heavyweight:	Antonio Tarver (bronze)
Heavyweight:	Nate Jones (bronze)

CANOE/KAYAK

Slalom Women's Kayak: Dana Chladek (silver)

CYCLING

Women's Mountain Biking:	Susan DeMattei (bronze)
Men's Kilometer Time Trial:	Erin Hartwell (silver)
Men's Match Sprint:	Marty Nothstein (silver)

DIVING

Women's 10m Platform: Mary Ellen Clark (bronze)
Men's 3m Springboard: Mark Lenzi (bronze)

EQUESTRIAN

Show Jumping:	Leslie Burr-Howard (team silver)
	Anne Kursinski (team silver)
	Peter Leone (team silver)
	Michael Matz (team silver)
Three-Day Event:	Bruce Davidson (team silver)
	Jill Henneberg (team silver)
	David O'Connor (team silver)

	Karen O'Connor (team silver)
Individual Three-Day Event:	Kerry Millikin (bronze)
Dressage:	Robert Dover (team bronze)
	Lois "Michelle" Gibson (team bronze)
	Steffen Peters (team bronze)
	Guenter Seidel (team bronze)

FOOTBALL (SOCCER)

Women's Soccer:	Michelle Akers (team gold)
	Brandi Chastain (team gold)
	Joy Fawcett (team gold)
	Julie Foudy (team gold)
	Carin Gabarra (team gold)
	Mariel "Mia" Hamm (team gold)
	Mary Harvey (team gold)
	Kristine Lilly (team gold)
	Shannon MacMillan (team gold)
	Tiffeny Milbrett (team gold)
	Carla Overbeck (team gold)
	Cynthia "Cindy" Parlow (team gold)
	Tiffany Roberts (team gold)
	Briana Scurry (team gold)
	Tisha Venturini (team gold)
	Staci Wilson (team gold)

GYMNASTICS

Women's Artistic Team:	Amanda Borden (team gold)
	Amy Chow (team gold)
	Dominique Dawes (team gold)
	Shannon Miller (team gold)
	Dominique Moceanu (team gold)
	Jaycie Phelps (team gold)
	Kerri Strug (team gold)
Women's Balance Beam:	S. M. (gold)
Women's Floor Exercise:	D. D. (bronze)
Women's Uneven Bars:	A. C. (silver)
Men's Parallel Bars:	Jair Lynch (silver)

JUDO

Men's 157 lbs.:   James Pedro (bronze)

ROWING

Women's Lightweight Doubles:	Teresa Z. Bell (team silver)
	Lindsay Burns (team silver)
Women's Coxless Pair:	Karen Kraft (team silver)
	Melissa "Missy" Schwen (team silver)
Men's Lightweight Four:	William Carlucci (team bronze)
	David Collins (team bronze)
	Jeffrey Pfaendtner (team bronze)
	Marcus Schneider (team bronze)
Men's Quad Sculls:	Jason Galles (team silver)
	Brian Jamieson (team silver)
	Eric Mueller (team silver)
	Timothy Young (team silver)

SHOOTING

Women's Double Trap:	Kimberly Rhode (gold)
Men's Trap:	Josh Lakatos (silver)
	Lance Bade (bronze)

SOFTBALL

Women's Softball: Laura Berg (team gold)
Gillian Boxx (team gold)
Sheila Cornell (team gold)
Lisa Fernandez (team gold)
Michele Granger (team gold)
Lori Harrigan (team gold)
Dionna Harris (team gold)
Kim Ly Maher (team gold)
Leah O'Brien (team gold)
Dorothy "Dot" Richardson (team gold)
Julie Smith (team gold)
Michele Smith (team gold)
Shelly Stokes (team gold)

Daniale "Dani" Tyler (team gold)
Christa Williams (team gold)

SWIMMING

Women's 100m Backstroke:	Beth Botsford (gold)
	Whitney Hedgepeth (silver)
Women's 200m Backstroke:	W. H. (silver)
Women's 100m Breaststroke:	Amanda Beard (silver)
Women's 100m Butterfly:	Amy Van Dyken (gold)
	Angel Martino (bronze)
Women's 50m Freestyle:	A. V. D. (gold)
Women's 100m Freestyle:	A. M. (bronze)
Women's 200m Breaststroke:	A. B. (silver)
Women's 400m Freestyle Relay:	A. B. (team gold)
	Catherine Fox (team gold)
	Lisa Jacob (team gold)
	A. M. (team gold)
	Jenny Thompson (team gold)
	Melanie Valerio (team gold)
	A. V. D. (team gold)
Women's 400m IM:	Allison Wagner (silver)
Women's 400m Medley Relay:	B. B. (team gold)
	C. F. (team gold)
	W. H. (team gold)
	A. M. (team gold)
	Kristine Quance (team gold)
	J. T. (team gold)
	A. V. D. (team gold)
Women's 800m Freestyle:	Brooke Bennett (gold)
	Trina Jackson (team gold)
	L. J. (team gold)
	Annette Salmeen (team gold)
	Sheila Taormina (team told)
	Cristina Teuscher (team gold)
	J. T. (team gold)
	Ashley Whitney (team gold)
Men's 50m Freestyle:	Gary Hall (silver)

Men's 100m Backstroke:	Jeff Rouse (gold)
Men's 200m Backstroke:	William "Tripp" Schwenk (silver)
Men's 100m Breaststroke:	Jeremy Linn (silver)
Men's 100m Freestyle:	G. H. (silver)
Men's 200m Butterfly:	Tom Malchow (silver)
Men's 400m Freestyle Relay:	Josh Davis (team gold)
	David Fox (team gold)
	Gary Hall (team gold)
	John Hargis (team gold)
	Jon Olsen (team gold)
	Brad Shumacher (team gold)
	Scott Tucker (team gold)
Men's 400m IM:	Tom Dolan (gold)
	Eric Namesnik (silver)
Men's 400m Medley Relay:	Brad Bridgewater (team gold)
	J. D. (team gold)
	Kurt Grote (team gold)
	G. H. (team gold)
	Mark Henderson (team gold)
	J. L. (team gold)
	J. R. (team gold)
	William "Tripp" Schwenk (team gold)
Men's 800m Freestyle Relay:	Ryan Berube (team gold)
	J. D. (team gold)
	Joe Hudepohl (team gold)
	E. N. (team gold)
	B. S. (team gold)

SYNCHRONIZED SWIMMING

Women's Team:	Suzannah Bianco (team gold)
	Tammy Cleland (team gold)
	Rebecca "Becky" Dyroen-Lancer (team gold)
	Heather Pease (team gold)
	Emily Porter-LeSueur (team gold)
	Jill Savery (team gold)
	Nathalie Schneyder (team gold)
	Heather Simmons-Carrasco (team gold)

Jill Sudduth (team gold)
Margot Thien (team gold)

TENNIS

Women's Singles: Lindsay Davenport (gold)
Women's Doubles: Gigi Fernandez (gold)
                Mary Joe Fernandez (gold)
Men's Singles: Andre Agassi (gold)

VOLLEYBALL

Beach Volleyball: Charles "Karch" Kiraly (team gold)
                Kent Steffes (team gold)
                Michael "Mike" Dodd (team silver)
                Michael "Mike" Whitmarsh (team silver)

WRESTLING

125.5 lbs.:   Kendall Cross (gold)
136.5 lbs.:   Tom Brands (gold)
149.5 lbs: Townsend Saunders (silver)
220 lbs.:   Kurt Angle (gold)
286 lbs.:   Bruce Baumgartner (bronze)
Greco-Roman 114.5 lbs.: Brandon Paulson (silver)
Greco-Roman 125.5 lbs.: Dennis Hall (silver)
Greco-Roman 286 lbs.. Siamak "Matt" Ghaffari (silver)

YACHTING

Soling: (Skipper) Jeff Madrigali (team bronze)
       (Crew) Jim Barton (team bronze)
       (Crew) Joseph "Kent" Massey (team bronze)
Europe: Courtenay Becker-Dey (bronze)

Names of Your Favorite Soap Opera Characters

The soap opera is an American art form, bringing to the lives of its viewers romance, intrigue, fantasy, adventure, thrills, suspense, laughter, and the overall feeling of "And I thought *I* had problems!"

Since the 1970s, the soaps have come into their own in terms of popularity and sophistication. Most are on for an hour a day, five days a week. Many are very real reflections of life and deal with issues of the day. In many ways the soaps make an impact on their viewers' lives. They influence styles of dress and hair; they help with problem-solving and, yes, even with naming babies!

Imaginative and distinctive names used on soap operas show up on health departments' "most popular name" lists. Tiffany and Nicole are just two examples of those names whose origins can be traced to characters on daytime serials.

We've compiled a list of the most interesting soap opera characters' names from both past and present. Last names change quite often on the soaps, so please forgive us if and when we're not totally up-to-date.

Ready to take a look at how these names rate for your little character?

Lights! Camera! Action!

ALL MY CHILDREN

Female Characters

Brooke English
Hayley Vaughan
Ceara Connor Hunter
Claudette Montgomery
Opal Cortlandt
Angelique Marick
Erica Kane
Leora Sanders
Noelle Keaton
Livia Frye
Dixie Larson
Marestella LaTour
Devon Shepherd
Margo Flax
Daisy Cortlandt
Silver Kane
Skye Chandler
Bianca Montgomery
Galen Henderson
Taylor Roxbury-Cannon
Kelsey Jefferson
Anita Santos
Liza Colby

Male Characters

Trevor Dillon
Trask Bodine
Jeremy Hunter
Kent Bogard
Derek Frye
Palmer Cortlandt
Dimitri Marick
Travis Montgomery
Wade Matthews
Lucas Barnes
Thadeus "Tad" Martin
Wyatt Coles
Brandon Kingsley
Langley Wallingford
Nigel Fargate
Jackson Montgomery
Adam Chandler
Edmund Grey
Noah Keefer
Mateo Santos

ANOTHER WORLD

Female Characters

Frankie Frame
Maggie Cory
Josie Watts
Lorna Devon
Felicia Gallant
Sharlene Frame
Paulina Cory Carlino
Sofia Carlino
Rachel Cory Hutchins

Male Characters

Gabe McNamara
Rafael Santierro
Jake McKinnon
Morgan Winthrop
Grant Harrison
Cass Winthrop
Tomas Rivera

AS THE WORLD TURNS

Female Characters	*Male Characters*
Jade Sullivan	Darryl Crawford
Courtney Baxter	Nels Andersson
Dawn Stewart	Duncan McKechnie
Iva Snyder	Kent Bradford
Lucinda Walsh	Holden Snyder
Connor Walsh	Gavin Kruger
Cricket Montgomery	Gunnar Stenbeck
Dana Lambert	Kirk Andersson
Ariel Aldrin	Linc Lafferty
Charmane McColl	Tucker Foster
Lily Grimaldi	Dustin Donovan
Sierra Estaben	Tad Channing
Sabrina Hughes	Earl Mitchell
Taylor Baldwin	Tonio Reyes
Olivia Wycroft	Grant Colman
Lyla Montgomery Peretti	Gar Kramer
Nikki Graves	Diego Santana
Carly Tenney	Lamar Griffin
Dani Andropolous	Ryder Hughes
Zoe Crane	Hal Munson
Margo Hughes	Cal Stricklyn

THE BOLD AND THE BEAUTIFUL

Female Characters	*Male Characters*
Felicia Forrester	Ridge Forrester
Macy Forrester	Jake MacLaine
Darla	Clarke Garrison
Margo Lynley Spencer	Blake Hayes
Brooke Logan	Thorne Forrester
Kristen Forrester	Storm Logan
Faith Roberts	Saul Feinberg
Taylor Hayes	Zack Hamilton
Bridget Forrester	Pierre Jourdan
Lauren Fenmore	Grant Chambers

Jasmine Malone   Sly Donovan
                                      Dylan Shaw

THE CITY

Female Characters	*Male Characters*
Sydney Chase	Buck Huston
Tess Wilder	Jacob Foster
Zoey	Bernardo Castro
Jocelyn Brown	Gino Soleito
Carla Soleito	
Azure C.	

DAYS OF OUR LIVES

Female Characters	*Male Characters*
Glynnis Turner	Marcus Hunter
Calliope Jones	Tanner Scofield
Carly Kiriakis	Bo Brady
Savannah Wilder	Roman Brady
Marlena Evans-Brady	Stefano DiMera
Daphne DiMera	Speed Selejko
Trista Evans	Shane Donovan
Jeri Clayton	Kellam Chandler
Brooke Hamilton	Maxwell Jarvis
Delia Abernathy	Woody King
Kayla Brady	Hart Bennett
Nikki Wade	Franco Kelly
Hope Brady	Brady Black
Lexie Carver	Lucas Roberts
Vivian Alamain	Ivan Marais
Tess Janings	Jonah Carver
Valery Grant	Austin Reed
Desiree McCall	Mickey Horton
	Brett Fredricks

GENERAL HOSPITAL

Female Characters	*Male Characters*
Kira Faulkner	Harlan Barrett
Felicia Cummings Jones	Mitch Williams
Lila Quartermaine	Noah Drake
Dominique Taub	Cesar Faison
Jade Soong	Blackie Parrish
Tiffany Hill Donely	Connor Olivera
Robin Scorpio	Duke Lavery
Ruby Anderson	Frisco Jones
Jessie Brewer	Chase Murdock
Augusta McLeod	Gordon Grey
Dorne Fleming	Finian O'Toole
Holly Sutton Scorpio	Cameron Faulkner
Tanya Roskov Jones	Derek Barrington
Louisa (Lou) Swenson	Lord Rama
Celia Quartermaine	Grant Putnam
Keesha Ward	Crane Tolliver
Simone Hardy	Justus Ward
Carly Roberts	Lucky Spencer
Dara Jensen	Reginald Jennings
Maxie Jones	Nikolas Cassadine
Lois Cerullo Ashton	Jasper "Jax" Jacks
	Sonny Corinthos

GUIDING LIGHT

Female Characters	*Male Characters*
Chelsea Reardon	Ross Marler
Nadine Cooper Lewis	Dylan Shayne Lewis
Violet Penfield	Quinton Chamberlain
Eleni Cooper Spaulding	Warren Andrews
Reva Shayne Cooper	Hart Jessup
Harley Cooper	Kyle Sampson
India von Halkein	Hawk Shayne
Holly Lindsey Reade	Clay Tynan
Roxie Shayne	Fletcher Reade

Blake Thorpe Marler
Maeve Stoddard
Gilly Grant
Kit Vested
Linell Conway
Viola Stapleton
Hillary Bauer
Brandy Shelooe
Calla Matthews
Nola Reardon Chamberlain
Marah Lewis
Bridget Reardon
Vanessa Chamberlain Reardon
Dahlia Crede
Nell Cleary

Jackson Freemont
Hampton Speakes
Dean Blackford
Justin Marler
Logan Stafford
Derek Colby
Cameron Stewart
Rusty Shayne
Floyd Parker
Griffin Williams
Marcus Williams

ONE LIFE TO LIVE

Female Characters

Cassie Callison Carpenter
Meri Lynn Dennison
Rika Price
Dorian Lord
Clover Wilde
Lana McClain
Luna Moody
Didi O'Neill
LeAnn Demerest
Sadie Gray
Gwendolyn Abbott
Edwina Lewis
Gretel Cummings
Katrina Karr
Courtney Wright
Jinx Rollins
Delilah Buchanan Garretson
Marty Saybrooke
Carlotta Vega
Andy Harrison

Male Characters

Brad Vernon
Troy Nichols
Victor Lord
Cord Roberts
Talbot Huddleston
Asa Buchanan
Marco Dane
Hudson King
Marcello Salta
Hunter Guthrie
Carlo Hesser
Rafe Garretson
Cain Rogan
Trent Chapin
Clint Buchanan
Giles Morgan
Alec Lowndes
Drew Buchanan
Cristian Vega
Dylan Moody

Nora Gannon Buchanan   Antonio Vega
Blair Manning

THE YOUNG AND THE RESTLESS

Female Characters	*Male Characters*
Christine "Cricket" Blair	Clint Radison
Leanna Newman	Rex Sterling
Lauralee Brooks	Jazz Jackson
Salena Wiley	Miguel Rodriguez
Dina Abbott	Jared Markson
Mamie Johnson	Nathan Hastings
Drucilla Barber Winters	Snapper Foster
Boobsie Caldwell	Brock Reynolds
Nikki Newman	Warner Wilson
Casey Reed	Jed Andrews
April Stevens	Lance Prentiss
Faren Connor	Brent Davis

Names of Fictional
Characters

While working on this chapter, we noticed that many of the classics, as well as popular literature and Broadway plays and musicals, have been made into movies. So, when there is a movie based on a book or play, we've listed the name of the fictional character, followed by the actor or actress who played the part. That way, if you're interested in a character's name for your baby, you'll know there's a film you can rent to see and hear the name in action.

Of course, in the case of the classics, you can always get a copy of the book and read it. That's what fourteen-year-old Susan Weaver was doing—reading F. Scott Fitzgerald's *Great Gatsby* for her English class—when she came across a name that she felt truly embodied her personality. So right then and there, at the Ethel Walker School, a prestigious all-girl boarding school in Simsbury, Connecticut, the young woman changed her name to Sigourney Weaver.

Demi Moore and Bruce Willis named their daughter Scout, the name of Atticus Finch's daughter in *To Kill a Mockingbird*. John Travolta's son is Jett, the name of the character played by James Dean in *Giant*. We're guessing that the fictional characters inspired these celebrities when they named their children. We hope they'll inspire you, too.

NOTE: There's *no way* we can include all of literature's greatest classics, or all the best movies. So we've included here our favorite names, books, plays, and movies. Hope they work for you as well!

"A" IS FOR ALIBI, by Sue Grafton
   Kinsey Millhone (female detective)

THE ACCIDENTAL TOURIST, based on the novel by Anne
Tyler
   Macon Leary . . . William Hurt
   Muriel Pritchett . . . Geena Davis

THE AGE OF INNOCENCE, by Edith Wharton
   Newland Archer

ALIEN, screenplay by Dan O'Bannon
   Ripley . . . Sigourney Weaver

ALL ABOUT EVE, based on a novel by Mary Orr
   Eve Harrington . . . Anne Baxter
   Margo Channing . . . Bette Davis
   Addison De Witt . . . George Sanders

ANNIE HALL, screenplay by Woody Allen and Marshall
Brickman
   Annie Hall . . . Diane Keaton
   Alvy Singer . . . Woody Allen

AROUND THE WORLD IN 80 DAYS, based on a novel by
Jules Verne
   Phileas Fogg . . . David Niven
   Aouda . . . Shirley MacLaine

BACK TO THE FUTURE, screenplay by Robert Zemeckis
and Bob Gale
   Marty McFly . . . Michael J. Fox

BATMAN, based on the characters created by Bob Kane
   Bruce Wayne (Batman) . . . Michael Keaton
   Jack Napier (the Joker) . . . Jack Nicholson

BEACHES, based on the novel by Iris Rainer Dart
   C. C. Bloom . . . Bette Midler
   Hillary Whitney . . . Barbara Hershey

BELL, BOOK AND CANDLE, based on the play by James
Van Druten
    Shepherd Henderson . . . James Stewart
    Gilliam Holroyd . . . Kim Novak

BEVERLY HILLS COP, screenplay by Daniel Petrie
    Axel Foley . . . Eddie Murphy

BIG, screenplay by Anne Spielberg and Gary Ross
    Josh Baskin . . . Tom Hanks

BORN YESTERDAY, based on the play by Garson Kanin
    Billie Dawn . . . Judy Holiday

BREAKFAST AT TIFFANY'S, based on the novel by
Truman Capote
    Holly Golightly . . . Audrey Hepburn

BRIGADOON, based on the musical by Alan Jay Lerner
    Fiona Campbell . . . Cyd Charisse

THE BROTHERS KARAMAZOV, based on the novel by
Fyodor Dostoyevski
    Dmitri Karamazov . . . Yul Brynner
    Fyodor Karamazov . . . Lee J. Cobb
    Alexey Karamazov . . . William Shatner
    Katya . . . Claire Bloom

BUS STOP, based on the play by William Inge
    Cherie . . . Marilyn Monroe
    Bo . . . Don Murray
    Virgil . . . Arthur O'Connell

BUTTERFIELD 8, based on the novel by John O'Hara
    Gloria Wandrous . . . Elizabeth Taylor
    Weston Liggett . . . Laurence Harvey
    Bingham Smith . . . Jeffrey Lynn

THE CARPETBAGGERS, based on the novel by Harold Robbins
   Jonas Cord . . . George Peppard
   Nevada Smith . . . Alan Ladd

CASABLANCA, based on an unproduced play by Murray Burnett and Joan Allison
   Rick Blaine . . . Humphrey Bogart
   Ilsa Lund Laszlo . . . Ingrid Bergman

CAT BALLOU, based on the novel by Roy Chanslor
   Cat Ballou . . . Jane Fonda
   Kid Shelleen/Strawn . . . Lee Marvin
   Clay Boone . . . Michael Callan

CAT ON A HOT TIN ROOF, based on the play by Tennessee Williams
   Maggie . . . Elizabeth Taylor
   Brick . . . Paul Newman

CATCHER IN THE RYE, by J. D. Salinger
   Holden Caulfield
   Phoebe Caulfield

CHARADE, based on a story by Peter Stone and Marc Behm
   Alexander Dyle, Adam Canfield, Peter Joshua, and Bryan
      Cruikshank . . . Cary Grant
   Reggie Lampert . . . Audrey Hepburn
   Hamilton Bartholomew . . . Walter Matthau

CIMARRON, based on the novel by Edna Ferber
   Yancey Cravat . . . Richard Dix
   Sabra Cravat . . . Irene Dunne

THE COLOR PURPLE, based on the novel by Alice Walker
   Celie . . . Whoopi Goldberg
   Sofia . . . Oprah Winfrey
   Shug Avery . . . Margaret Avery

CONAN THE BARBARIAN, screenplay by John Milius and Oliver Stone

Conan . . . Arnold Schwarzenegger
Thulsa Doom . . . James Earl Jones
Valeria . . . Sandahl Bergman
Rexor . . . Ben Davidson

CYRANO DE BERGERAC, based on Brian Hooker's translation of the play by Edmond Rostand
Cyrano de Bergerac . . . Gerard Depardieu
Roxanne Robin . . . Anne Brochet

DADDY LONG LEGS, based on the play and novel by Jean Webster
Jervis Pendleton . . . Fred Astaire
Julie . . . Leslie Caron

DIAMONDS ARE FOREVER, based on the novel by Ian Fleming
James Bond . . . Sean Connery
Tiffany Case . . . Jill St. John
Plenty O'Toole . . . Lana Wood

THE DIRTY DOZEN, based on the novel by E. M. Nathanson
Tassos Bravos . . . Al Mancini
Victor Franko . . . John Cassavetes
Glenn Gilpin . . . Ben Carruthers
Robert Jefferson . . . Jim Brown
Pedro Jiminez . . . Trini Lopez
Roscoe Lever . . . Stuart Cooper
Archer Maggott . . . Telly Savalas
Vernon Pinkley . . . Donald Sutherland
Samson Posey . . . Clint Walker
Seth Sawyer . . . Colin Maitland
Joseph Wladislaw . . . Charles Bronson

DOCTOR ZHIVAGO, based on the novel by Boris Pasternak
Lara . . . Julie Christie
Yuri . . . Omar Sharif
Tonya . . . Geraldine Chaplin

DRIVING MISS DAISY, based on the play by Alfred Uhry
Daisy Werthan . . . Jessica Tandy
Hoke Colburn . . . Morgan Freeman

EAST OF EDEN, based on the novel by John Steinbeck
  Cal . . . James Dean
  Abra . . . Julie Harris

E.T.—THE EXTRA-TERRESTRIAL, screenplay by Melissa Mathison
  Elliott . . . Henry Thomas
  Gertie . . . Drew Barrymore

ETHAN FROME, by Edith Wharton
  Ethan Frome
  Zenobia "Zeena" Frome

THE EXORCIST, based on the novel by William Peter Blatty
  Regan MacNeil . . . Linda Blair

THE FALCON AND THE SNOWMAN, based on the novel by Robert Lindsey
  Daulton Lee . . . Sean Penn
  Christopher Boyce . . . Timothy Hutton

FEAR OF FLYING, by Erica Jong
  Isadora Wing

FLAMINGO ROAD, based on the play by Robert Wilder and Sally Wilder
  Lane Bellamy . . . Joan Crawford
  Fielding Carlisle . . . Zachary Scott
  Titus Semple . . . Sydney Greenstreet

FATAL ATTRACTION, screenplay by James Dearden
  Alex Forrest . . . Glenn Close
  Dan Gallagher . . . Michael Douglas

FORT APACHE, suggested by the story "Massacre" by James Warner Bellah
  Kirby York . . . John Wayne
  Owen Thursday . . . Henry Fonda
  Philadelphia Thursday . . . Shirley Temple

FOR WHOM THE BELL TOLLS, based on the novel by Ernest Hemingway
  Robert Jordan . . . Gary Cooper
  Maria . . . Ingrid Bergman
  Pilar . . . Katrina Paxinon
  Pablo . . . Akim Tamiroff

GHOST, screenplay by Bruce Joel Rubin
  Molly Jensen . . . Demi Moore
  Sam Wheat . . . Patrick Swayze
  Oda Mae Brown . . . Whoopi Goldberg

GHOSTBUSTERS, screenplay by Dan Ackroyd and Harold Ramis
  Peter Venkman . . . Bill Murray
  Raymond Stantz . . . Dan Ackroyd
  Egon Spangler . . . Harold Ramis
  Dana Barrett . . . Sigourney Weaver

GIANT, based on the novel by Edna Ferber
  Leslie Lynnton Benedict . . . Elizabeth Taylor
  Bick Benedict . . . Rock Hudson
  Jett Rink . . . James Dean
  Luz Benedict . . . Mercedes McCambridge

GONE WITH THE WIND, based on the novel by Margaret Mitchell
  Rhett Butler . . . Clark Gable
  Scarlett O'Hara . . . Vivien Leigh
  Ashley Wilkes . . . Leslie Howard
  Melanie Hamilton . . . Olivia De Havilland
  India Wilkes . . . Alicia Rhett

THE GREAT GATSBY, based on the novel by F. Scott Fitzgerald
  Nick Carraway . . . Sam Waterston
  Daisy Buchanan . . . Mia Farrow
  Tom Buchanan . . . Bruce Dern
  Jay Gatsby . . . Robert Redford
  Jordan Baker . . . Lois Chiles
  Myrtle Wilson . . . Karen Black

GREEN CARD, screenplay by Peter Weir
  Bronte Mitchell . . . Andie MacDowell

GREEN MANSIONS by W. H. Hudson
  Rima

GUYS AND DOLLS, based on the musical by Jo Swerling
and Abe Burrows, from a story by Damon Runyon
  Sky Masterson . . . Marlon Brando
  Sarah Brown . . . Jean Simmons

HARVEY, based on the play by Mary C. Chase
  Elwood P. Dowd . . . James Stewart
  Veta Louise Simmons . . . Josephine Hull

HAWAII, based on the novel by James A. Michener
  Jerusha Bromley . . . Julie Andrews
  Rafer Hoxworth . . . Richard Harris

HOME ALONE, screenplay by John Hughes
  Kevin McAllister . . . Macauley Culkin

THE HOUSE OF SEVEN GABLES, by Nathaniel Hawthorne
  Hepzibah Pyncheon
  Clifford Pyncheon
  Jaffrey Pyncheon
  Phoebe Pyncheon

INDIANA JONES AND THE TEMPLE OF DOOM, screen-
play by Williard Huyck and Gloria Katz
  Indiana Jones . . . Harrison Ford
  Willie Scott . . . Kate Capshaw

IN HARM'S WAY, based on the novel by James Bassett
  Rockwell Torrey . . . John Wayne

KINGS ROW, based on the novel by Henry Bellamann
  Randy Monoghan . . . Ann Sheridan
  Parris Mitchell . . . Robert Cummings
  Drake McHugh . . . Ronald Reagan
  Cassandra Tower . . . Betty Field

KLUTE, screenplay by Andy K. Lewis and Dave Lewis
  Bree Daniel . . . Jane Fonda

THE LAST PICTURE SHOW, based on the novel by Larry McMurtry
  Sonny Crawford . . . Timothy Bottoms
  Duane Jackson . . . Jeff Bridges
  Jacy Farrow . . . Cybill Shepherd

THE LITTLE FOXES, by Lillian Hellman
  Regina Giddens

THE LITTLE MERMAID, screenplay by John Musker and Ron Clements
  Ariel . . . animated mermaid

LITTLE WOMEN, based on the novel by Louisa May Alcott
  Meg March . . . Frances Dee
  Jo March . . . Katharine Hepburn
  Beth March . . . Jean Parker
  Amy March . . . Joan Bennett

THE LITTLEST REBEL, based on the play by Edwin Burke
  Virgie Cary . . . Shirley Temple

LONESOME DOVE, by Larry McMurtry
  Augustus McCrae
  Woodrow Call
  Jake Spoon
  Lorena Wood
  Clara Allen

LOVE STORY, based on the novel by Erich Segal
  Jenny Cavilleri . . . Ali MacGraw
  Oliver Barrett IV . . . Ryan O'Neal

LOVING, by Danielle Steele
  Bettina Daniels
  Ivo Stewart

THE MAN WHO CAME TO DINNER, based on the play by
George S. Kaufman and Moss Hart
  Sheridan Whiteside . . . Monty Woolley

THE MARK OF ZORRO, based on the story "The Curse of
Capistrano" by Johnston McCulley
  Diego Vega . . . Tyrone Power
  Lolita Quintero . . . Linda Darnell
  Esteban Pasquale . . . Basil Rathbone
  Inez Quintero . . . Gale Sondergaard
  Fray Felipe . . . Eugene Pallette

THE MISFITS, screenplay by Arthur Miller
  Gay Langland . . . Clark Gable
  Roslyn Taber . . . Marilyn Monroe
  Perce Howland . . . Montgomery Clift

MOONSTRUCK, screenplay by John Patrick Shanley
  Loretta Castorini . . . Cher

THE MUSIC MAN, based on the musical by Meredith
Willson
  Harold Hill . . . Robert Preston
  Marian Paroo . . . Shirley Jones
  Marcellus Washburn . . . Buddy Hackett
  Eulalie Mackechnie Shinn . . . Hermione Gingold
  Amaryllis . . . Monique Vermont
  Winthrop Paroo . . . Ronny Howard

NATIONAL VELVET, based on the novel by Enid Bagnold
  Velvet Brown . . . Elizabeth Taylor
  Mi Taylor . . . Mickey Rooney

NINE TO FIVE, screenplay by Colin Higgins and Patricia
Resnick
  Judy Bernley . . . Jane Fonda
  Violet Newstead . . . Lily Tomlin
  Doralee Rhodes . . . Dolly Parton

ON THE BEACH, based on the novel by Nevil Shute
Dwight Towers . . . Gregory Peck
Moira Davidson . . . Ava Gardner

PAPER MOON, based on the novel *Addie Pray* by Joe David Brown
Moses Pray . . . Ryan O'Neal
Addie Loggins Pray . . . Tatum O'Neal
Trixie Delight . . . Madeline Kahn

THE PHILADELPHIA STORY, based on the play by Philip Barry
Dexter Haven . . . Cary Grant
Tracy Lord . . . Katharine Hepburn

PRETTY WOMAN, screenplay by J. F. Lawton
Vivian Ward . . . Julia Roberts
Edward Lewis . . . Richard Gere

THE PRINCE OF TIDES, based on the novel by Pat Conroy
Savannah Wingo . . . Melinda Dillon
Sallie Wingo . . . Blythe Danner
Lila Wingo . . . Kate Nelligan
Chandler Wingo . . . Brandlyn Whitaker

REQUIEM FOR A HEAVYWEIGHT, screenplay by Rod Serling
Mountain Rivera . . . Anthony Quinn
Maish Rennick . . . Jackie Gleason

THE RETURN OF THE NATIVE, by Thomas Hardy
Diggory Venn
Damon Wildeve
Thomasin Yeobright
Clement "Clym" Yeobright
Eustacia Vye

ROCKY, screenplay by Sylvester Stallone
Rocky Balboa . . . Sylvester Stallone
Adrian . . . Talia Shire
Apollo Creed . . . Carl Weathers

SABRINA, based on the play *Sabrina Fair* by Samuel Taylor
Sabrina Fairchild . . . Audrey Hepburn
Linus Larrabee . . . Humphrey Bogart

THE SANDS OF TIME, by Sidney Sheldon
Lucia
Graciella
Megan
Teresa

THE SCARLET LETTER, based on the novel by Nathaniel
Hawthorne
Hester Prynne . . . Demi Moore

SCRUPLES, by Judith Krantz
Billy Winthrop Orsini, born Wilhelmina Hunnenwell
  Winthrop
Spider Elliot, born Peter Elliot
Valentine O'Neill
Maggie MacGregor, born Shirley Silverstein

SEASON OF PASSION, by Danielle Steele
Kaitlin "Kate" Harper
Felicia "Licia" Norman
Tygue Harper (male)

SEVEN BRIDES FOR SEVEN BROTHERS, based on the
story "The Sobbin' Women" by Stephen Vincent Benét
Alice . . . Nancy Kilgas
Dorcas . . . Julie Newmeyer
Liza . . . Virginia Gibson
Milly . . . Jane Powell
Ruth . . . Ruta Kilmonis
Martha . . . Norma Doggett
Sarah . . . Betty Carr
Adam . . . Howard Keel
Benjamin . . . Jeff Richards
Caleb . . . Matt Mattox
Daniel . . . Marc Platt
Ephraim . . . Jacques d'Amboise

Frank . . . Tommy Rall
Gideon . . . Russ Tamblyn

SHOW BOAT, based on the novel by Edna Ferber and the musical by Oscar Hammerstein II and Jerome Kern
Magnolia Hawks . . . Kathryn Grayson
Gaylord Ravenal . . . Howard Keel

THE SILENCE OF THE LAMBS, based on the novel by Thomas Harris
Hannibal Lecter . . . Anthony Hopkins
Clarice Starling . . . Jodie Foster

A STAR IS BORN, based on a story by William A. Wellman and Robert Carson
Vicki Lester, born Esther Blodgett . . . Judy Garland
Norman Maine . . . James Mason

STAR WARS, screenplay by George Lucas
Luke Skywalker . . . Mark Hamill
Princess Leia . . . Carrie Fisher
Han Solo . . . Harrison Ford
Obi-wan Kenobi . . . Alec Guinness
Darth Vader . . . David Prowe, with voice of James Earl Jones

STEEL MAGNOLIAS, based on the play by Robert Harling
M'Lynn Eatenton . . . Sally Field
Truvy Jones . . . Dolly Parton
Ouiser Boudreaux . . . Shirley MacLaine
Annelle Dupuy Desoto . . . Darryl Hannah
Claree Belcher . . . Olympia Dukakis
Shelby Eatenton Latcherie . . . Julia Roberts

THE SUN ALSO RISES, based on the novel by Ernest Hemingway
Jake Barnes . . . Tyrone Power
Brett Ashley . . . Ava Gardner

SWEET BIRD OF YOUTH, based on the play by Tennessee Williams
  Chance Wayne . . . Paul Newman
  Heavenly Finley . . . Shirley Knight

TEENAGE MUTANT NINJA TURTLES, screenplay by Todd W. Langen and Bobby Herbeck
  Raphael . . . Josh Pais
  Michelangelo . . . Michelan Sisti
  Donatello . . . Leif Tilden
  Leonardo . . . David Forman
  April O'Neil . . . Judith Hoag

TERMS OF ENDEARMENT, based on the novel by Larry McMurtry
  Aurora Greenway . . . Shirley MacLaine
  Emma Horton . . . Debra Winger
  Garrett Breedlove . . . Jack Nicholson
  Flap Horton . . . Jeff Daniels

THE THORN BIRDS, based on a novel by Colleen McCullough
(This is the cast of the ABC-TV miniseries.)
  Meggie Cleary . . . Rachel Ward
  Fiona "Fee" Cleary . . . Jean Simmons
  Ralph de Bricassart . . . Richard Chamberlain
  Rainier Hartheim . . . Ken Howard
  Luddie Miller . . . Earl Holliman
  Justine O'Neill . . . Mare Winningham
  Luke O'Neill . . . Bryan Brown
  Dane O'Neill . . . Philip Anglim
  Vittorio Contini-Verchese . . . Christopher Plummer

THE THREE SISTERS, by Anton Chekhov
  Olga
  Masha
  Irina

TO KILL A MOCKINGBIRD, based on the novel by Harper Lee
  Atticus Finch . . . Gregory Peck

Scout Finch . . . Mary Badham
Jem Finch . . . Philip Alford
Dill Harris . . . John Megna

UNCLE BUCK, screenplay by John Hughes
Buck Russell . . . John Candy
Tia Russell . . . Jean Kelly
Maizy Russell . . . Gaby Hoffman
Miles Russell . . . Macauley Culkin
Chanice Kobolowski . . . Amy Madigan

VALLEY OF THE DOLLS, based on the novel by Jacqueline Susann
Neely O'Hara . . . Patty Duke
Lyon Burke . . . Paul Burke

THE WIZARD OF OZ, adapted from the novel by L. Frank Baum
Dorothy . . . Judy Garland
Hunk (Scarecrow) . . . Ray Bolger
Zeke (Cowardly Lion) . . . Bert Lahr
Hickory (Tin Woodman) . . . Jack Haley
Glinda . . . Billie Burke
Oz . . . Frank Morgan

WORKING GIRL, screenplay by Kevin Wade
Tess McGill . . . Melanie Griffith
Jack Trainer . . . Harrison Ford
Katherine Parker . . . Sigourney Weaver

WUTHERING HEIGHTS, based on the novel by Emily Brontë
Heathcliff . . . Laurence Olivier
Catherine . . . Merle Oberon
Nellie . . . Flora Robson
Hindley . . . Hugh Williams

ZORBA THE GREEK, based on the novel by Nikos Kazantzakis
Alexis Zorba . . . Anthony Quinn

Something to Sing About
Lyrical Names

> "She has eyes that men adore so
> And a torso, even more so."
> —From "Lydia, the Tattooed Lady"

Okay, okay, so "Lydia, the Tattooed Lady" isn't a beautiful ballad that opens the floodgates of one's most romantic memories. But from experience, I can tell you that I love it when I'm introduced to someone and they sing that song to me. It means they know my name—and it becomes unlikely that they'll forget it. Plus, not only is it a good icebreaker, but I get more attention than people whose names are not associated with songs.

> —Lydia Hope Wilen

So there you have it . . . an unsolicited testimonial in favor of giving your child a name worth singing about!

With the help of the Billboard Research Service, here are all the songs we uncovered to start you thinking (and singing!) about the right name for your child. When you go through the list, be prepared for a sentimental stream of memories to flow by as you spot some of your old favorites. Whenever possible, we've listed one or more of the song's recording artists to make it easier for you to find the song in your local music store. And now, you're ready to play "Name That Tune with a Name!"

SONGS WITH GIRLS' NAMES

Song	*Recording Artist*
Sweet ADELINE	
ALICE Blue Gown	
ALICE in Wonderland	Neil Sedaka
ALLISON	Elvis Costello
AMANDA	Boston; Waylon Jennings
AMAPOLA	Helen O'Connell
Once in Love with AMY	Ray Bolger
ANASTASIA	Pat Boone; Roger Williams
ANGIE	Rolling Stones
ANGIE Baby	Helen Reddy
ANNIE	(from Broadway show of same title)
ANNIE's Song	John Denver
Dreamboat ANNIE	Heart
AUBREY	Bread
BARBARA Polka	
BARBARA ANN	Beach Boys; Regents
BERNADETTE	Four Tops
BERNADINE	Pat Boone
BESS You Is My Woman	(from Broadway show *Porgy and Bess*)
BETH	Kiss
Sweet BETSY from Pike	
BETTY Co-Ed	
My Girl BILL	Jim Stafford
BILLIE JEAN	Michael Jackson
BOBBIE SUE	Oak Ridge Boys
BONNIE Came Back	Duane Eddy
I've Got BONNIE	Bobby Rydell
My BONNIE	Beatles and Tony Sheridan
BRANDY	Scott English
CANDIDA	Dawn
CANDY	Iggy Pop & Kate Pierson
CANDY's Room	Bruce Springsteen
CAROL	Chuck Berry

Song	*Recording Artist*
Oh, CAROL	Neil Sedaka
CAROLINE, No	Brian Wilson
Sweet CAROLINE	Neil Diamond
CARRIE	Europa; Cliff Richards
CARRIE ANN	Hollies
CATERINA	Perry Como
Close to CATHY	Mike Clifford
CECILIA	Simon & Garfunkel
Sweet CHARITY	(from Broadway show of same title)
Hush, Hush Sweet CHARLOTTE	(from film of same title)
CHARMAINE	
CHERRY, CHERRY	Neil Diamond
CHLOE	Elton John
CINDY's Birthday	Johnny Crawford
CINDY, Oh, CINDY	Eddie Fisher; Vince Martin
CINNAMON	Derek
CLAIR	Gilbert O'Sullivan
CLAUDETTE	Everly Brothers
CLEMENTINE	Bobby Darin; Weavers
Oh My Darling CLEMENTINE	
CORINNA, CORINNA	Ray Peterson
DAISY, DAISY	
DAISY JANE	America
Darlin' DANIELLE Don't	Henry Lee Summer
DELILAH	Tom Jones
Modern Day DELILAH	Van Stephenson
DELTA DAWN	Helen Reddy
DENISE	Randy & the Rainbows
DIANA	Paul Anka
DIANE	Bachelors
Little DIANE	Dion
DINAH	Danny Kaye
Hello, DOLLY!	(from Broadway show of same title); Louis Armstrong

Song	*Recording Artist*
DOMINIQUE	
DONNA	Richie Valens
DOTTIE	Danny & the Juniors
Come On EILEEN	Dexy's Midnight Runners
I Still See ELISA	(from Broadway show *Paint Your Wagon*)
ELVIRA	Oak Ridge Boys
EMILY	(from film *The Americanization of Emily*)
For EMILY	Simon & Garfunkel
EMMA	Hot Chocolate
FANNIE (Be Tender with My Love)	Bee Gees
FANNIE MAE	Buster Brown
FANNY	(from film of same title)
FRANCENE	ZZ Top
GEORGY Girl	(from film of same title)
GIGI	(from film of same title)
GINA	Johnny Mathis
GINNY Come Lately	Brian Hyland
GLORIA	Shadows of Knight; Laura Branigan; Them; Doors
Amazing GRACE	
GUINNEVERE	
Hard Hearted HANNAH	
Hi Hi HAZEL	Gary & the Hornets
Hooray for HAZEL	Tommy Roe
HEATHER Honey	Tommy Roe
HELENA Polka	
HONEY (I Miss You)	
HONEY (I'm in Love with You)	
IDA, Sweet as Apple Cider	Eddie Cantor
Goodnight, IRENE	Weavers
JAMIE	Eddie Holland; Ray Parker, Jr.
JANE	Jefferson Starship
JANET	Commodores

Song	Recording Artist
The Ballad of JAYNE	L.A. Guns
JEAN	Oliver
JEANNIE with the Light Brown Hair	
JEANNIE's Packin' Up	(from Broadway show *Brigadoon*)
Little JEANNIE	Elton John
JENNIE LEE	Jan & Arnie
JENNY	Danny Kaye
JENNY, JENNY	Little Richard
JEZEBEL	Frankie Lane
JILL	Gary Lewis & the Playboys
JO ANN	Playmates
JOANNA	Kool & the Gang
JOANNE	Michael Nesmith
JOLENE	Dolly Parton
JOSEPHINE	Bill Black's Combo
My Girl JOSEPHINE	Fats Domino
JOSIE	Steely Dan
JUDY in Disguise (with Glasses)	John Fred & His Playboy Band
Suite: JUDY Blue Eyes	Crosby, Stills & Nash
JULIA	Beatles
JULIE, Do Ya Love Me	Bobby Sherman
Oh, JULIE	Crescendos
O KATHARINA	
Sister KATE	
I'll Take You Home Again, KATHLEEN	
KATHY-O	Diamonds
K-K-K-KATY	
LAURA	(from film of same title)
Think of LAURA	Christopher Cross
LAURIE (Strange Things Happen . . .)	Dickey Lee
LEAH	Roy Orbison
LAYLA	Eric Clapton
Sweet LEILANI	

Song	*Recording Artist*
LILI MARLENE	
LILY of the Valley	
I Saw LINDA Yesterday	Dickey Lee
LINDA	Jan & Dean; Buddy Clarke
LOLA	Kinks
Whatever LOLA Wants	(from Broadway show *Damn Yankees*)
Sweet LORRAINE	Kay Starr
LOUISE	Maurice Chevalier
LUCILLE	Everly Brothers; Kenny Rogers
LUCY in the Sky with Diamonds	Beatles; Elton John
Watch Out for LUCY	Eric Clapton
LULU's Back in Town	
LYDIA, the Tattooed Lady	Groucho Marx; Burl Ives
MABEL's Waltz Song	(from operetta *The Pirates of Penzance*)
MAGGIE	Redbone
When You and I Were Young, MAGGIE	
MAME	(from Broadway show of same title)
MANDY	Barry Manilow; Johnny Mathis
MARGIE	
MARIA	(from Broadway shows *The Sound of Music*; *West Side Story*)
MARIA ELENA	Los Indios Tabajaras
MARIAN the Librarian	(from Broadway show *The Music Man*)
C'mon MARIANNE	Four Seasons; Donny Osmond
MARIANNE	Hilltoppers; Terry Gilkyson
MARIE	Bachelors
MARLENA	Four Seasons

Song	*Recording Artist*
Mostly MARTHA	Crew Cuts
Along Comes MARY	Association
MARY's a Grand Old Name	
MARY's Prayer	Danny Wilson
Proud MARY	Creedence Clearwater Revival
Take a Message to MARY	Everly Brothers
MARY ANN	
MARY JANE	Rick James
MARY LOU	Ronny Hawkins
MATILDA	Harry Belafonte
Twistin' MATILDA	Jimmy Soul
Waltzing MATILDA	
Sweet MAXINE	Doobie Brothers
MELINDA	
MICHELLE	Beatles; David & Jonathan
Thoroughly Modern MILLIE	(from film of same title)
Good Golly Miss MOLLY	Little Richard; Swinging Blue Jeans
MONA LISA	Conway Twitty; Nat "King" Cole
NADIA's Theme	(from soap opera *The Young and the Restless*)
NADINE (Is It You)	Chuck Berry
NANCY with the Laughing Face	Frank Sinatra
No, No NANETTE	(from Broadway show of same title)
Wait Till the Sun Shines, NELLIE	
NELLY Was a Lady	
NOLA	Billy Williams
PAMELA	Toto
PATRICIA	Perez Prado
Hey PAULA	Paul & Paula
PEG	Steely Dan
PEG o' My Heart	
PEGGY SUE	Buddy Holly
POLLY Wolly Doodle	Burl Ives

Song	*Recording Artist*
RAMONA	Nat "King" Cole
REBECCA Came Back from Mecca	Burl Ives
Walk Away RENEE	Four Tops
Help me RHONDA	Beach Boys
RIKKI Don't Lose That Number	Steely Dan
Lovely RITA	Beatles
RONI	Bobby Brown
RONNIE	Four Seasons
ROSALIE	
ROSANNA	Toto
Honeysuckle ROSE	
My Wild Irish ROSE	
Rambling ROSE	
ROSE of Washington Square	Barbra Streisand
Second Hand ROSE	Barbra Streisand
ROSEMARIE, I Love You	
ROSIE, You Are My Posie	
ROXANNE	Police
ROXIE	(from Broadway show *Chicago*)
RUBY	Ray Charles
RUBY Baby	Dion
RUBY ANN	Marty Robbins
SADIE, SADIE, Married Lady	(from Broadway show and film *Funny Girl*)
My Gal SAL	
Lay Down SALLY	Eric Clapton
SALLY	Grand Funk Railroad
Long Tall SALLY	Pat Boone; Little Richard
SANDY	Ronny & the Daytonas; Larry Hall; Dion
SANDY's Song	Dolly Parton
SARA	Fleetwood Mac; Starship
SARA Smile	Daryl Hall & John Oates
SHANNON	Henry Gross
Oh SHEILA	Ready for the World
SHEILA	Tommy Roe

Song	Recording Artist
Oh SHERRIE	Steve Perry
SHERRY	Four Seasons
Letter from SHERRY	Dale Ward
STELLA by Starlight	
Sweet SUE, Just You	
SUSAN	Buckinghams
O, SUSANNA	
If You Knew SUSIE	Eddie Cantor
Wake Up Little SUSIE	Everly Brothers; Simon & Garfunkel
SUZANNE	Journey
TAMMY	Debbie Reynolds
JUSTINE	Righteous Brothers
TARA's Theme	(from the film *Gone with the Wind*)
TINA MARIE	Perry Como
TRACY	Cuff Links
TRACY's Theme	Spencer Ross
VALERIE	Steve Winwood
VENUS	Bananarama; Shocking Blue
VERONICA	Elvis Costello
VICTORIA	Kinks
I'm Coming VIRGINIA	
WENDY	Beach Boys

SONGS WITH BOYS' NAMES

Song	Recording Artist
You Can Call Me AL	Paul Simon
ALEXANDER's Ragtime Band	
ALFIE	Cher; Dionne Warwick
ARTHUR's Theme	Christopher Cross
BEN	Michael Jackson
BILL	(from Broadway show *Show Boat*)
He's Just My BILL	

Song	*Recording Artist*
Soliloquy (My Boy BILL)	(from Broadway show *Carousel*)
Ode to BILLIE JOE	Bobby Gentry
BILLY	Kathy Linden
BILLY Boy	
BRIAN's Song	(from TV film of same title)
BRUCE	Rick Springfield
CHARLIE Is My Darling	Carmen McRae
CHARLIE My Boy	
DANIEL	Elton John
DANNY Boy	
DUNCAN	Paul Simon
EDDIE My Love	Teen Queens; Chordettes
ELI's Coming	Three Dog Night
ELMER's Tune	
FERNANDO	Abba
FRANKIE	Connie Francis
FREDERIC's Song	(from the operetta *Pirates of Penzance*)
Blow, GABRIEL, Blow	
I'm Just Wild About HARRY	
Dance with Me, HENRY	Georgia Gibbs
Hit the Road JACK	Ray Charles & the Raelets
JESSE	Roberta Flack; Carly Simon
JIMMY	(from Broadway show of same title)
Go, JIMMY, Go	Jimmy Clanton
Ragtime Cowboy JOE	David Seville & the Chipmunks
JOEY	Concrete Blonde
Big Bad JOHN	Jimmy Dean
Where Do You Work-A, JOHN?	
JOHNNY Loves Me	Shelley Fabares
JOHNNY One Note	Judy Garland
Oh JOHNNY, Oh JOHNNY Oh!	Bonnie Baker
When JOHNNY Comes Marching Home	

Song	*Recording Artist*
Who's JOHNNY	El DeBarge
JOSHUA Fit the Battle of Jericho	Traditional
Hey JUDE	Beatles; Wilson Pickett
Hats Off to LARRY	Del Shannon
Mr. LEE	Bobbettes
Meet Me in St. Louis, LOUIS	Judy Garland
MACK the Knife	Bobby Darin
Message to MICHAEL	Dionne Warwick
MICHAEL	Highwaymen
MICHAEL, Row the Boat Ashore	Weavers
MICKEY	Toni Basil
Go Down, MOSES	
NORMAN	Sue Thompson
OLIVER	(from Broadway show of same title)
Tall PAUL	Annette
QUENTIN's Theme	Charles Randolph Greane Sound
ROCKY	Austin Roberts
RUDY's Rock	Bill Haley & His Comets
Lovin' SAM (The Sheik of Alabam)	
SAM	Olivia Newton-John
Watching SCOTTY Grow	Bobby Goldsboro
A Boy Named SUE	Johnny Cash
SUNNY	
Ready TEDDY	Little Richard
TEDDY	Connie Francis
TIMOTHY	Buoys
Little WALTER	Tony! Toni! Tone!
Little WILLY	Sweet
ZORBA the Greek	Herb Alpert & the Tijuana Brass

Celebrities . . .
Their Names,
Once Upon a Time

Would Maurice Micklewhite have won an Academy Award in 1986 if he hadn't changed his name to Michael Caine? Would Steveland Morris be the sunshine of your life if he hadn't changed his name to Stevie Wonder? Would a film called *Pal Come Home* have been a box office hit if Pal's owner hadn't changed the dog's name to Lassie? On a scale from one to ten, how would you rate Mary Cathleen Collins? Would she be a ten if she hadn't changed her name to Bo Derek? In other words, would the celebrities who changed their names have "made it" *without* changing their names? Of course there's no way of knowing, but what you can find out from the list below is who was who, and what their name of choice currently is.

Professional Name	*Name at Birth*
Kareem Abdul-Jabbar	Ferdinand Lewis Alcindor, Jr.
Alan Alda	Alphonse D'Abruzzo
Muhammad Ali	Cassius Marcellus Clay, Jr.
Woody Allen	Allen Stewart Konigsberg
June Allyson	Ella Geisman
Julie Andrews	Julia Elizabeth Wells
Ann-Margret	Ann-Margret Olsson

Beatrice Arthur	Bernice Frankel
Lauren Bacall	Betty Joan Perske
Anne Bancroft	Annemarie Italiano
Brigitte Bardot	Camille Javal
Warren Beatty	Henry Warren Beaty
Tony Bennett	Antonio Dominick Benedetto
Robby Benson	Robert Segal
Bono (U2's lead singer)	Paul Hewson
Victor Borge	Borge Rosenbaum
David Bowie	David Robert Hayward-Jones
Beau Bridges	Lloyd Vernet Bridges III
Morgan Brittany	Suzanne Cupito
Charles Bronson	Charles Buchinsky
Mel Brooks	Melvin Kaminsky
George Burns	Nathan Birnbaum
Raymond Burr	William Stacey Burr
Ellen Burstyn	Edna Rae Gillooly
Michael Caine	Maurice Joseph Micklewhite
Dyan Cannon	Samille Diane Friesen
Kate Capshaw	Kathleen Sue Nail
Diahann Carroll	Carol Diahann Johnson
Ray Charles	Ray Charles Robinson
Chevy Chase	Cornelius Crane Chase
Cher	Cherilyn Sarkisian La Piere
Alice Cooper	Vincent Furnier
Elvis Costello	Declan Patrick McManus
Ted Danson	Edward Bridge Danson III
Tom Cruise	Thomas Cruise Mapother IV
John Denver	Henry John Deutschendorf, Jr.
Bo Derek	Mary Cathleen Collins
Angie Dickinson	Angeline Brown
Bo Diddley	Elias McDaniel
Kirk Douglas	Issur Danielovitch Demsky
Patty Duke	Anne Marie Duke
Faye Dunaway	Dorothy Faye Dunaway
Bob Dylan	Robert Zimmerman
Dale Evans	Frances Octavia Smith
Morgan Fairchild	Patsy Ann McClenny
Jodie Foster	Alicia Christian Foster
Redd Foxx	John Elroy Sanford
Zsa Zsa Gabor	Sari Gabor

James Garner	James Baumgarner
Crystal Gayle	Brenda Gail Webb
Whoopi Goldberg	Caryn Johnson
Elliot Gould	Elliot Goldstein
Lee Grant	Lyova Haskell Rosenthal
Buddy Hackett	Leonard Hacker
Hammer	Stanley Burrell
Margaux Hemingway	Margot Hemingway
Audrey Hepburn	Edda van Heemstra Hepburn-Ruston
Pee-wee Herman	Paul Reubens
Hulk Hogan	Terry Jean Bollette
Bob Hope	Leslie Townes Hope
Englebert Humperdinck	Arnold Dorsey
Lauren Hutton	Mary Laurence Hutton
Mick Jagger	Michael Phillip Jagger
Elton John	Reginald Kenneth Dwight
Tom Jones	Thomas Jones Woodward
Diane Keaton	Diane Hall
Michael Keaton	Michael Douglas
Chaka Khan	Yvette Marie Stevens
Ben Kingsley	Krishna Bhanji
Lassie	Pal
Spike Lee	Shelton Jackson Lee
Jay Leno	James Leno
Jerry Lewis	Joseph Levitch
Sophia Loren	Sofia Scicolone
Madonna	Madonna Louise Ciccone
Karl Malden	Mladen Sekulovich
Walter Matthau	Walter Matuschanskayasky
Meat Loaf	Marvin Lee Adax
Toni Morrison	Chloe Wofford
Kate Nelligan	Patricia Colleen Nelligan
Mike Nichols	Michael Igor Peshkowsky
Jack Nicholson	John Joseph Nicholson
Chuck Norris	Carlos Ray Norris
Tony Orlando	Michael Anthony Orlando Cassavitis
Pocahontas	Mataoka
Jack Palance	Walter Palahnuik
Minnie Pearl	Sarah Ophelia Colley Cannon

Gregory Peck	Eldred Gregory Peck
Michelle Phillips	Holly Michelle Gilliam
Jane Powell	Suzanne Burce
The Artist Formerly Known as Prince	Prince Rogers Nelson
Robert Redford	Charles Robert Redford, Jr.
Della Reese	Deloreese Patricia Early
Burt Reynolds	Burton Leon Reynolds, Jr.
Debbie Reynolds	Mary Frances Reynolds
Ginger Rogers	Virginia McMath
Roy Rogers	Leonard Slye
Mickey Rooney	Joe Yule, Jr.
Mickey Rourke	Philip André Rourke
Sade	Helen Folasade Adu
Telly Savalas	Aristoteles Savalas
Jane Seymour	Joyce Penelope Frankenberg
Omar Sharif	Michael Shalhoub
Charlie Sheen	Carlos Irwin Estevez
Brooke Shields	Christa Brooke Camille Shields
Dinah Shore	Frances Rose Shore
Neil Simon	Marvin Neil Simon
Sissy Spacek	Mary Elizabeth Spacek
Mickey Spillane	Frank Morrison
Ringo Starr	Richard Starkey
Cat Stevens	Steven Georgian
Connie Stevens	Concetta Ann Ingola
Shadoe Stevens	Terry Ingstad
Sting	Gordon Matthew Sumner
Meryl Streep	May Louise Streep
Barbra Streisand	Barbara Joan Streisand
Donna Summer	La Donna Andrea Gaines
Marlo Thomas	Margaret Julian Thomas
Lily Tomlin	Mary Jean Tomlin
Garry Trudeau	Garretson Beckman Trudeau
Tina Turner	Anna Mae Bullock
Twiggy	Leslie Hornby
Conway Twitty	Harold Lloyd Jenkins
Mike Wallace	Myron Leon Wallace
Sigourney Weaver	Susan Weaver
Gene Wilder	Jerry Silbermann

Stevie Wonder	Steveland Morris
Jane Wyman	Sarah Jane Fulks
Tammy Wynette	Virginia Wynette Pugh

What the Celebrities
Name Their Kids

Kathie Lee and Frank Gifford named their son Cody after the
Cleveland Browns' tackle Cody Risien. After this, you're on
your own when it comes to why the rest of the celebrities mentioned in this chapter chose the names they did for their children.

Meryl Streep, whose real name is Mary Louise Streep, took
the traditional approach, naming her children Grace, Henry,
Mary, and Louisa. As to the opposite of traditional—that's what
Frank Zappa went for when he zapped his kids with the names
Moon Unit, Dweezil, Ahmet Emuukha Rodan, and Diva.

As you'll see when you go through our extensive list, most
celebs chose names for their children that are closer to traditional than way out.

NOTE: To the celebrities who have more children than we have
listed, our apologies. Next time, send us an announcement!

To get you started, here's a Pop Quiz and a Mom Quiz. See
how many celebs you can match up with the name(s) of their
children. (Correct answers can be found on the following pages,
under the celebrities' names, which are listed alphabetically.)

POP QUIZ

1) Sylvester Stallone   a) Ezra Samuel
2) Harry Connick, Jr.   b) Jett
3) Michael J. Fox   c) Sam (son), twins: Schuyler
                                   and Aquinnah
4) Tom Cruise   d) Georgia Tatom

5)	Alec Baldwin	e)	(3 boys) Sage Moon Blood, Seth, and Seargeoh, and Sophia Rose
6)	Paul Reiser	f)	Brawley King
7)	Michael Douglas	g)	Annie, Joe, and Lily
8)	Nick Nolte	h)	Ireland Eliesse
9)	John Travolta	i)	Cameron Morrell (boy)
10)	Kevin Costner	j)	Isabella and Connor (boy)

MOM QUIZ

1)	Michelle Pfeiffer	a)	Annie Maude
2)	Bette Midler	b)	Dexter (girl)
3)	Reba McEntire	c)	Sophie Frederica Alohilani
4)	Pamela Anderson	c)	Alexa Ray and Jack Paris
5)	Rosie O'Donnell	e)	Claudia Rose and John Henry
6)	Glenn Close	f)	Clementine (Clemmy) and twins: Molly Ariel and Cyrus Zachariah
7)	Cybill Shepherd	g)	Parker Jaren (boy)
8)	Diane Keaton	h)	Bobbi Christin
9)	Christie Brinkley	i)	Shelby (boy)
10)	Whitney Houston	j)	Brandon

CELEBRITIES' CHILDREN'S NAMES

Brooke Adams	Josie Lynn
Alan Alda	Eve, Elizabeth, and Beatrice
Kim Alexis	Jamie (boy)
Debbie Allen	Vivian
Kirstie Alley and Parker Stevenson	William True and Lily Price
Harry Anderson	Dashiell and Eva Fay
Pamela Anderson and Tommy Lee	Brandon
Ursula Andress and Harry Hamlin	Dimitri
Prince Andrew and Sarah (Fergie), the Duchess of York	Beatrice Elizabeth Mary and Eugenie Victoria Helena
Julie Andrews	Emma Kate

Arthur Ashe and Jeanne Moutoussamy (a photographer)	Camera (girl)
Ed Asner	Kathryn, twins Liza and Matthew, and Charlie
Lauren Bacall and Humphrey Bogart	Stephen and Leslie Howard (girl)
and Jason Robards, Jr.	Sam
Kevin Bacon and Kyra Sedgewick	Travis Sedg and Sosie Ruth
Alec Baldwin and Kim Basinger	Ireland Eliesse
Stephen Baldwin	Alaia (girl)
Mikhail Baryshnikov and Jessica Lange	Alexandra (Sasha)
and Lisa Rinehart	Peter, Anna Katerina, and Sofia-Luisa
Ellen Barkin and Gabriel Byrne	Jack and Romy
Meredith Baxter and David Birney	Kate and twins Mollie Elizabeth and Peter David Edwin
Amanda Bearse	Zoe
Ed Begley, Jr.	Amanda and Nick
Harry Belafonte	Adrienne, Shari, Gina, and David
Annette Bening and Warren Beatty	Kathlyn
Tony Bennett	D'Andrea (boy), Deagal (boy), Joanna, and Antonia
Robby Benson and Karla DeVito	Lyric (girl) and Zephyr (boy)
Marisa Berenson	Starlite Melody
Candice Bergen and Louis Malle	Chloe
Corbin Bernsen and Amanda Pays	Oliver and twins Henry and Angus
Valerie Bertinelli and Eddie Van Halen	Wolfgang
Lisa Bonet	Zoe
Sonny Bono	Chesare

with Cher	Chastity
Debbie Boone	twins Dustin (girl) and Gabrielle, Jordan Alexander, and Tessa
Bjorn Borg	Robin (boy)
Timothy Bottoms	Bartholomew
David Bowie and Angela Burnet	Zowie (now known as Joey)
Bruce Boxleitner	Lee Davis and Sam
with Melissa Gilbert	Michael Garrett
Marlon Brando	Christian Devi, Miko (boy), Rebecca, Tehoto (boy), and Cheyenne Tarita (girl)
Conni Marie Brazelton	Michael Samarie (girl)
David Brenner	Cole (boy) and Slade Lucas Moby (boy)
Jeff Bridges	Hayley Rose, Isabelle, and Jessica
Christie Brinkley and Billy Joel	Alexa Ray
and Ricky Taubman	Jack Paris
Garth Brooks	Taylor Mayn Pearl (girl)
Mel Brooks	Stefanie, Nicholas, and Edward
with Anne Bancroft	Maximilian
Carol Burnett	Carrie Louise, Jody Ann, Erin, and Kate
David Byrne	Malu Valentine
Kate Capshaw	Jessica
with Steven Spielberg	Sasha (girl), Sawyer (boy), and Theo
David Carradine	Calista (girl) and Kansas (girl)
with Barbara Hershey	Free, who then changed his name to Tom
Keith Carradine	Martha Plimpton
with Sandra Will	Cade Richmond (boy), and Sorel (girl)
James Carville and Mary Matalin	Matalin Mary
Shaun Cassidy	Caitlin and John
Prince Charles and Princess Diana	William Arthur Philip Louis and Henry (Harry) Charles Albert David

Chevy Chase	Caley (girl), Emily, Cydney, and Cathalene
Cher and Greg Allman and Sonny Bono	Elijah Blue Chastity
Jackson Browne	Ethan
Linda Carter	James Clifford
Michael Chiklis (*The Commish*)	Autumn Isabella
Neneh Cherry	Tyson (girl)
Rae Dawn Chong	Morgan (boy)
Jill Clayburgh and David Rabe	Lily and Michael
Glenn Close	Annie Maude
Dabney Coleman	Kelly (girl), Randolph, and Mary
Margaret Colin and Justin Deas	Sam and Joe
Joan Collins and Anthony Newley and Ron Kass	Tara and Anthony Katherine
Phil Collins	Lillie
Alice Cooper	Calico
Harry Connick, Jr., and Jill Goodacre	Georgia Tatom
Jimmy Connors	Aubree (girl) and Brett David
Bill Cosby	Erika Ranee, Erinn Charlene, Ennis William, Ensa Camille, and Evin Harrah
Kevin Costner	Annie, Joe, and Lily
Lindsay Crouse and David Mamet	Willa
Tom Cruise and Nicole Kidman	Isabella and Connor (boy)
Billy Crystal	Jennifer and Lindsay
Jane Curtin	Tess
Jamie Lee Curtis and Christopher Guest	Annie and Thomas Haden
Willem Dafoe and Elizabeth LeCompte	Jack
Roger Daltrey	Rosie Lea and Willow Amber
Tyne Daly and Georg Stanford Brown	Beatris, Elizabeth, and Kathryne

Faith Daniels	Andrew Steven and Alyx Ray (girl)
Jeff Daniels	Ben
Blythe Danner and Bruce Paltrow	Gwyneth and Jake
Ted Danson	Alexis and Kate
Tony Danza	Catherine Ann and Emily Lynn
Pam Dawber and Mark Harmon	Sean and Ty Christian
Jonathan Demme	Ramona
Catherine Deneuve and Marcello Mastroianni	Chiara-Charlotte
Robert De Niro	Raphael Eugene
Brian Dennehy	Cormac (boy) and Sarah
John Denver	Anna Kate and Jessie Belle
Brian DePalma and Gale Ann Hurd	Lolita
Rick Derringer	Mallory Loving
Neil Diamond	Marjorie, Flyn, Jesse (boy), and Micah (boy)
Danny DeVito and Rhea Perlman	Grace, Jacob, and Lucie
Joan Didion and John Gregory Dunne	Quintana Roo
Kirk Douglas	Michael, Joel, Peter, and Eric
Michael Douglas	Cameron Morrell (boy)
Lesley-Anne Down and William Friedkin	Jack
Richard Dreyfuss	Benjamin, Emily, and Harry
Patrick Duffy	Padraic (boy) and Connor (boy)
Faye Dunaway and Terry O'Neill	Liam
Sheena Easton	Jake and Skylar (girl)
Britt Ekland and Slim Jim Phantom	Thomas Jefferson
Gordon Elliott	Angus Alexander
Nora Ephron and Carl Bernstein	Jacob Walker and Max Ephron
Louise Erdrich and Michael Dorris	Pallas (girl) and Persia (girl)
Julius Erving	Jazmin

Gloria Estefan	Nayib (boy)
Emilio Estevez and Carey Salley	Paloma and Taylor Levi (boy)
Chris Evert and Andy Mill	Alex (boy)
Mia Farrow	Tam and Isaiah
and Andre Previn	Fletcher, twins Matthew Phineas and Sascha Villiers, Lark Song, Daisy, and Soon-Yi (girl)
and Woody Allen	Dylan O'Sullivan (girl), Satchel O'Sullivan (boy), and Moses Amadeus
Carrie Fisher	Billie Cathryn
Harrison Ford	Benjamin and Willard
with Melissa Mathison	Malcolm
Michael J. Fox and Tracy Pollan	Sam (son), twins: Schuyler and Aquinnah
Andy Garcia	(girls) Dominik, Allesandra, and Daniela
Leeza Gibbons	
and Chris Quinten	Jordan (girl)
and Stephen Meadows	Troy Stephen
Mel Gibson	twins Christian and Edward, Hannah, and William
Kathie Lee and Frank Gifford	Cody Newton (boy) and Cassidy Erin (girl)
Melissa Gilbert	Dakota Mayi (boy)
and Bruce Boxleitner	Michael Garrett
Wayne Gretzky and Janet Jones	Paulina and Ty
Melanie Griffith	Alexander
and Don Johnson	Dakota (girl)
and Antonio Banderas	Stella del Carmen
George Hamilton and Alana Hamilton Stewart	Ashley Steven
Tom Hanks	Colin and Elizabeth
and Rita Wilson	Chester and Truman Theodore
Mel Harris	Byron and Madeline
Phil Hartman	Sean (boy) and Birgen (girl)

Goldie Hawn
  and Bill Hudson   Kate Garry and Oliver
  and Kurt Russell   Wyatt
Patty Hearst   Gillian Catherine and
                         Lydia Marie
Hugh Hefner   Marston (boy) and Cooper (boy)
Mariel Hemingway   Dree Louise and Langley Fox
                         (girl)
Gregory Hines   Zachary, Daria, and Jessica
Dustin Hoffman and
  Anne Byrne   Karina and Jennifer
  and Lisa Gottsegen   Jacob, Rebecca, Maxwell, and
                         Alexandra
Whitney Houston and
  Bobby Brown   Bobbi Christin (girl)
Ron Howard   twins Jocelyn and Paige
Mary Beth Hurt and
  Paul Schrader   Molly
William Hurt   Alex and Sam
Billy Idol   Willem Wolfe
Iman and Spencer
  Haywood   Zulekha (girl)
Mick Jagger
  and Bianca Jagger   Jade (girl)
  and Marsha Hunt   Karis (girl)
  and Jerry Hall   Elizabeth Scarlett, James Leroy
                         Augustine, and Georgia May
                         Ayeesha
Don Johnson
  and Patti D'Arbanville   Jesse (boy)
  and Melanie Griffith   Dakota (girl)
Earvin "Magic" Johnson   Earvin Johnson III
James Earl Jones   Flynn Earl
Rickie Lee Jones   Charlotte Rose
Erica Jong   Molly Miranda
Wynonna Judd   Elijah and Pauline Grace
Raul Julia   Benjamin and Raul Sigmund
Lainie Kazan   Jennifer
Diane Keaton   Dexter (girl)
Michael Keaton   Sean

Kevin Kline and
  Phoebe Cates   Owen Joseph
Kris Kristofferson   Johnnie and Casey (girl)
Cheryl Ladd   Jordan Elizabeth
Christine Lahti   Wilson and twins: Emma and Joe
Tom Landry   Thomas, Kitty, and Lisa
Jessica Lange and
  Mikhail
  Baryshnikov
  and Sam Shepard   Alexandra (Sasha)
                                Hannah Jane and Samuel
                                  Rogers IV
Lucy Lawless   Daisy
Martin Lawrence   Jasmine Page
Annie Lennox   (girls) Lola and Tali
Sugar Ray (Ray
  Charles) Leonard   Ray Charles
John Lithgow   Nathan and Phoebe
Kenny Loggins   Cody (boy) and Crosby (boy)
Shelley Long   Juliana
George Lucas   Katie
Susan Lucci   Andreas Martin and Liza Victoria
Joan Lunden   Jamie (girl), Lindsay (girl), and
                                  Sarah Emily

Paul and Linda
  McCartney   James Louis, Mary, and Stella
Reba McEntire   Shelby (boy)
Ali MacGraw and
  Robert Evans   Joshua
Ralph Macchio   Julia and Daniel
Madonna and
  Carlos Leon   Lourdes Marie Ciccone
Barbara Mandrell   Matthew, Jaime (girl), and
                                  Nathaniel

Andrea Marcovicci and
  Daniel Reichert   Alice Wolfe
Wynton Marsalis   Wynton Jr. and Simeon
Marlee Matlin   Sarah Rose
John Mellencamp   Justice (girl), Teddi Jo (girl)
  and (model)
  Elaine Irwin   Hud and Speck Wildhorse (boy)
Bette Midler   Sophie Frederica Alohilani

Dennis Miller	Holden (boy)
Demi Moore and Bruce Willis	(girls) Rumer Glenn, Scout LaRue, and Tallulah Belle
Melba Moore	Charli (girl)
Kate Mulgrew	Ian Alexander
Eddie Murphy	Bria and Miles Mitchell
Bill Murray	Homer and Luke
Joe Namath	Jessica Grace
Liam Neeson and Natasha Richardson	Micheál Richard Antonio and Daniel Jack
Brigitte Neilsen and Mark Gastineau	Marcus
Tracy Nelson and Billy Moses	Remington (girl)
Olivia Newton-John	Chloe Rose
Jack Nicholson	Lorraine Broussard and Raymond
Nick Nolte	Brawley King
Chuck Norris	Mike and Eric
Ken Olin and Patricia Wettig	Clifford and Roxanne
Ryan O'Neal and Farrah Fawcett	Tatum and Griffin Redmond James Fawcett
Tatum O'Neal and John McEnroe	Kevin John and Sean Timothy
Tony Orlando	John and Jenny Rose
Marie Osmond	Stephen James
Rosie O'Donnell	Parker Jaren (P. J.) (boy)
Peter O'Toole	Lorcan (boy), Pat, and Kate
Catherine Oxenberg	India (girl)
Chazz Palminteri and Gianna Renaudo	Dante Lorenzo (boy)
Mandy Patinkin	Isaac and Gideon
Jane Pauley and Garry Trudeau	twins Rachel and Ross, and Thomas
Sean Penn and Robin Wright	Dylan (girl) and Hopper Jack
Anthony Perkins and Berry Berenson	Elvis Brooke and Osgood Robert

Ron Perlman	Blake Amanda
Michelle Pfeiffer and David E. Kelley	Claudia Rose and John Henry
John Phillips and Genevieve Waite	Bijoux (girl) and Tamerlaine
Michelle Phillips	Austin Devereux (boy) and Chynna
Annie Potts	James Powell and Isaac Harris
Maury Povich with Connie Chung	Susan and Amy Matthew Jay
Priscilla Presley	Navarone Anthony
Bill Pullman	Maesa (girl), Jack, and Louis
Paul Reiser	Ezra Samuel
James Danforth and Marilyn Quayle	Tucker Danforth, Benjamin Eugene, and Mary Corinne
Phylicia and Ahmad Rashad	Condola Phylea
Lynn Redgrave and John Clarke	Benjamin B., Kelly B., and Annabel Lucy
Christopher Reeve and Gae Exton and Dana Morosini	Alexandra and Matthew Owen
Mary Lou Retton	Shayla Rae
Burt Reynolds and Loni Anderson	Quinton
Keith Richards and Patti Hansen	Alexandria and Theodore Dupree
John Ritter	Carly, Jason, and Tyler
Geraldo Rivera	Isabella Holmes
Tom Robbins	Fleetwood Starr
Tony Roberts	Nicole
Kenny Rogers	Christopher
Diana Ross	Ross Arne (boy), Chudney Lane (girl), Rhonda Suzanne, and Tracee Joy
Isabella Rossellini	Elettra-Ingrid
Victoria Rowell and Wynton Marsalis	Maya (girl) Jasper Armstrong
Kurt Russell and Season Hubley	Boston (boy)

and Goldie Hawn	Wyatt
Theresa Russell and Nicolas Roeg	Max and Statten Jack
Bob Saget	Aubrey and Lara
Susan St. James	Sunshine (girl) and Harmony (boy)
and Dick Ebersole	Charlie and William
Susan Sarandon and Franco Amarri	Eva Maria Livia
and Tim Robbins	Jack Henry and Miles Guthrie Tomalin
Caroline Kennedy Schlossberg	Rose Kennedy and Tatiana Celia
Arnold Schwarzenegger and Maria Shriver	Katherine Eunice and Christina Aurelia
Steven Seagal and Miyako Fujitani	Ayako and Kentaro
and Kelly LeBrock	Annaliza, Dominic, and Arissa
and Arissa Wolf	Savannah
Tom Selleck and Jilly Mack	Hannah
Jane Seymour	Katharine Jane (Katie)
Charlie Sheen	Cassandra
Cybill Shepherd	Clementine (Clemmy) and twins Molly Ariel and Cyrus Zachariah
Martin Short	Katherine and Oliver
Carly Simon and James Taylor	Benjamin Simon
Paul Simon	Harper (boy)
Helen Slater	Hannah Nika
Grace Slick	China
Jaclyn Smith	Gaston and Spencer Margaret
Patti Smith	Jesse Paris (girl) and Jackson Frederick
Will Smith	Trey (boy)
Paul Sorvino	Mira, Amanda, and Michael
Sissy Spacek	Schuyler Elizabeth
Steven Spielberg and Amy Irving	Max Samuel

and Kate Capshaw	Sasha (girl), Sawyer (boy), Theo, and Mikaela George (girl)
Bruce Springsteen and Patti Scialfa	Evan James and Jessica Rae
Sylvester Stallone	Sage Moon Blood (boy), Seth, and Seargeoh (boy)
and Jennifer Flavin	Sophia Rose
Mary Steenburgen and Malcolm McDowell	Charlie and Lillie
Rod Stewart	
and Kelly Emberg	Ruby
and Alana Hamilton Stewart	Sean Roderick and Kimberly
and Rachel Hunter	Renee and Liam
Sting	Joe and Kate
and Trudie Styler	Jake, Brigitte Michael (girl, called Mickey), Eliot (girl), and Giacomo Luke Summer (boy)
Oliver Stone	Sean
Darryl Strawberry	Diamond Nicole
Meryl Streep	Grace Jane, Henry, Mary Willa, and Louisa
Barbra Streisand and Elliott Gould	Jason Emanuel
Sally Struthers	Samantha
Donna Summer	Mimi
Keifer Sutherland	Sarah
Meshach Taylor	Tamar, Tariq, Yasmine, and Esmé (all girls)
Philip Michael Thomas and Sheila DeWindt	India Serene and Melody
Richard Thomas	Richard Francisco and triplets Barbara Ayala, Gwyneth Gonzales, and Pilar Alma
Lea Thompson and Howard Deutch	Madeline
Charlene Tilton	Cherish
John Travolta	Jett
Alex Trebek	Matthew Alexander
Donald Trump and Ivana Trump	Donald, Ivanka, and Eric

and Marla Trump	Tiffany
Tanya Tucker	Presley Tanita (girl) and Beau Grayson
Kathleen Turner	Rachel Ann
Mike Tyson	Rayna (girl)
Tracey Ullman	Mabel Ellen
Lindsay Wagner	Alex and Dorian Henry
Rachel Ward and Bryan Brown	Matilda and Rosie
Jill Whelan	Harrison Robert
Billy Dee Williams	Corey Dee (boy) and Hanako (girl)
Robin Williams	Zachary, Zelda, and Cody Alan
Vanessa Williams	Melanie and Jillian
Marianne Williamson	India Emmaline
Bruce Willis and Demi Moore	Rumer Glenn (girl), Tallulah Belle, and Scout LaRue (girl)
Debra Winger and Timothy Hutton	Emanuel Noah
Henry Winkler	Max and Zoe Emily
Stevie Wonder	Aisha (girl), Keita (boy), and Mumtaz (boy)
Pia Zadora and Meshulem Riklis	Christopher and Kady
Paula Zahn	Haley
Frank Zappa	Moon Unit, Ahmet Emuukha Rodan, Dweezil, and Diva

Favorites over the Years

America has long been a melting pot of races and religions—and, therefore, names. One of the most active and populated melting pots is New York City. It is for that reason we're listing (in order of popularity) the most frequently chosen names for newborns, according to New York City birth records, starting with the most recent list available at the time of this printing.

For the first time, the New York City Health Department has analyzed the top ten most popular boys' and girls' names by ethnicity. And this caused some surprises. For instance, while Michael was the most popular boy's name overall (as it has been for at least a decade and a half), Kevin was number one for baby boys listed on their birth certificates as Hispanic or Asian. For the third year in a row, Ashley was the most popular girl's name among all baby girls. This first ethnic breakdown shows it was also tops among baby girls listed on their birth records as Hispanic or black.

John dropped off the top-ten list for the first time in anyone's memory and moved down to twelfth, changing places with Brandon.

Note: In case you're wondering, Elvis has almost dropped off the pop charts completely. In 1993, fifty-two babies were named Elvis in New York City; only half as many, twenty-six, were in 1994.

Most Popular Baby Names by Mother's Ethnicity, NYC, 1994

NYC TOTAL	HISPANIC	BLACK	WHITE	ASIAN
GIRLS				
1 Ashley	Ashley	Ashley	Jessica	Michelle
2 Jessica	Stephanie	Jasmine	Nicole*	Jennifer
3 Stephanie	Jennifer	Danielle	Samantha	Stephanie
4 Samantha	Jessica	Brittany	Sarah	Sarah*
5 Amanda	Kimberly	Tiffany	Amanda	Tiffany*
6 Nicole	Amanda	Alexis	Danielle	Jessica
7 Jennifer	Samantha	Brianna	Rachel	Samantha
8 Michelle	Tiffany	Diamond	Emily	Christine*
9 Tiffany	Katherine	Jessica	Alexandra*	Jenny*
10 Danielle	Michelle	Crystal	Stephanie*	Vivian
Total: 65,452	21,431	19,346	18,483	5,461
BOYS				
1 Michael	Kevin	Christopher	Michael	Kevin
2 Christopher	Jonathan	Michael	Joseph	David
3 Kevin	Christopher	Brandon	Matthew	Jason
4 Anthony	Jose	Anthony	Daniel	Daniel*
5 Jonathan	Michael	Joshua	Nicholas	Michael*
6 Daniel	Luis	Justin	Christopher	Andrew
7 Joseph	Anthony	Kevin	John	Jonathan
8 Matthew	Joshua	James	Anthony	Christopher
9 David	Brandon	Jonathan	David	Justin
10 Brandon	Christian	David	Andrew	Jeffrey
Total: 68,205	22,049	19,846	19,719	5,806

Note: Total includes other and unknown ethnicities.

Girls 1991	Boys	Girls 1986	Boys
Stephanie	Michael	Jessica	Michael
Ashley	Christopher	Jennifer	Christopher
Jessica	Jonathan	Stephanie	Jonathan
Amanda	Anthony	Nicole	Anthony
Samantha	Joseph	Christina	David
Jennifer	Daniel	Amanda	Daniel

*Tied

Girls 1991	Boys	Girls 1986	Boys
Nicole	David	Melissa	Joseph
Michelle	Matthew	Tiffany	John
Mclissa	Kevin	Danielle*	Jason
Christina	John	Elizabeth*	Andrew

Girls 1983	Boys	Girls 1980	Boys
Jennifer	Michael	Jennifer	Michael
Jessica	Christopher	Jessica	David
Melissa	Jason	Melissa	Jason
Nicole	David	Nicole	Joseph
Stephanie	Daniel	Michelle	Christopher
Christina	Anthony	Elizabeth	Anthony
Tiffany	Joseph	Lisa	John
Michelle	John	Christina	Daniel
Elizabeth	Robert	Tiffany	Robert
Lauren	Jonathan	Maria	James

Girls 1976	Boys	Girls 1964	Boys
Jennifer	Michael	Lisa	Michael
Jessica	David	Deborah	John
Nicole	John	Mary	Robert
Melissa	Christopher	Susan	David
Michelle	Joseph	Maria	Steven
Maria	Anthony	Elizabeth	Anthony
Lisa	Robert	Donna	William
Elizabeth	Jason	Barbara	Joseph
Danielle	James	Patricia	Thomas
Christine	Daniel	Ann(e)*	Christopher*
		Theresa*	Richard*

Girls 1948	Boys	Girls 1928	Boys
Linda	Robert	Mary	John
Mary	John	Marie	William
Barbara	James	Annie	Joseph
Patricia	Michael	Margaret	James
Susan	William	Catherine	Richard
Kathleen	Richard	Gloria	Edward
Carol	Joseph	Helen	Robert

*Tied

Girls	1948	Boys		Girls	1928	Boys
Nancy		Thomas		Teresa		Thomas
Margaret		Stephen		Joan		George
Diane		David		Barbara		Lewis

Girls	1898	Boys
Mary		John
Catherine		William
Margaret		Charles
Annie		George
Rose		Joseph
Marie		Edward
Esther		James
Sarah		Louis
Frances		Francis
Ida*		Samuel

*Tied

By Virtue of . . .
Virtuous Names

During the time of the Puritans—the 1500s and 1600s—many children (mostly baby girls) were given very meaningful names—in fact, names of virtue.

Although the trend never caught on to any great extent, some of these virtuous names remain popular to this day. My (Lydia's) middle name is Hope. When Joan went through a "feeling-cheated" phase because she didn't have a middle name, she decided to give herself a virtuous name as well. Her kid sister was Hope, so she chose Faith. It never really took, and within a short time Joan dropped the middle name. For weeks our parents joked about their daughter not wanting to *keep the Faith*.

If the thought of endowing your child with a name of virtue is an appealing one, here are the best of the batch.

Amity	Grace	Modesty
Bliss	Harmony	Patience
Charity	Honor	Prudence
Clarity	Hope	Serenity
Constance	Joy	Unity
Courage	Justice	Verity
Faith	Learned	
Felicity	Mercy	

The Way the Wind Blows
Names of Hurricanes

The National Hurricane Center near Miami, Florida, keeps a constant watch on the oceanic storm-breeding areas for tropical disturbances that may develop into hurricanes. If a disturbance intensifies into a tropical storm—with rotary circulation and wind speeds above thirty-nine miles per hour—the Center officially gives that storm a name.

According to the U.S. Department of Commerce's National Weather Service, short, distinctive names given in written—as well as spoken—communications are quicker and less subject to error than the older and more cumbersome identification methods (which involved latitude-longitude readings). These advantages are especially important when hundreds of widely scattered stations, airports, coastal bases, and ships at sea are hurriedly exchanging detailed storm information.

For several hundred years, hurricanes in the West Indies were named after the saint whose feast day it was when the hurricane developed. Before the end of the nineteenth century, an Australian meteorologist began giving women's names to tropical storms. And in 1953, our nation's weather services began using women's names for storms. Wait a second! Why should only *women* be associated with the destructive climactic forces of nature? So in the late seventies the weather service started applying men's names as well.

Come rain or come shine, your baby needs a name. The fact that these are hurricane names may appeal to you, or you may want to know these names just so that you can stay away from them. We can't *forecast* your feelings, but we can give you the names of hurricanes. (Please note that the names for the

Atlantic and Eastern Pacific Storms are rotated every six years, so that the names for 1992 were also the names for 1986 and will be the names for 1998, 2004, and so forth. The names for the Central Pacific Tropical Cyclones start with the first name on List 1 and continue to the last one on List 4—no matter how many years that may take. They then pick up the first name on List 1, and proceed onward once again. Also be aware that the National Weather Service retires names of those hurricanes, storms, or cyclones that have done terrible damage and taken lives. Two such names are Bob and Hugo.)

Since hurricanes affect other nations and are tracked by the weather bureaus of countries other than the United States, many of the names, especially the Eastern Pacific ones, have an international flavor. These more exotic names are agreed upon during international meetings of the World Meteorological Organization.

Also notice that the letters Q, U, X, Y, and Z are not used in the Atlantic Storms list; the letters Q and U are not used in the Eastern Pacific Storms lists. The reason given by the National Weather Service is "the scarcity of names beginning with those letters." (Obviously, they haven't seen *this* book!)

Before you weather the storm, we'd like to share with you the name of the meteorologist who gave us most of this information. He is the Hurricane and Winter Storm Programs Coordinator on the national level for the U.S. National Weather Service and his name is "*Rain*er Dombrow*sky*."

ATLANTIC STORMS

1995	1996	1997	1998	1999	2000
Allison	Arthur	Ana	Andrew*	Arlene	Alberto
Barry	Bertha*	Bill	Bonnie	Bret	Beryl
Chantal	Cesar	Claudette	Charley	Cindy	Chris
Dean	Dolly	Danny	Danielle	Dennis	Debby
Erin	Edouard	Erika	Earl	Emily	Ernesto
Felix	Fran*	Fabian	Frances	Floyd	Florence
Gabriello	Gustav	Grace	Georges	Gert	Gordon
Humberto	Hortense*	Henri	Hermine	Harvey	Helene
Iris	Isidore	Isabel	Ivan	Irene	Isaac

*Name is being retired

Jerry	Josephine	Juan	Jeanne	Jose	Joyce
Karen	Klaus	Kate	Karl	Katrina	Keith
Luis	Lili	Larry	Lisa	Lenny	Leslie
Marilyn	Marco	Mindy	Mitch	Maria	Michael
Noel	Nana	Nicholas	Nicole	Nate	Nadine
Opal	Omar	Odette	Otto	Ophelia	Oscar
Pablo	Paloma	Peter	Paula	Philippe	Patty
Roxanne	Rene	Rose	Richard	Rita	Rafael
Sebastien	Sally	Sam	Shary	Stan	Sandy
Tanya	Teddy	Teresa	Tomas	Tammy	Tony
Van	Vicky	Victor	Virginia	Vince	Valerie
Wendy	Wilfred	Wanda	Walter	Wilma	William

EASTERN PACIFIC STORMS

1995	1996	1997	1998	1999	2000
Agatha	Adrian	Aletta	Adolph	Alma	Andres
Blas	Beatriz	Bud	Barbara	Boris	Blanca
Celia	Calvin	Carlotta	Cosme	Cristina	Carlos
Darby	Dora	Daniel	Dalilia	Douglas	Delores
Estelle	Eugene	Emilia	Erick	Elida	Enrique
Frank	Fernanda	Fabio	Flossie	Fausto	Fefa
Georgette	Greg	Gilma	Gil	Genevieve	Guillermo
Howard	Hilary	Hector	Henriette	Hernan	Hilda
Isis	Irwin	Ileana	Ismael	Iselle	Ignacio
Javier	Jova	John	Juliette	Julio	Jimena
Kay	Knut	Kristy	Kiko	Kenna	Kevin
Lester	Lidia	Lane	Lorena	Lowell	Linda
Madeline	Max	Miriam	Manuel	Marie	Marty
Newton	Norma	Norman	Narda	Norbert	Nora
Orlene	Otis	Olivia	Octave	Odile	Olaf
Paine	Pilar	Paul	Priscilla	Polo	Pauline
Roslyn	Ramon	Rosa	Raymond	Rachel	Rick
Seymour	Selma	Sergio	Sonia	Simon	Sandra
Tina	Todd	Tara	Tico	Trudy	Terry
Virgil	Veronica	Vincente	Velma	Vance	Vivian
Winifred	Wiley	Willa	Winnie	Wallis	Waldo
Xavier	Xina	Xavier	Xina	Xavier	Xina
Yolanda	York	Yolanda	York	Yolanda	York
Zeke	Zelda	Zeke	Zelda	Zeke	Zelda

*Name is being retired.

CENTRAL PACIFIC TROPICAL CYCLONES

List 1

Akoni   (Ah-koh´-nee)
Ema   (Eh´-mah)
Hana   (Hah´-nah)
Io   (Ee´-oo)
Keli   (Keh´-lee)
Lala   (Lah´-lah)
Moke   (Moh´-keh)
Nele   (Neh´-leh)
Oka   (Oh´-kah)
Peke   (Peh´-keh)
Uleki   (Oo-leh´-kee)
Wila   (Vee´-lah)

List 2

Aka   (Ah´-kah)
Ekeka   (Eh-keh´-kah)
Hali   (Hah´-lee)
Iniki*   (Ee-nee´-kee)
Keoni   (Keh-on´-nee)
Li   (Lee)
Mele   (Meh´-leh)
Nona   (Noh´-nah)
Oliwa   (Oh-lee´-vah)
Paka   (Pah´-kah)
Upana   (Oo-pah´-nah)
Wene   (Weh´-neh)

List 3

Alika   (Ah-lee´-kah)
Ele   (Eh´-leh)
Huko   (Hoo´-koh)
Ioke   (Ee-oh´-keh)
Kika   (Kee´-kah)
Lana   (Lah´-nah)
Maka   (Mah´-kah)
Neki   (Neh´-kee)
Oleka   (Oh-leh´-kah)
Peni   (Peh´-nee)
Ulia   (Oo-lee´-ah)
Wali   (Wah´-lee)

List 4

Ana   (Ah´-nah)
Ela   (Eh´-lah)
Halola   (Hah-loh´-lah)
Iune   (Ee-oo´-neh)
Kimo   (Kee´-moh)
Loke   (Loh´-keh)
Malia   (Mah-lee´-ah)
Niala   (Nee-ah´-lah)
Oko   (Oh´-koh)
Pali   (Pah´-lee)
Ulika   (Oo-lee´-kah)
Walaka   (Wah-lah´-kah)

NOTE: All letters in the Hawaiian language are pronounced, including even double or triple vowels.

*Name is being retired.

Introduction to the
Main Name List

Here's what our A-to-Z listing of names is all about: Each name, from the most ancient appellations to the most contemporary cognomens, is listed and then followed by its origin. We've classified the origins quite broadly, not distinguishing Low German from Middle German, or Middle Low German from Middle High German. To us, it's all German—just as English is English, not Old English or Anglo-Saxon.

After the name and origin, we offer each name's meaning. We found many names to have several meanings along with several origins. We've chosen to present the most positive meanings we could find, and listed them with the appropriate origins.

Although it's interesting to know the early meanings of names, we feel that *today's* association with names is more important. After years of interviews and observation, we think that, to a degree, people are influenced by what others expect of them because of their name's stereotypical image. For instance, you wouldn't expect to be saved by a lifeguard named Melvin or served by a flight attendant named Yetta. How many accountants are called Biff? How many book-keepers Bambi?

There are exceptions. We mustn't forget that there was a heroic military leader named *Norman* (Schwarzkopf) and a sexy, raunchy pop-culture superstar named *Madonna*.

So, we suggest you pay attention to the way your contemporaries react to a name, at least as much as—or more than—you are influenced by the name's original meaning.

In some cases, the name, its origin, and meaning are

followed by a little more information about the name or about a person who has the name. Many of those entries tell you a celebrity's professional name and the name he or she was given at birth. We think it's intriguing to know a successful person's professional name—the name they *chose*—and what it was changed from. (If you too think it's intriguing, be sure to check out the chapter "Celebrities . . . Once Upon a Time.") Although most of the people we feature in the main list of names are in show business, we do have politicians, writers, artists, and others. We've chosen just a smattering of these names simply because if we went into detail with each and every name, you would need a derrick to lift the book—and much more than nine months to go through it!

Following the name, its origin, and meaning (and, in some cases, anecdotal information) are variations of the name, including shortened or lengthened versions, foreign versions, nicknames, and various spelling options.

Our goal is to help you find the perfect name for your perfect little baby. Our method: giving you the greatest choice of names. If we've succeeded, we'd love to hear from you. Please send us a birth announcement with the good news—and the good name.

Every good wish,

Joan Wilen and Lydia Wilen
P. O. Box 416
Ansonia Station
New York, NY 10023

A-to-Z
Girls' Names

A

Aba—Ghanaian: Girl born on Thursday
Abbie—See: Abigail
Abena/Abina—African: A girl born on Tuesday
Abigail—Hebrew: Born of a joyous father
Abageal, Abbe, Abbey, Abbi, Abbie, Abigayle, Abby, Abbye
Abira—Hebrew: Strong
Abra—Hebrew: Earth Mother
Acacia—Greek: Naive
Cacia, Casee, Casey, Casi, Casia, Kaci, Kacia, Kacie
Acantha—Greek: Thorny
Ada—English: Prosperous, happy; German: Noble
Adda, Addie, Aida
Adah—Hebrew: Crown, ornament
Addia, Addy
This was a very popular name in the 1800s because of the famous actress/writer Adah Isaacs Mencken.
Adamma—Nigerian: Child of beauty
Adara—Greek: Beauty; Arabic: Virgin
Adelaide—German: Noble, kind; Place name: Capital of South Australia
Adala, Adalia, Adalie, Adaline, Adel, Adela, Adele, Adelia, Adelina, Adelind, Adelinda, Adeline, Adella, Adila, Dalina, Daline, Del, Delin, Delina, Della, Delly
Adeline—See: Adelaide
Adelle—See: Adelaide
Adelpha/Adelphe—Greek: Sisterly, beloved sister
Adena/Adina—Greek: Noble, delicate, gentle
Adolpha—German: Defender of honor
Adolfina, Adolphina, Adolphine, Dolfine, Dolphina
Adoncia—Spanish: Sweet

Adoree—Latin: To adore, worthy of divine worship
Adora, Adoria, Doree, Dori, Doria, Dorie, Dory

Adrienne—French: Dark one; Latin: From the Adriatic
Adria, Adrian, Adriana, Adriane, Adrianna

Agatha—Greek: Kind, good
Agathe, Agathia, Aggie, Aggy, Gatha
This name is seen on many bookshelves because of the famous mystery writer Agatha Christie.

Agnes—Greek: Pure person
Aggy, Agna, Agnella, Agnese, Agnesa, Annis, Ina, Nessa

Ahava—Hebrew: Loved one
Ahuda, Ahuva

Aida—See: Ada

Aileen—Greek: Light
Ailene, Ailey, Alene, Aline, Allie, Eileen, Eleen, Eleena, Ileana, Ileane, Ileanna, Ilene, Iliana, Illeane, Illianna, Leana, Lena, Liana, Lina

Aiyana—Native American: Eternal bloom

Alanna—Celtic: Fair, beautiful; Hawaiian: Awakening
Alaine, Alana, Alane, Alayne, Allene, Allena, Allyn

Alarice/Allaryce—German: Ruler of all
Alar, Alarica, Alrica

Alba—See: Alberta

Alberta—English: Noble, brilliant
Alba, Albertina, Albertine, Ali, Allie, Ally, Berrie, Berry, Berta, Elberta, Elbertina, Elbertine

Alda—German: Rich

Alex/Alix—See: Alexandra

Alexandra—Greek: Defender of humankind
Alejandra, Alessandra, Alex, Alexa, Alexina, Alexine, Alexis, Ali, Alix, Alixe, Alyx, Lexi, Lexie, Lexy, Sandra, Sondra, Zandi, Zandra, Zandy
The first woman known to have this name was Queen Alexandra of Judea, who died in 69 B.C.

Alfonsine/Alphonsine—German: Noble family
Alfee, Alfi, Alfie, Alfy, Alonsa, Alphy, Fonsie

Alfreda/Alfrieda—German: Psychically in tune
Alfreta, Elfrida, Elfrieda

Ali/Allie/Ally—Nickname for names beginning with "Al"; *Ali* is also given as an Arabic name, "from Allah"

Alice—Greek: Truth

Aleta, Aletha, Alethea, Alicea, Alicia, Alisha, Alison, Allis, Allison, Allyce, Allys, Allyson, Alyce

It's a name used frequently in the arts, such as in Lewis Carroll's Alice in Wonderland; *Booth Tarkington's* Alice Adams; *the films* Alice Doesn't Live Here Anymore, *starring Ellen Burstyn, and* Alice, *starring Mia Farrow; and, now in syndication, the TV series "Alice," starring Linda Lavin.*

Alida—Latin: Small winged one; Place name: An ancient city in Asia Minor noted for the manufacture of beautiful clothing.

Aleda, Aleta, Aletta, Alette, Alleda, Allida, Dela, Dila, Leda, Lida, Lita, Lyda, Lyta

Aliza—Hebrew: Joy

Aleeza, Alizah

Allegra—Italian: Joyous

Allison—See: Alice

Alma—Italian: Soul, spirit, warmhearted; Latin: Nourishing, bountiful

The ancient Romans called several goddesses Alma Mater (it meant nourishing or bounteous mother). Today, we call the school(s) we attended our alma mater.

Almira—Arabic: Princess, the exalted

Almera, Almyra, Elmira, Mera, Mira

Alpha—Greek: First one

Althea—Greek: Healthy, wholesome

Altheda, Althy, Thea

American tennis player Althea Gibson was the first black person to win a major tennis championship—she won the women's singles title at both the U.S. Open and at Wimbledon in 1957 and 1958.

Alva—Latin: White

Alvera—Latin: The all-truthful

Alvina—German: Noble friend

Alvinia, Elvena, Elvina, Vina

Alyssa—Greek: Logical

Alissa, Alyssum, Elissa, Ilyssa, Lissa, Lyssa

Amanda—Latin: Lovable

Amandee, Amandine, Amandis, Manda, Mandi, Mandie, Mandy, Mandye

In 1728, poet James Thompson wrote "Spring," which contained these two memorable lines:
"And thou, Amanda, come, pride of my song!
Formed by the Graces, loveliness itself."

Amarinda—Greek: Long lived
Amara, Mara, Rinda

Amaris—Hebrew: Whom God has promised

Amaryllis—Greek: Refreshing stream
Rilla, Ryllis

Amber—French: A deep-yellow jewel
Amberlie, Amby

Ambrosina—Greek: Immortal
Ambrosine, Brosina

Amelia—German: Industrious, stirring
Amalia, Amalie, Amelie, Amilia, Emelia, Emelie, Emelina, Mell, Millia
Amelia Earhart, the first female pilot to cross the Atlantic, certainly lived up to the meaning of this name.

Amelinda—Spanish: Beloved

Amethyst—Greek: An anti-intoxicant
This purple gemstone was and still is thought to have powers that can remedy drunkenness.

Amira—Arabic: Highborn girl
Amera, Amerah, Amirah, Amyra, Amyrah, Mera, Mira

Amity—Latin: Friendly

Amy—Latin: Beloved
Aimee, Amie, Amoret, Amoretta, Amorette, Amorita, Amye

Anastasia—Greek: Of the resurrection
Anastasie, Asia, Nastassia, Stacey, Stacie, Stacy, Stasia, Tacey, Tasia
This name belonged to the daughter of Russia's last czar, Nicholas II; her story has been popularized in books, plays, and films. After the Russian royal family was massacred in 1918, many theories about Anastasia's escape and survival emerged.

Andrea—Latin: Womanly
Andee, Andi, Andra, Andreana, Andria, Andriana, Andy

Anemone—Greek: Wind flower
In Greek legend, the nymph with this name was pursued by the wind and changed into a delicate flower.

Angel—See: Angela

Angela—Greek: Angel, messenger
Angel, Angele, Angelica, Angelika, Angelina, Angeline, Angelique, Angelot, Angey, Angie, Anjelica, Anjelika

Anica/Anika—Spanish: Graceful

Anita—See: Ann/Anne

Ann/Anne—Hebrew: Graceful
Ana, Anetta, Anina, Anisa, Anita, Anitra, Anna, Annette, Anney, Annick, Annie, Annina, Annisa, Anny, Anushka, Anya, Ayn
This name is known as "the names of queens," and for good reason: Anne, queen of Great Britain and Ireland; Anne of Austria; Anne of Brittany; Anne of Denmark; Anne Boleyn of England; Empress Anna of Russia; and, in modern times, Princess Anne of England.

Annabel—Hebrew: Beautiful, graceful
Annabella, Annabelle

Annamarie—Hebrew: Graceful, wished-for child (it's a combination of Ann and Mary)
Annemarie, Annamaria, Annemaria

Annette—See: Ann/Anne

Annora—Latin: Honor
Annorah, Anora, Anorah

Anthea—Greek: Flowerlike

Antoinette—See: Antonia

Antonia—Latin: Priceless
Antoinette, Antonetta, Antonette, Netta, Nettie, Netty, Tona, Toni, Tonia, Tonie, Tony, Tonya

Apollonia—Greek: Belonging to Apollo, the Greek god of sunlight, music, medicine, prophecy, and poetry

April—Latin: Open to the sun
Averel, Averil, Averyl, Avril

Arabella—Latin: Fair and beautiful altar
Ara, Arabela, Arabele, Arabelle

Ardelia—Latin: Zealous, ardent
Arda, Ardel, Ardella, Ardelle, Ardith, Ardra

Arden—Celtic: Lofty, eager
Arda, Ardena, Ardene

Ardis/Ardyce—Latin: Fervent, eager

Arela/Arella—Hebrew: Angel

Aretha—Greek: The best
Areta, Retha
Talk about the best *and you'd have to talk about Aretha
Franklin, the "Queen of Soul."*

Ariana—Latin; Very holy, or pleasing one
Ari, Ariadna, Ariadne
Ariana was the mythological princess of ancient Crete.

Aricia—Greek: Princess of the royal blood of Athens
In Racine's version of Phaedra, *Aricia is Hippolytus's lover.*

Ariel—Hebrew: Lioness of God
Ariell, Ariella, Arielle

Arlen—See: Arlene

Arlene—Celtic: A pledge
Arla, Arlana, Arleana, Arleen, Arlen, Arlena, Arlette, Arlie,
Arline, Arlise, Arliss, Arly, Arlyn, Arlyne, Arlynn, Arlyss

Armina—Latin: Of high degree
Armeda, Armida, Arminda, Armine, Armyn

Arnelle—Latin: The eagle rules
Arnella, Arnetta, Arnette

Artemis—Greek: Moon goddess
Artema, Artemisa, Artemise, Artie

Asha—Swahili: Life

Ashira—Hebrew: Wealthy

Ashley—English: From the ash-tree meadow
Ashlee, Ashleigh, Ashlie, Ashly

Asia—See: Anastasia

Astera—Greek: Star
Asta, Astra, Astre, Astrea, Astria

Astred/Astrid—Norse: Divine strength

Athena—Greek: Goddess of wisdom, reason, and purity

Aubrey—German: Elf-wise ruler
Aubrianna, Aubrianne, Aubrie, Aubry

Audrey—German: Noble
Audi, Audie, Audra, Audre, Audrea, Audreanna, Audree,
Audrie, Audrielle, Audrina, Audrine, Audris, Audry

Augusta—Latin: High, revered
Auguste, Augustina, Augustine, Austina, Gus, Gussie, Gussy,
Gusta, Gusti
*Roman emperors took the title "Augustus" when they took
the throne, while "Augusta" was the title of honor given to
their female kin (mothers, wives, daughters, and sisters).*

Aura—Greek: Breath of air
  Aural, Aure
Aurelia—Latin: Golden
  Aurea, Aurel, Aurelie, Aurie, Aurilla
Aurora—Latin: Goddess of the dawn
  Aurore, Rora, Rori, Rorie, Rory
Autumn—Nature name: From the autumn/fall season
Ava—Latin: Bird
Avis—German: Refuge in war; Latin: Bird
  This name is famous because of the car-rental company.
Aviva—Hebrew: Springtime, youthfulness, freshness
  Avivah, Viva
Ayla—Hebrew: Oak tree
  In Jean Auel's best seller, The Clan of the Cave Bear, *the
  Cro-Magnon heroine is called Ayla.*
Azalea—Greek: Dry; English: Name of a flower
Aziza—Arabic: Beloved; Swahili: Very beautiful
Azura—French: Blue sky
  Azora, Azure, Azurine

B

Babette—See: Barbara
Bambalina—Italian: Little one
  Bambee, Bambi, Bambie
Bambi—See: Bambalina
Baptista—Latin: Baptizer
  Baptiste, Batista
Bara—Hebrew: To select
  Bari, Barra
Barbara—Greek: A stranger
  Bab, Babbie, Babette, Babita, Babs, Barb, Barbary, Barbe,
  Barbee, Barberi, Barbetta, Barbette, Barbey, Barbi, Barbie,
  Barbra, Barby, Barbye, Bobbee, Bobbi, Bobbie
  *This is considered a power name for women: Barbra (née
  Barbara) Streisand, Barbara Walters, Barbara Bush. The
  name also enjoys favor with young girls because of the doll
  Barbie.*
Barika—Swahili: Successful
Barrie—Irish: Spearlike
Basha—Polish: A stranger

Basilia—Greek: Regal
Basile, Basilie, Basille

Bathilda/Bathilde—German: Commanding maiden of war

Bathsheba/Batsheva—Hebrew: Daughter of an oath, seventh daughter

Beatrice—Latin: She brings joy, bestower of blessings
Bea, Beatrisa, Beatrix, Beatriz, Beattie, Beatty, Bebe, Trix, Trixi, Trixie, Trixy
How true when you think of the joy Beatrix Potter, author of Peter Rabbit *(among other tales), has brought to so many for so long.*

Becky—See: Rebecca

Bedelia—French: Strength

Belinda/Belynda—Spanish: Beautiful

Bella—Italian: Beautiful
Bel, Bela, Belah, Belia, Belita, Bell, Belle, Belva, Belvia

Bellanca—Greek: Stronghold; Italian: Blonde

Benedicta—Latin: Blessed; Spanish: Well spoken
Benedetta, Benedette, Benita, Bennie

Berdine—German: Shining from within

Bernadette—German: Courageous as a bear
Bernadene, Bernadetta, Bernadette, Bernadina, Bernadine, Bernadinia, Bernetta, Bernie, Bernie, Bernita, Berny
The Song of Bernadette, *the book and film about the saintly visionary, popularized the name in the early 1940s.*

Bernice—Greek: Carrier of victory
Bernice, Berni, Bernie, Berny, Bernyce, Bernye, Berrie, Berry

Bertha—German: Glorious one
Berta, Berte, Berthe, Berti, Bertia, Bertie, Bertina, Bertine, Berty
This was a popular name in Victorian times, when it was also the name of a wide, ruffled—and concealing!—lace collar worn on low-cut dresses. A huge slot machine payoff in Las Vegas is known as a Big Bertha.

Beryl—Greek: Crystal clear
Berry, Beryle, Berylee, Berylla, Rylla

Bessie—See: Elizabeth

Beth—Hebrew: House of God
Bethel

Bethany/Bethani—Place name: A village near Jerusalem
   Bethanie, Bethenee
Betsy—See: Elizabeth
Betty—See: Elizabeth
Beulah—Hebrew: Married woman
   The biblical term for Israel is Land of Beulah.
Beverly—English: From the meadow of the beavers
   Bev, Beverlee, Beverlie, Bevvy, Buffy
Bevin—Irish: Sweet singing maiden
Bianca—See: Blanche
Bibi—Arabic: Lady
Billie/Billy—German: Wise protector
   Billee, Billeena, Billi
Bina—Hebrew: Intelligence
Birdie—English: Little bird
   Bird, Birdella, Birdena, Birdene, Birdita
Blain/Blaine—Irish: Slender
   Blane, Blayne
Blair/Blaire—Celtic: Place; Scottish: Field of battle
Blaise—Latin: Stammers
   Blaize, Blayze, Blaze
Blake—English: Fair haired and pale
   Blakelee, Blakelie, Blakely
Blanche—French: Fair, pale
   Bianca, Blanca, Blancia, Blanka, Blinni, Blinnie, Blinny
   Playwright Tennessee Williams immortalized the name with
   the character Blanche DuBois in A Streetcar Named Desire.
Blessing—English: A blessing
Bliss—English: Perfect joy
Blossom—English: Flower, bloom
Blythe—English: Cheerful one
   Blithe, Bly, Blyth
Bo—Chinese: Precious
   Thanks to actress Bo Derek, this name is thought of as "a
   ten."
Bobbie/Bobby—See: Barbara, Roberta
Bonita—Spanish: Pretty little one
Bonnie—Latin: Good one; Scottish: Charming, pretty
   Bona, Bonna, Bonnee, Bonni, Bonnibella, Bonnibelle,
   Bonny

Brandy/Brandi—Dutch: Fine wine
  Brandee, Brandice, Brandie, Brandyce, Brandyn
Brenda—German: Sword, fire stoker
Brenna—Celtic: Dark haired
Brett—Irish: From Britain
  Bret, Bretta, Brit, Britt, Britta, Brittany, Britte
Briana—Celtic: Strong
  Brea, Breanne, Bree, Bria, Brianna, Brianne, Brielle, Brina,
  Bryana, Bryanna
Bridget—Irish: Mighty, spirited
  Berget, Biddi, Biddie, Biddy, Birgitta, Bridgie, Bridie,
  Brigid, Brigida, Brigit, Brigitta, Brigitte, Brita
Brina/Bryna—Slavic: Protector
Bronwen/Bronwyn—Welsh: White bosomed
Brook/Brooke—English: To break out, bubbling stream
  *Model Brooke Shields has inspired many parents over the
  last decade to bestow this name upon their little girls.*
Brunella—German: Wise, brown-haired woman
  Brunetta, Brunilla
Bryna—Irish: Strength
Brynn—Irish: Heights
  Bryn, Bryna, Brynna, Brynelle
Bunnie/Bunny—English: small rabbit

C

Cadence—Latin: Melodious
  Cadenza, Cadi, Cadie, Cady
Cai—Vietnamese: Female
Caitlin—See: Catherine
Calandra—Greek: Lark
  Cal, Calandre, Calandria, Calla, Calli, Callie, Cally
Calantha/Calanthe—Greek: Lovely blossom
Caledonia—Latin: From Scotland
Caley—Gaelic: Slender
  Caela, Caila, Cailley, Caleigh, Cayla, Cayley
Calida—Spanish: Loving, ardent
  Caleda, Callida
Calista—Greek: Most beautiful
  Callise, Callistra

Callan—German: Chatter
   Calli, Callie, Cally
Camelia—Latin: A beautiful flower
Camille—Latin: Handmaiden
   Cam, Camilia, Camilla, Cammi, Cammie, Cammila,
   Cammy
   For a good cry, see the film classic Camille, *with Greta
   Garbo playing the title role.*
Candice—Greek: Pure, glowing white
   Candace, Candee, Candi, Candida, Candide, Candie, Candis,
   Candra, Candy, Candyce, Kandace, Kandie, Kandy
   *The success of the sitcom "Murphy Brown," starring Can-
   dice Bergen, awakened an interest in the names Murphy and
   Candice.*
Candida/Candide—See: Candice
Caprice—Italian: Whimsical, unpredictable
   Cappi, Cappy, Capri
Cara—Latin: Dear one
   Carah, Cari, Carita, Kara, Karah
Caress—French: Tender touch
   Caressa, Carress, Carressa, Charis
Carey—Welsh: Loving
   Caree, Cari, Carie, Carrey, Carri, Carrie, Carry, Cary
Carina—Spanish: Little darling
   Carena, Carin, Carine, Carinna
Carla—See: Carol/Carole
Carmel—Hebrew. God's vineyard; Place name: Mount
   Carmel, in Israel overlooking the Mediterranean
   Carmela, Carmella
Carmen—Spanish: Rosy red; Latin: Song
   Carmin, Carmina, Carmine, Charmaine
   *There's not only a song for Carmen, but an entire opera by
   Bizet.*
Carnation—Latin: Flesh colored; English: Name of a flower
Carnelian—Latin: A red gem
Carol/Carole—French: Song for rejoicing
   Carey, Cari, Carla, Carleen, Carlen, Carlene, Carlin, Car-
   lina, Carline, Carlita, Carly, Carlyn, Carlynne, Caro, Carola,
   Carolin, Carolina, Caroline, Carolyn, Carolyne, Carri,
   Carrie, Carroll, Charyl, Cheryl, Cherylynne, Karla, Karole,
   Karolina, Karoly, Sheryl

Caroline—See: Carol/Carole

Caron—French: Pure

Carrie—See: Carol/Carole

Casey—See: Acacia

Cassandra—Greek: A prophetess for humankind
Cass, Cassandre, Cassandry, Cassia, Cassondra, Sanda, Sandee, Sandi, Sandie, Sandra, Sandy, Sondra

Cassidy—Irish: Curly haired

Casta—Latin: Modest, pure
Castara, Casti, Casty

Catherine—Latin: Woman of purity (Also see: Katherine)
Caitlin, Caitlyn, Caitrin, Caitrine, Carin, Caryn, Catarina, Catarine, Catharina, Cathee, Catherina, Cathi, Cathie, Cathleen, Cathlene, Cathryn, Cathrynne, Cathrynnia, Cathy, Catriona, Caty, Caye, Trina

Cathleen—See: Catherine

Cecania—German: Free

Cecilia—Latin: One who cannot see
Cacillia, Cacille, Ceci, Cecil, Cecile, Cecily, Ceil, Celee, Celia, Celie, Cicely, Cissi, Cissie, Cissy, Sisillia, Sisillya
*Despite its meaning, this name has seen its share of fame:
it's in poems by Pope and Dryden, in Chaucer's* Canterbury
Tales, *in paintings by Raphael and Rubens, in a hit song of
the 1920s, and in a song sung by Simon & Garfunkel.*

Celandine—Greek: Swallow

Celeste—Latin: Heavenly
Cele, Celeka, Celena, Celene, Celesta, Celestee, Celestina, Celestine, Celestyn, Celestyna, Celina, Celinda, Celinka

Celia—See: Cecelia

Cella—Italian: Free one

Cerelia—Latin: Of the spring

Cerise—French: Cherry
Carise, Charise, Charrissee

Chandra—Hindi: Of the moon
Chandara, Chandria, Chandry

Chantal—French: Sing out loud
Chantalle, Chantel, Chantelle

Chara—Greek: Joy

Charissa—Greek: Graceful
Char, Chari, Charie, Charis, Charisse

Charity—Latin: Benevolent, loving
Charita, Charry
Thanks to Neil Simon's play and film, it's hard to hear this name without thinking of Charity Blackstock, better known as "Sweet Charity."

Charlotte—German: Strong but feminine
Carlota, Carlote, Carlotie, Carlotta, Carlotte, Char, Charla, Charleen, Charlene, Charlotta, Charmaine
If the film Hush, Hush, Sweet Charlotte *comes to mind, you can replace that thought with English novelist Currer Bell, the pen name used by Charlotte Brontë.*

Charmaine—See: Carmen, Charlotte

Charmian—Greek: Source of joy

Charo—Spanish: Nickname meaning "little Rosa"

Chastity—Latin: Purity
Sonny and Cher gave their daughter this name in 1969.

Chaya—Hebrew: Life

Chelsea—English: Port, landing place
Chelsee, Chelsey, Chelsie, Chelsy

Chenoa—Native American: White dove

Cher—French: Dear one
Chere, Cheri, Cherice, Cherie, Cherye, Sher, Shere, Sherri, Sherrie, Sherry

Cheryl—See: Carol/Carole

Chesna—Slavic: Peaceful
Ches, Chessa, Chessy, Chezna

Chiquita—Spanish: Little girl
Chickee, Chickie, Chicky
Anyone with this name is sure to be top banana!

Chloe—Greek: New grass
Chlo, Clo, Cloe, Cloey

Chloris/Cloris—Greek: Pale flower
Actress Cloris Leachman has brought attention to this name ever since she appeared on "The Mary Tyler Moore Show."

Cho—Japanese: Butterfly

Cholena—Native American (Delaware): Bird

Christabelle—Greek: Fair Christian
Christabel, Christabell, Christabella, Christobella, Christobelle

Christina/Christine—Greek: Christian one
Caristina, Caristine, Chris, Chrisa, Chrissi, Chrissie, Chrissy,

Christa, Christiana, Christiane, Christie, Christy, Chryste, Cris, Crissi, Crissie, Crissy, Cristina, Cristine, Cristy, Kris, Kristina, Kristine, Tina

Chrysanthemum—Greek: A gold flower

Cicely—See: Cecilia

Cinderella—French: Little one of the ashes
Cindee, Cindie, Cindy
The children's classic fairy tale has made this name symbolize happy endings.

Cindy—See: Cinderella, Cynthia, Lucinda

Cipriana—Italian: From Cyprus
Cipriann, Cypriana, Cyprienne

Clair/Claire—See: Clara

Clara—Greek: Bright, clear
Clair, Claira, Claire, Clarabelle, Clare, Clareta, Claretta, Clarette, Clarice, Clarie, Clarinda, Clarissa, Clarita, Clary, Clarye, Klara

Claudia—Latin: Lame one
Claude, Claudetta, Claudette, Claudina, Claudine, Claudy
Despite its unfortunate meaning, this name is one of the oldest surviving names in Britain and became quite popular in France because of Queen Claude.

Cleantha/Cliantha—Greek: Glory flower

Clementine—Greek: Merciful one
Clem, Clemence, Clemency, Clementia, Clementina, Clemenza, Clemmie

Cleopatra/Cleo—Greek: Famed
The most famous woman to have this name was the queen of Egypt—that is, until Elizabeth Taylor!

Clio/Cleo—Greek: Proclaimer

Clorina—Persian: Renowned

Cloris—See: Chloris

Clothilda—German: Notable war maid
Clotilda, Clotilde, Tilda, Tildie, Tildy

Clover—English: Fragrant flower

Cody—English: Pillow
Codey, Codi, Codie

Colette—Latin: Victorious
Coletta, Collatte, Collie
Sidonie Gabrielle Colette (1873–1954) was the famous French novelist who used only her surname, Colette.

Colleen—Irish: Girl
Collene, Colline, Collyne
Columba—Latin: Dove
Columbia, Columbina, Columbine
Comfort—Latin: To strengthen
Conception—Latin: Beginning
Concepcion, Conceptiona
Concha—Greek: Shell
Conchetta, Conchette, Conchita
Connie—See: Constance
Constance—Latin: Firmness, steadfastness
Conni, Connie, Conny, Constancia, Constancy, Constantia,
Constanza, Konstanza, Konstanze
Consuela—Spanish: Wonderful friend
Consolata, Consuelo
Cora—Greek: Maiden
Coretta, Corette, Corey, Cori, Corina, Corinna, Corinne,
Corissa, Corisse, Corrine, Corry, Corynna, Kora, Koran,
Koren, Kori, Kory
Corabelle—Greek: Beautiful maiden
Corabell, Corabella
Coral—Latin: Coral from the sea
Coralie, Coralina, Coraline
Corazon—Spanish: Heart
*Because of the dramatic events in the Philippines in 1986,
which resulted in the presidency of Corazon Aquino, the
name Corazon is now known worldwide and represents
"courage" as well as "heart."*
Cordelia—Welsh: Sea jewel; Celtic: Daughter of the sea
Corda, Cordella, Cordelle, Cordie, Cordy
*According to old Welsh legend, Cordelia was the daughter
of Ler, King of the Sea. Appropriately enough, Shakespeare
named one of King Lear's daughters Cordelia.*
Coretta—See: Cora
Corinna/Corinne—See: Cora
Corliss—English: Cheerful
Corlie
Cornelia—Latin: Womanly virtue
Cornela, Cornelie, Cornelle
Cosette—German: Pet lamb
Cossetta, Cozette

Cosima—Greek: Order, harmony
Courtney—English: Of the court
  Courtlynn
Crescent—Latin: To increase, to create
  Cres, Crescence, Crescencia, Cresentia, Cressie, Cressy
Crystal—Latin: Clear as ice
  Chrystal, Cryssie, Crystie, Krystal
Cybela/Cybele—Greek: Divine Mother
Cybil—See: Sibyl
Cymbaline—Celtic: Lord of the sun
Cynara—Greek: Thistle plant
Cynthia—Greek: Moon
  Cinda, Cindee, Cindi, Cindy, Cyndie, Cyndy, Cynthie
Cyrena—Greek: From Cyrene (ancient African capital)
  Cyra, Cyri
Cyrilla—Latin: Lordly, proud
  Cerella, Cira, Ciri, Cirilla, Cyri

D

Dacey—American English: Southern girl
Dacia—Place name: In ancient Rome, the region north of the Danube
Dagmar—Danish: Joy of the land
  This was the name of a queen of Denmark.
Dahlia/Dalia—Norse: From the valley
  This is also an exotic flower named for Dahl, a Swedish botanist.
Daisy—English: Name of a flower
  Daisee, Daisie
  The name became very popular in the 1890s when Henry Dacre wrote the song that starts: "Daisy, Daisy, give me your answer, do! I'm half crazy, all for the love of you." Picking off the petals of a daisy is said to determine whether "(s)he loves me" or "(s)he loves me not."
Dakota/Dakotah—Native American (Sioux): Friend
Dale—German: Valley dweller
  Dael, Daile, Dalena, Dayle
Dalila—Swahili: Gentle
Dallas—German: Playful; Scottish: From the meadows of the valley

Dama—Latin: Gentle lady

Damaris—Greek: Gentle, trusting
Damara

Damiana—Greek: One who tames
Damiana is an herb that some believe has aphrodisiacal properties.

Damita—Spanish: Little noble lady

Dana—Celtic: Mother of the gods
Danae, Danella, Danelle, Danice

Danica—Slavic: Morning star

Daniela/Daniele—Hebrew: Judged by God
Danella, Danelle, Danetta, Danette, Dani, Dania, Danice, Danicee, Daniella, Danielle, Danita, Danna, Danni, Dannia, Dannie, Danny

Daphne—Greek: Laurel tree
Daffi, Daffie, Daffy, Daffye, Daphna, Daphnie, Daphney, Daphny
Novelist Daphne du Maurier helped popularize this name.

Dara—Hebrew: Heart of wisdom; English: Compassion
Daralice, Daralise, Dareen

Darby—Irish: Free person
Darbiana, Darbianne, Darbie, Darbra

Darcie—Celtic: Dark girl; French: Of the fortress
Darcee, Darcy, Darsey, Darsy

Dardanella—Greek: Feminine of Dardanos, a son of Zeus

Daria/Darya—Greek: Possessing wealth

Darlene—French: Little darling
Darell, Darelle, Darla, Darleen, Darline, Darly, Darryl, Darylle

Darryl—See: Darlene

Davida—Hebrew: Beloved one
Daveda, Davene, Davina, Davita, Devina, Veda, Vida

Dawn—English: Daybreak

Daya/Dayah—Hebrew: Bird

Deanna—See: Diana

Deborah—Hebrew: Bee, to speak kind words
Deb, Debbi, Debbie, Debby, Debi, Debora, Debra, Devora, Devore

Deirdre—Irish: Raging one; English: Young girl
Dede, Dee, Deidra, Deidre, Derdre, Didi, Didie, Dierdra, Dierdre

Delicia—Latin: Delightful one
Delica, Delice, Delight, Delize, Delizia

Delilah—Hebrew: Poor, heir; Arabic: Guide, leader
Dalila, Delila, Lila, Lilah

Della—Greek: Visible; German: Noble
Dehlia, Delea

Delma—Spanish: Of the sea; German: Noble protector

Delpha—Greek: Dolphin
Delphi, Delphine, Delphina, Delfine

Delta—Greek: The fourth
Delta Burke made a name for herself as one of the original four "Designing Women" on the popular sitcom.

Demetria—Greek: Of Demeter, Greek goddess of the harvest
Demeter, Demetra, Demetri, Demetrice, Demetris, Demi, Demmi, Dimitra

Demi—See: Demetra
Actress Demi Moore, born Demi Guynes, knows that an unusual first name worked for her. Maybe that's why she and husband Bruce Willis named their daughters Rumer Glenn, Scout LaRue, and Tallulah Belle.

Dena—English: From the valley

Denise—French: Follower of Dionysus, the Greek god of wine
Denni, Dennie, Denny, Dennye, Denyse

Desdemona—Greek: Ill-fated one
Desdemonda, Desmona

Desire/Desiree—French: Hoped for, long awaited
Desideria, Desirata

Deva—Hindi: Divine

Devona—English: Defender

Devora—See: Deborah

Diamanta—French: Like a diamond
Diamante, Diamond, Diamonique

Diana/Diane—Latin: Divine, bright one
Deana, Deandra, Deane, Deanna, Dede, Dee, Deena, Deenie, Dena, Di, Diahnn, Dian, Diandra, Dianna, Dianne, Didi, Dyan, Dyana, Dyane, Dyanna, Dyanne
Diana Spencer brought new appeal to the name when she married Great Britain's Prince Charles in 1981 and became Diana, Princess of Wales.

Diantha/Dianthe—Greek: Divine flower

Dillian—Latin: Worshiped one
   Dilli, Dilliana
Dilys—Welsh: Genuine
Dina—See: Dinah, Geraldina/Geraldine
Dinah—Hebrew: Judgment
   Dina, Dinorah, Dyna, Dynah
   The song says it all: "Dinah, is there anyone finer?"
Dionne—Greek: Daughter of heaven
   Dion, Diona, Dione, Dionna, Dyon, Dyonne
Dita—Czech: Rich gift
Dixie—American English: Girl from the South; Norse: Active
   sprite
Dodie—Hebrew: Beloved
   Doda, Dodi, Dody
Dollie/Dolly—See: Dorothy
Dolores—Spanish: Sorrowful one
   Delores, Deloris, Dolorita, Doloritas
Dominique—French: Belonging to God
   Dom, Domeniga, Domina, Domine, Dominga, Domini,
   Dominica, Dominiqua
Donata—Italian: Gift from God
Donna—Italian: Woman worthy of respect
   Dona, Donee, Donella, Donia, Donie, Donni, Donny
Dora—Greek: Gift
   Doral, Doralea, Doralyn, Doralynn, Dorelai, Dorella, Dorelle,
   Doretta, Dorette, Dori, Dorian, Dorita, Doro
Dorcas—Greek: Gazelle
   Dorcia
Dorena/Dorene—French: Golden girl
   Doreen, Doreena, Dorina, Dorine
Doria—Greek: From the sea
Dorinda—Greek: Beautiful one
Doris—Greek: From the sea
   Dori, Dorice, Dorisa, Dorita, Dorri, Dorrie, Dorris, Dorry,
   Dory, Dorys, Dorysa
Dorothy—Greek: God's gift
   Dolley, Dolli, Dollie, Dolly, Dorotea, Doroteya, Dorothea,
   Dorothee, Dortha, Dorthy, Dot, Dotti, Dotty
   *All forms of this name were popular in the United States in
   the early 1800s, thanks to trendsetting first lady Dorothea
   Payne Madison, better known as Dolley Madison.*

Drew—Greek: Masculine
Actress Drew Barrymore drew our attention to this name when she played the little girl in the 1982 film E.T.
Drina—Spanish: Helper of humankind
Drusilla—Greek: Eyes of innocence
Dru, Druci, Drucie, Drucilla, Drucy, Drusie, Drusy
Dulcie—See: Dulcinea
Dulcinea—Spanish: Sweet
Delcina, Delcine, Dulce, Dulcea, Dulcet, Dulcia, Dulcie, Dulcine, Dulcy
The woman with this sweet name helped Don Quixote dream the impossible dream in The Man of La Mancha.
Dyani—Native American: Deer
Dyna—Greek: Powerful

E

Earlene—English: A title of nobility
Eartha—English: Child of the earth
Erda, Erta
The exotic singer/actress Eartha Kitt made this name known in America.
Easter—English: Of the springtime
Ebony—English: Symbol of black beauty
Echo—Greek: Repeated sound
In mythology, Echo was a nymph whose love for Narcissus was unrequited. She pined away for his affection until only her voice remained . . . remained . . . remain . . . rema . . . .
Edana—Celtic: Fiery one
Edda—English: Rich, prosperous
Eden—Hebrew: Pleasure
Edina—English: Prospering, joyful
Edith—English: Wonderful gift
Eda, Ede, Edeva, Edi, Edie, Edita, Editha, Edithe, Ediva, Edy, Edyth, Edythe, Eydie
This name was held by two of our country's first ladies: Edith Kermit Carow (wife of Theodore Roosevelt) and Edith Bolling Galt (wife of Woodrow Wilson).
Edlyn—English: Of the nobility
Edmonda—English: Rich protector
Edmondia, Edmunda

Edna—Hebrew: Delightful, renewal
  Eadie, Eadna, Eddi, Eddie
  Edna Ferber, novelist (Giant) *and playwright* (Show Boat),
  *is the most famous Edna in America—especially among
  crossword-puzzle creators!*
Edwina—English: Rich friend
  Eadwina, Eadwyne, Edwinette, Win, Winnie
Efrona—Hebrew: Sweet-singing bird
Efia—Fante (African): Born on a Friday
Eileen—Irish: Glowing light; Also see: Aileen
  Eilene, Ileen, Ilene
Elaine—Greek: A light
  Elana, Elane, Elani, Elayna, Elayne, Laina, Laine, Lainie,
  Layna, Layne, Laynie
Eleanor—French: Brilliant light
  Elanor, Elanora, Elanore, Eleanora, Eleanore, Elenora,
  Elenore, Elinor, Elinore, Elladine, Ellc, Elna, Elnora, Elnore,
  Elora, Elore, Leanor, Lenorc, Leonora, Leonore, Nora, Norah
  *Question: Can you name a first lady and a song that both
  have the initials E. R.? Answer: Eleanor Roosevelt and
  "Eleanor Rigby," respectively.*
Electra/Elektra—Greek: Shining star
Eleora/Eliora—Hebrew: The Lord is my light
Elissa/Elyssa—See: Elizabeth
Elita—French: Special one
Eliza—See: Elizabeth
Elizabeth—Hebrew: Consecrated to God, oath of God
  Babette, Belita, Bess, Besse, Bessie, Bessy, Beth, Betsey, ·
  Betsy, Betta, Bette, Betti, Bettina, Bettine, Betty, Betze,
  Elisabeth, Elisabetta, Elissa, Eliza, Elizabet, Helsa, Lisette,
  Lissie, Lizabet, Lizabeth, Lizzie, Lizzy
  *This regal name is associated with European royalty, but
  American royalty also favors the name. Do you know who
  Elizabeth Bloomer Warren Ford is? We knew her as Betty
  Ford when she was our first lady. President James Monroe
  was married to an Elizabeth—Elizabeth Kortright, whose
  nickname was Eliza. President Andrew Johnson's wife was
  born with the name Eliza—Eliza McCardle—and let's not
  forget Bess Wallace, wife of President Harry S. Truman.*
Ella—English: Elfin
  Eletta, Elette, Elli, Ellie, Elly, Ellye

Say "Ella" to anyone who loves jazz and they'll assume you're referring to the great Ella Fitzgerald, inducted into the Jazz Hall of Fame in 1985.

Ellen/Ellyn—Greek: Light

As you proceed through the "E" list of names, you'll see several first ladies mentioned, and there are two right here: Ellen Lewis Herndon, wife of Chester Arthur, and Ellen Louise Axson, first wife of Woodrow Wilson.

Elma—Greek: Pleasant

Eloisa/Eloise—See: Louisa/Louise

Elsa—German: Noble woman
   Elsey, Elsie

Elvira—German: Elfin charm
   Elva, Elve, Elvera, Elvina, Elvire, Elwire, Elwirea

Elysia—Latin: Blissful, rapturous
   Elisa, Elise, Elyse, Ilise, Ilysa, Ilyse

Emalia/Emelia—Latin: Flatterer

Emerald/Emeraud—French: A green jewel

Emily—German: Industrious one
   Amalea, Amalia, Amalie, Amelia, Amelie, Ameline, Amelita, Emelda, Emelina, Emeline, Emelita, Emera, Emilia, Emilie, Emiline, Emlyn, Emma, Emmaline, Emmalyn, Emmey, Emmy, Emmye

This is a name of some pretty industrious writers: Emily Dickinson, who wrote some eighteen hundred poems, and Emily Brontë, who is best known for her novel Wuthering Heights.

Emma—See: Emily

Emmanuella/Emmanuelle—Hebrew: God is among us

Endora—Hebrew: Fountain

If you don't personally know anyone with this name, yet it still seems familiar to you, it may be because you've watched "Bewitched," the TV sitcom in which Samantha's mother (Agnes Moorehead) was called Endora.

Enid—Celtic: Purity

Enola—French: Ennobled

Erica/Erika—Norse: Eternal ruler, the queenly
   Ericha, Rica, Ricka, Ricki, Rickie, Ricky, Rikki

In keeping with the name's definition, Erica Kane, the leading character on "All My Children," seems to be the

eternal queen of daytime TV. Susan Lucci has played that
part since January 5, 1970.

Erin—Irish: Peace
  Erinn, Erinna, Erinne, Eryn

Erma—See: Irma

Ernestine—German: Earnest one
  Erna, Ernesta, Ernestina, Tina

Esmeralda/Esmerelda/Ezmerelda—Greek: Precious jewel
  Esmie, Ezmie

Esperanza—Spanish: Hope

Estelle—Latin: Star
  Estel, Estele, Estell, Estella, Estrelita, Estrelite, Estrella,
  Stella, Stellita

Esther—Hebrew: Star
  Essie, Essy, Essye, Ester, Etti, Ettie, Etty

Ethel—German: Noble
  Ethelda, Ethelin, Etheline, Ethyl

Etta—German: Little, tiny

Eudora —Greek: Priceless gift

Eugenia—Greek: Wellborn
  Eugenie, Geena, Gena, Gene, Genia, Genie, Gennie

Eulalia—Greek: Articulate, well spoken
  Eula, Eulalie, Eulaylia, Lallie, Lally

Eunice—Greek: Happy victory
  Unice, Younice

Euphemia/Euphemie Greek: Of great fame
  Effie, Effy, Ephemia, Ephie, Euphemy

Eurydice—Greek: Broad separation

Eustacia—Latin: Fruitful
  Stacey, Staci, Stacie, Stacy, Tacia, Tacie

Evangeline—Greek: Proclaimer of good news
  Angel, Angie, Evan, Evangelina

Eve—Hebrew: Life giving
  Eba, Eva, Evaleen, Evalene, Evelina, Eveline, Evelyn,
  Evey, Evie, Evita, Evonne, Evy
  Here we could discuss Eve, the first woman, or the films The
  Three Faces of Eve *and* All About Eve. *But since a lot of*
  pregnant women will be reading this, we've chosen a
  thought-provoking theory called the Eve Principle. It's the
  idea that all fetuses initially are female, until a biological

*process occurs in the womb, making about half of them
male.*

Evelyn—See: Eve

Ezrela—Hebrew: Reaffirmation of belief in God

F

Fabia—Latin: Bean grower

Faith/Fayth—Latin: The believing, the faithful

Fallon—Irish: In charge

Fancie/Fancy—Greek: Imagination

Fannie/Fanny—See: Frances

Farrah—English: Lovely, attractive; Arabic: Happy
*Farrah Fawcett burst on the scene in 1976 to star in
"Charlie's Angels." And if you meet a Farrah today,
chances are that she was born at the end of the seventies.*

Fatima—Muslim: Descendant of the wife of the prophet
Mohammed

Faun/Fawn—Latin: Young deer

Fay/Faye—French: Fairy, magical creature
Fayette, Fayine, Fayne
Fay Wray was the leading lady in the original film version of
King Kong.

Fayme—French: Held in high esteem

Fedora—See: Theodora

Felda—German: From the field

Felicia—Latin: Happy
Felice, Felicie, Felicity, Felidad, Felita, Feliza, Felizia

Fenella/Finella—Celtic: White shouldered
Fionulla, Fynola

Fern—English: Wing, feather, fern plant

Fernanda—Spanish: World traveler, adventurer
Ferdinanda, Ferdinande, Fernandetta, Fernandette, Fernandia, Fernandina

Fidela—Latin: Faithful one
Fidelia, Fidelita, Fidelity

Fifi—See: Josephine

Filomena/Philomena—Greek: Loving, harmony

Fiona/Fionna—Irish: Ivory skinned

Fira—English: Fiery

Flavia—Latin: Blond one

Flora—Latin: Flower
Fleur, Flo, Flor, Flore, Florella, Floria, Florie, Floris, Florrie, Florry

Florence—Latin: Flowering, successful
Floran, Florance, Florancia, Florentia, Flori, Florida, Florina, Florinda, Florine, Flossi, Flossie, Flossy
On July 4, 1820, Florence Nightingale was born and named for the city of her birth—Florence, Italy. She became the first and most famous of war nurses.

Flower—French: Blossom

Fortune—Latin: Destiny, chance
Fortuna, Fortunata

Frances—Latin: Free
Fan, Fanchetta, Fanchette, Fanchon, Fania, Fanni, Fannie, Fanny, Fanya, Fran, Francesca, Franci, Francie, Francine, Francisca, Francoise, Franki, Frankie, Frannie, Franny, Frannye
First lady Frances Folsom was the wife of President Grover Cleveland.

Francesca—See: Frances

Francine—See: Frances

Franki/Frankie—See: Frances

Frayda/Frayde—Yiddish: Joy

Freda/Freida/Frieda—See: Frederica

Frederica—German: Peaceful ruler
Federa, Federe, Federicka, Freda, Fredda, Freddie, Freddy, Frederique, Freida, Frida, Frieda, Fryda, Ricki, Rickie, Ricky, Rikki
This name was created by the followers of Frederick the Great, the eighteenth-century king of Prussia, who wanted to honor their king by naming their newborn daughters after him.

Freya—Norse: Highborn lady
In Norse mythology Freya is the goddess of love and beauty.

Fritzi/Fritzie—German: Benevolent ruler

Frodina/Frodine—German: Learned friend

Fulvia—Latin: Golden haired

G

Gabrielle—Hebrew: Woman of God
Gabey, Gabella, Gabi, Gabie, Gabriela, Gabriele, Gabriella, Gabrilla, Gaby, Gavra, Gavrale, Gavrell, Gavrella

Gaia—Greek: The earth

Gail—English: Lively
Gael, Gaela, Gale, Galey, Galie, Gayla, Gayle, Gayleen, Gaylene, Gaylia

Gala—Spanish: From Gaul

Galatea—Greek: Milky white

Galina/Galinka—Russian: White light

Galya/Galye—Hebrew: God has redeemed

Gana—Hebrew: Garden
Gania, Ganya

Ganesa—Hindi: Good luck

Gardenia—Early American English: Beautiful scented flower
The flower is named after the American botanist Dr. Alexander Garden (1730–91).

Garland—French: Wreath of flowers

Garnet—German: A dark red jewel
Garnetta, Garnette, Garnettia

Gavrilla—Hebrew: Heroine

Gay/Gaye—French: Merry

Gayora—Hebrew: Valley of light

Gelasia—Greek: Inclined to laughter
Gela, Gelacey, Gelasie, Lacey, Lacie, Lacy, Lasia

Gemina—Greek: Twin
Gemie, Gemini, Geminie, Mina

Gemma—Italian: Jewel

Gena—See: Eugenia, Gina

Gene—See: Eugenia

Genevieve—See: Guinevere

Georgia—Latin: Earth lover
Georgeanna, Georgeanne, Georgena, Georgene, Georgette, Georgey, Georgianna, Georgianne, Georgie, Georgina, Georgine, Georgy, Jorja, Jorji, Jorjie, Jorjy
Artist Georgia O'Keeffe was born in Wisconsin but named for the southern state.

Geraldine—German: Mighty with a spear

Deena, Deenie, Deeny, Dina, Geralda, Geraldina, Gerarda, Gerarde, Gerardetta, Gerardette, Geri, Gerri, Gerrie, Gerry, Giralda, Giralde, Giraldina, Giraldine, Jeri, Jerrie, Jerry
Geraldine (Gerry) Ferraro, the first woman to run for the vice presidency, was named for her brother, Gerald, who had died in an accident two years before she was born.

Geranium—Greek: Crane (the bird, not the machinery!)

Gerda—German: Protected one

Germaine—French: From Germany
Germa, Germain, Germana, Germane, Germayne, Jermaine, Jermayne

Gertrude—German: Spear maiden
Gerta, Gerti, Gertie, Gertrud, Gertruda, Gerty, Truda, Trude, Trudel, Trudi, Trudie, Trudy, Trudye
Who'd have thought that Gertie, the most familiar form of this old-fashioned name, would be the name of Elliot's kid sister (played by Drew Barrymore) in the film E.T.*?*

Geva—Hebrew: Hill

Ghislaine—German: Sweet pledge

Gianina—Italian: God is gracious
Gia, Gianetta, Giannina, Ginetta, Ginette, Giovana, Giovanna, Giovanne

Gigi—See: Gilberta

Gilana—Hebrew: Joy
Geela, Gila, Gilada, Gilah, Gilia, Gillie, Gilly

Gilberta—German: Brilliant
Gigi, Gilberte, Gilbertina, Gilbertine

Gilda—English: Covered with gold

Gillian—Latin: Young child
Gillee, Gilli, Gillie, Gilly, Gillye

Gina—Japanese: Silvery
Geena, Gena

Ginat—Hebrew: Garden

Ginger—Latin: The ginger spice
It's the nickname of Virginia Rogers, best known for her dance routines with Fred Astaire.

Giselle—German: Pledge
Gisela, Gisele, Giselia, Gizel, Gizela, Gizelle, Sella, Zella, Zelly

Gita—Slavic: Pearl

Gladys—Latin: Sword

Glad, Gladey, Gladie, Gladsy, Gleda, Gledy

Glenda—Irish: From the valley

Glendan, Glendane, Glendeen, Glendene, Gleni, Glenina, Glenine, Glenna, Glennis, Glyn, Glyna, Glynis, Glynisa, Glynnis, Glynnisa, Glynny

Gloria—Latin: Glory

Glorey, Glori, Glorian, Gloriann, Glorianna, Glorianne, Glorien, Glory, Glorya

Glynis/Glynnis—See: Glenda

Godiva—English: Gift of God

Golda—English: Gold

Goldan, Goldey, Goldi, Goldie, Goldina, Goldy

Golda Meir became prime minister of Israel in 1969.

Grace—Latin: Graceful one, favor, blessing

Gracella, Gracia, Gracie, Gracielle, Grata, Gratia, Gratiana, Gratiane, Grayce, Graycey, Graycia, Gracy

Actress Grace Kelly did a lot to inspire parents to name their daughters Grace, and even more so when she became Princess Grace of Monaco.

Greer—Scottish: Watchwoman

Gregoria—Greek: The awakened

Greta/Gretta—Greek: Pearl

Grata, Gretal, Gretchen, Gretel, Gretyl

Gretchen—See: Greta/Gretta

Griselda—German: War heroine

Griseldies, Grishilda, Grizel, Grizelda, Grizella, Selda, Zelda

Guenevere/Guinevere—Welsh: White wave

Genevieva, Genevieve, Genevra, Genna, Genni, Gennie, Gennifer, Genny, Ginevra, Ginevre, Guenevera, Guenn, Guinn, Guinna, Guinnavere, Zenavere, Zenevera, Zenevieve

Gulla—Norse: Divine sea

Gunda—Scandinavian: Battle maiden

Gwendolyn—Welsh: White browed, fair

Gwen, Gwendolen, Gwendolin, Gwenna, Gwenni, Gwenny, Gwennye, Gwyna, Gwyndolin, Gwyned, Gwyneth, Gwynne

Gypsy—English: Wanderer

Ask your parents about Gypsy Rose Lee, a wonderful character and the inspiration for the award-winning musical play and film Gypsy.

Gytha—English: Gift

H

Habiba—Arabic: Lover

Hadara—Hebrew: Bedecked in beauty

Hadassa/Hadassah—Hebrew: Flowering myrtle
Dassa, Dassi
Hadassah is best known as a Jewish women's philanthropic organization.

Haidee—Greek: Honored, well behaved

Hailey—Scottish: Hero; English: Field of hay
Hailee, Haili, Haleigh, Hali, Haylee, Hayley, Haylie

Halfrida—German: Peaceful heroine

Hallie—Greek: Thinking of the sea
Hallee, Halli, Halley

Hana/Hanae—Japanese: Blossom

Hanele/Hannele—Hebrew: Merciful

Hannah—Hebrew: Graceful
Hana, Hanna, Hanni, Hannie, Hanny, Hannye

Happi/Happy—English: Delighted

Harlene—English: Meadow of the hares
Harlee, Harleen, Harley, Harlie

Harmony—Latin: Unity, in tune

Harriet—French: Ruler of the home
Harra, Harre, Harri, Harrie, Harrietta, Harriette, Harriot, Hatti, Hattie, Hatty

Hattie—See: Harriet

Hazel—English: Forceful authority

Heather—English: Shrub with violet flowers

Hedda—German: Strife
Heda, Hedara, Hedarina, Hedde, Heddi, Heddie, Heddy, Hedvig, Hedwig, Hedy

Heidi—German: Noble, kind

Helaine/Helayne—See: Helen

Helen—Greek: Shining light
Helaine, Helayne, Helena, Helene, Helenka, Helli, Jelena, Jelene, Lainie
This was one of the most popular names in Greece and in Troy. It's also been popular in America for a long time. President William Howard Taft's first lady was Helen Herron. The first lady of the Broadway stage was Helen

Hayes. The first lady to make "I Am Woman" a hit song was Helen Reddy.

Helga—German: Religious

Helica/Helice—Greek: Spiral

Heloise—German: Glory, battle; French: Renowned fighter
The columnist Heloise has made her name synonymous with helpful household hints.

Helsa—English: Swan

Henrietta—German: Ruler of private property
Enrica, Enrice, Enrichetta, Enricia, Etta, Ettie, Etty, Hendrika, Henki, Henny, Henrie, Henrieta, Henriette, Henryetta, Hetty, Yetta

Hepzibah—Hebrew: Filled with joy

Hera—Latin: Queen

Hermione—Greek: Noble woman
Hermanie, Hermia, Hermina, Hermy

Hermosa—Latin: Lovely

Herta/Hertha—German: Mother Earth

Hesper—Greek: Evening star

Hester/Hesther—Greek and Hebrew: Star
Hettie, Hetty

Hilary/Hillary—Greek: Pleasant, cheerful

Hilda—German: Battle maiden
Hilde, Hildie, Hildy, Ilda, Ildie, Ildy

Hildegarde—German: Stronghold
Hildegarde is a famous chanteuse whose theme song is "Darling Je Vous Aime Beaucoup."

Hilma—German: Protection

Hinda—Hebrew: Deer

Hisa—Japanese: Long lasting
Hisae, Hisako, Hisayo

Hollace—English: From the holly tree
Hollis, Holly

Honey—English: Sweet one, sweet liquid from a bee

Honora—Latin: With honor
Honia, Honor, Honore, Honoria, Honorine, Nora, Norah

Hope—English: Optimistic expectation
This name was popular among the Puritans and was the name of the character played by Mel Harris on the TV series "thirtysomething."

Hortense—Latin: Gardener
  Hortencia, Hortensia, Hortie, Ortense
Huberta—German: Brilliant mind
Hulda—German: Loved one
  Huldie, Huldy
Hyacinth—Greek: A sweet-smelling flower; Also see: Jacinta
  Hyacindy, Hyacintha, Hyacinthia, Jacinta

I

Ida—English: Prosperous; German: Youthful; Norse: Diligent
  Idalina, Idaline, Idella, Idelle, Idetta, Idette, Idona, Idonia
  Ida Saxton was married to President William McKinley.
Idelia—German: Noble
Idola—Greek: Idolized
Ignacia—Latin: Ardent
  Ignatia, Ignea, Ignia, Nacia, Nacy
Ila—English: Insulated
Ilana—Hebrew: Tree
  Ileana, Ileane, Ileanna
Ilka—Slavic: Industrious
  Elka, Elke, Elky, Ilke, Ilkie, Ilky
Ilona—Hungarian: Beautiful
  Ilonka, Lona, Lonka
Ima—Japanese: Now, the present
Imelda Spanish: Powerful fighter
Imogene Latin: Image, blameless, innocent
  Emogen, Emogene, Emojean, Imogena
  *In the early days of television, Imogene Coca was Sid
  Caesar's brilliantly funny costar on "Your Show of Shows."*
Ina—See: Agnes
Ines/Inez—Greek: Chaste, pure
Inga/Inge—See: Ingrid
Ingrid—Norse: Hero's daughter
  Igna, Ingaberg, Inge, Ingeberg, Inger
  *When Swedish actress Ingrid Bergman made a name for
  herself in America, her very "foreign" name became a very
  familiar name to Americans.*
Iola—Greek: Violet colored
Iolana—Hawaiian: To soar like a hawk

Iona/Ione—Greek: Violet-colored stone
Irene—Greek: Peace
  Erena, Erene, Irena, Irenie, Ireny, Irina, Irine, Iriny
Iris/Irisa—Greek: Rainbow; English: Name of a flower
Irma/Erma—Latin: Noble; German: Power
  Ermina, Ermine, Irme, Irmina, Irminie
  Erma Bombeck, best-selling author and humor columnist,
  was syndicated in over one thousand newspapers and read
  by thirty million people throughout the world.
Irvette—English: Friend from the sea
Isabel—Spanish: Consecrated to God
  Isa, Isabeau, Isabelita, Isabella, Isabelle, Isobel, Isobela, Iso-
  bella, Isobelle, Issi, Issie, Issy, Izabel, Ysabel, Ysobel
  Isabella I, the queen of Castile and Aragon and wife of Fer-
  dinand II, financed Christopher Columbus's voyage to the
  New World.
Isadora/Isidora—Latin: Gift of Isis (the Egyptian moon
goddess)
  Sadora, Sadore, Zadora, Zohra
  Isadora Duncan was one of the world's most innovative
  dancers—and performed barefoot most of the time.
Isolda/Isolde—Welsh: Fair lady
  Isolte, Yseult, Yseulta, Ysolda, Ysolde
Ivah—Hebrew: God's gracious gift
Ivana—Hebrew: God is gracious
  Ivania, Ivanka, Ivanna, Ivannia
  Czechoslovakian-born Ivana Trump named her daughter
  Ivanka, which, in Czechoslovakian, is an affectionate way of
  saying "little Ivana."
Ivy—English: Clinging vines, a symbol of faithfulness
  Ivee, Ivi, Ivie, Ivye

J

Jacinta—Greek: Beautiful; Spanish: Hyacinth
  Jacanta, Jacenta, Jacente, Jacinda, Jacinte, Jacintha, Jacinthe,
  Jacinthia, Jacynthe, Jacynthy
Jackie—See: Jacqueline
Jacoba—Hebrew: Supplanter
  Jaci, Jacobina, Jacobine, Jacy, Jake, Jakee, Jakoba
Jacqueline—Hebrew: Supplanter

Jacki, Jackie, Jacklyn, Jackuelin, Jacky, Jaclyn, Jacque, Jacquetta, Jacquette, Jacqui, Jacquie, Jacquita, Jaquelina, Jaqueline, Jaquite, Jaquith, Jaquithe
This became a popular name for newborns in the 1960s after Jacqueline Bouvier Kennedy became our first lady.

Jada—Hebrew: Wise

Jade—Spanish: A jade gem
  Jadee, Jaeda, Jaida, Jaide, Jayde

Jael—Hebrew: Mountain goat, to ascend

Jaffa—Hebrew: Beautiful
  Jafit, Yaffa, Yaffit

Jaime—French: I love

Jamie—Hebrew: Supplanter

Jamila—Arabic: Beautiful
  Jameela, Jameelah, Jami, Jamilah, Jamilia, Jamille

Jan—See: Jane

Jane—Hebrew: God's gracious gift
  Jan, Jana, Janel, Janelle, Janet, Janetta, Janette, Jania, Janice, Janie, Janina, Janine, Janis, Janith, Janithe, Janithia, Janka, Janna, Jannel, Jannelle, Janot, Jayne, Jaynee
  The expression "plain Jane" has no meaning in today's world, what with the likes of women like Jane Pauley, Jane Curtin, Jane Fonda, and Jane Seymour.

Janet/Janice/Janis—See: Jane

Jardena—Hebrew: Flowing downward

Jarvinia—German: Keen intelligence

Jasmine—Persian: A fragrant flower
  Jasmina, Jasse, Jassey, Jassi, Jassie, Jassy, Yasmine

Jean—French: God is gracious
  Gene, Genia, Jeanee, Jeanette, Jeanie, Jeanne, Jeannetta, Jeannette

Jelena—Russian: Shining light

Jemima—Hebrew: Little dove
  Jamima, Jamime, Jamyma, Jemma, Jemmie, Jemmy, Mima, Yemima

Jenica—Hebrew: God is gracious
  Jenice, Jenicee, Jenicy

Jennifer—Welsh: White, fair
  Genna, Gennifer, Gennifera, Genny, Jen, Jena, Jenafer, Jenifer, Jenna, Jennee, Jenney, Jenny
  We think this name's unequaled popularity started more

than twenty years ago, with the phenomenal success of Erich Segal's book Love Story *(and the film of the same title), in which the female lead is named Jenny Cavilleri.*

Jenny—See: Jennifer

Jeremia—Hebrew: Exalted of the Lord
Jeremie, Jeremya, Jeremyea, Jerrey, Jerri, Jerry

Jessica—Hebrew: Wealthy
Jess, Jessa, Jessaca, Jessalin, Jessalyn, Jessaman, Jessamine, Jessamyn, Jesse, Jessee, Jessie, Jessy

Jewel—French: Precious stone
Jewela, Jewell, Jewelle, Jewelyn

Jezebel—Hebrew: Follower of idols

Jihan—Turkish: Universe

Jill—Greek: Youthful
Jillee, Jilli, Jillian, Jillie, Jilly, Jillye, Jyll
Jack and Jill went up the hill, to fetch a pail of water. . . .

Jo—See: Josephine

Joan—Hebrew: God's gracious gift
Joanie, Joann, Joanna, Joanne, Jo-Anne, Joany, Johanna, Johnna, Johnelle, Johnetta, Johnette, Jonetta, Jonette, Jonetty, Joni, Jonie, Jony
Joan is a female power name. Joan Crawford, Joan Collins, Joan Sutherland, Joan Baez, Joan Rivers, and Joan Lunden are all strong and powerful women.

Joann/Joanna/Joanne—See: Joan

Jobina—Hebrew: The persecuted
Jobee, Jobie, Joby, Jobyna

Jocelyn—Latin: Happy, joyful
Jocelen, Jocelin, Jocelina, Joceline, Joselin, Josselin, Josselyn

Jocosa—Latin: Playful
Jodetta, Jodette, Jodi, Jodia, Jodie, Jody

Jodi/Jody—See: Jocosa

Joelle—Hebrew: The Lord is willing
Jo-el, Joela, Joell, Joella, Joellen, Joellyn

Jolan—Hungarian: Violet blossom

Jolie—French: Pretty
Jolena, Jolene, Joli, Jolina, Joline, Joly

Jonina—Hebrew: Little dove

Jonita—Latin: Jovial

Jora—Hebrew: Autumn rain
   Jorah, Jori, Jory
Jordan—Hebrew: Flowing downward
   Jordaine, Jordana, Jordanne, Jordena, Jordyn, Joree, Jorey,
   Jori, Jorry, Jory
Josephine—Hebrew: She shall add
   Fifi, Fifine, Jo, Joeta, Joey, Josefa, Josefina, Josepha, Jose-
   phina, Josephiney, Josee, Josey, Josi, Josie, Josy
   *Napoleon's wife was Empress Marie Josèphe Rose, but
   everyone called her Josephine.*
Josie—See: Josephine
Joy—Latin: Joyfulness
   Joi, Joia, Joya, Joyann, Joyelle
Joyce—Latin: Joyous
   Joice, Joy, Joycee, Joycey, Joyci, Joycie, Joyous
Juanita—Spanish: God is gracious
   Anita, Juana
Jubilee—Latin: Joyful time
Judith—Hebrew: Praised one
   Judi, Judie, Judy, Judyth, Judythe
Judy—See: Judith
Julia—Latin: Youthful
   Jule, Julea, Julee, Juley, Juli, Juliana, Juliane, Juliann,
   Julianna, Julianne, Julie, Juliet, Julietta, Juliette, Julina,
   Juline, Julita, Julitta
June—Latin: Month of June, youthful
   Junella, Junetta, Junette, Junia, Junie, Juniet, Junieta, Junina
Juno—Latin: Queen of the heavens
Justine—Latin: Justice
   Giustina, Giustine, Justeen, Justina
   *Actress Justine Bateman from the hit sitcom "Family Ties"
   inspired a new interest in this turn-of-the-century name.*

K

Kali—Sanskrit: Energy
Kalika—Greek: Rosebud
Kalila—Arabic: Loved one
Kalinda—Sanskrit: Sun
Kama—Sanskrit: Love
Kamaria—African: Moonlike

Kamilia—Slavic: Sweet flower

Kara—See: Cara

Karen/Karin—Greek: Pure
Karena, Karene, Karina, Karine

Karida—Arabic: Virginal

Karima—Arabic: Noble, generous

Karli—Turkish: Covered with snow

Kate—See: Katherine

Katherine—Greek: Pure (Also see: Catherine)
Kass, Kassi, Kassia, Katalin, Kate, Katerina, Katerine, Katha, Katharine, Kathe, Kathee, Kathey, Kathie, Kathleen, Kathryn, Kathryna, Kathryne, Kathy, Kati, Katie, Katina, Katine, Katinka, Katrinka, Katuscha, Katuska, Katy, Katya, Kay, Kaye, Ketti, Kettia, Kit, Kittie, Kitty
This name is a classic throughout the Western world, and one of its most famous recipients is three-time Academy Award winner Katharine Hepburn.

Kathleen—See: Katherine

Kay—See: Katherine

Keely—Irish: Beautiful one

Kefira—Hebrew: Young lioness

Keiko—Japanese: Adored one

Kelda—Scandinavian: Clear mountain spring

Kelila—Hebrew: Crown of laurel
Kaile, Kayle, Kelula

Kelli/Kelly—Irish: Warrior woman
Kellee, Kelley, Kellie, Kellina

Kelsey—Norse: From the ship's island
Kelcee, Kelci, Kelcie, Kelsee, Kelsy

Kendra—English: Knowledge

Kerani—Indian: Sacred bells

Keren—Hebrew: Ray, beam

Kerensa—Cornish: Love
Karensa, Karenza, Kerenza

Kerry—Irish: Dark haired
Keri, Kerree, Kerrey, Kerri, Kerrie

Kezia—Hebrew: From Cassia
Kazia, Kessi, Kessie, Kessy, Kezzi, Kezzie, Kezzy, Kizzie, Kizzy
Cassia is the name of a group of trees and shrubs, one of which has cinnamonlike bark.

Kichi—Japanese: Fortunate

Kiki—Egyptian: Castor plant

Kimberley—English: From the meadow
Kim, Kimberlee, Kimberlie, Kimberly, Kimbie, Kimbra, Kimmee, Kimmi, Kimmie, Kimmy
Kimberly is the diamond-mining center in South Africa. The name also comes from kimberlite, a rock formation often containing diamonds.

Kineta—Greek: Active one

Kira/Kyra—Persian: Sun

Kirsten—Danish: Christian follower
Kirstan, Kirstane, Kirsti, Kirstie, Kirstin, Kirstina, Kirsty, Kirstyn

Kisa—Russian: Pussycat

Kitty—See: Katherine

Kizzy—Nickname for Kezia: (Also see: Kezia)
Kizzy was the name of one of the leading characters in the miniseries "Roots," which first aired on TV in 1977. Leslie Uggams played the part. Soon after the show's first airing, the name started appearing on birth certificates across the country.

Koko—Japanese: Stork (an Oriental symbol of longevity)

Kolina—Swedish: Maiden

Kora—See: Cora

Kristen—Norse: Christian follower
Krista, Kristel, Kristela, Kristella, Kristelle, Kristee, Kristi, Kristin, Kristina, Kristine, Krysta, Krystyn, Krystyna

Kumi—Japanese: Braid
Kumiko

Kyla/Kyle—Irish: Lovely

Kyna—Irish: Wise

Kyoko—Japanese: Mirror

L

Lacey/Lacie/Lacy—See: Gelasia

Laila—Arabic: Dark haired, night
Laili, Lailie, Layla, Lelia, Leyla

Lainie—See: Elaine, Helen

Lakeisha—Swahili: Favorite one
Lakecia, Lakeesha, Lakicia, Lekeesha, Lekeisha

Lala—Slavic: Tulip

Lalita—Sanskrit: Pleasing, charming

Lana—Latin: Woolly

Lanata, Lanetta, Lanette, Lanna, Lannata, Lanneta, Lanni, Lannie, Lanny

This name was popular in the 1940s and '50s when actress Lana Turner starred on the silver screen.

Lane—English: From the narrow road

Laney, Lani, Lanie, Layne, Laynie

Lara—Latin: Shining

This popular Russian name got the attention of expectant parents in America when the film Dr. Zhivago *was released in 1965. The part of Lara was played by Julie Christie, and the song "Lara's Theme" inspired many namings.*

Laraine—Latin: Sea bird

Larana, Larane, Larayne

Larissa—Greek: Cheerful, lighthearted

Laryssa, Larysse, Laryssia, Lissa, Lyssa

Lark—English: A songbird

Latoya—Spanish: Victorious one

This name is now a familiar one, thanks to singer LaToya Jackson.

Latricia—Latin: Of noble descent

Latrecia, Latreece, Latreshia, Latrice, Letrice, Letricia

Laura—Latin: Laurel wreath or crown

Laure, Laurette, Lauri, Laurice, Laurie, Lora, Loretta, Lorette, Lori, Lorita, Lorra, Lorray, Lorree, Lorrey, Lorrie

The Romans used the laurel wreath as a symbol of victory. They also believed that a laurel crown could protect them from lightning.

Laurel—Latin: Laurel tree

Laural, Laurall, Laurell

Lauren—Latin: Laurel wreath or crown

Laureen, Laureena, Laurena, Laurene, Loreen, Loren, Lorena, Lorene, Lorenza, Lorinda

This name became popular when actress Lauren Bacall became a star in the 1940s, when Lauren Tewes was on the TV series "The Love Boat" from 1977 to 1984, and when eighties supermodel and actress Lauren Hutton was splashed across the pages of magazines. Of course, fashion

designer Ralph Lauren (born Ralph Lefkowitz) has helped keep the name quite prominent.

Laurie—See: Laura

Laveda—Latin: Innocent one

Laverne/LaVerne—Latin: Springlike
Laverna, Laverney, Lavernia, Lavernie, Laverny, Lavernya

Lavinia/Lavinie—Latin: Purified, women of Rome
Lavena, Lavenia, Lavina, Levina, Levinia, Livinia, Lovinia

Leah—Hebrew: Weary
Lea, Leigha, Lia

Leala—French: Loyal one
Leal, Lealia, Leanna, Lelah, Loyale, Loyola

Leda/Leta—Greek: Lady, joy, gladness

Lee—English: From the meadow in the pasture (Also, a nick-name for names starting or ending with "Lee")
Leanna, Leeann, Leeanna, Leeanne, Leecynth, Leigh

Leeat—Hebrew: You are mine
Liat

Leeba/Liba—Yiddish: Beloved

Leila—Arabic: Born at night
Layla, Layle, Lela, Lelah, Leyla, Leylia

Leilani—Hawaiian: Heavenly flower

Lemuela—Hebrew: Consecrated to God

Lena/Lina—Latin: Temptress
Leni, Lenni, Lennie, Lenny

Lenore—See: Eleanor, Leonora

Leoda/Leota—German: Woman of the people

Leona—Latin: Lion
Leola, Leone, Leonelle, Leoney, Leonie, Leony, Leonya, Liona, Lionelle, Lionetta
The most famous owner of this name is real-estate/hotel magnate Leona Helmsley.

Leonora—Greek: Light
Leanor, Leanora, Leanore, Lenora, Lenore, Leonore

Leontine/Leontyne—Latin: Lionlike
Leontyn, Liontin, Liontine, Lyontin, Lyontine, Lyontyn, Lyontyne
In 1966, opera singer Leontyne Price was the first black person to open a New York Metropolitan Opera season.

Leslie—Scottish: From the gray fortress
Les, Lesley, Lesli, Lesly, Lezlee, Lezley, Lezlie, Lezly
Letha—Greek: Forgetfulness
Leticia/Letitia—Latin: Joy
Leta, Lethia, Letisha, Letishia, Letti, Lettie, Letty, Tish, Tisha
In the early 1800s, there was a first lady named Letitia—the wife of President John Tyler.
Levana/Levona—Latin: Rising sun
Levania, Levanna
Lewanna—Hebrew: Beaming white one, the moon
Lian/Liann—Chinese: Graceful willow
Liana/Liane—French: Binding
Libby—Hebrew: Oath of God
Lib, Libbee, Libbey, Libbie
Lida—Slavic: Beloved of the people
Lien—Chinese: Lotus
Lila/Lilah—See: Delilah
Lilac—Persian: Lilac flower
Lili/Lily—See: Lillian
Lilith—Hebrew: Spirit of the night; Assyrian: Storm goddess
Lilis, Lillis, Lillys, Lillyth, Lyllis, Lyllith
Lillian—Latin: Lily flower
Lil, Lili, Lillia, Lilian, Liliann, Lilli, Lillie, Lilly, Lillyan
Linda—Spanish: Pretty
Lin, Lindy, Lyn, Lynda, Lyndey, Lyndi, Lyndie, Lyndy
In the mid-1940s and throughout the 1950s, Linda was one of the most popular names in the U.S. Born during that time were Lynda Carter, Linda Evans, Linda Ellerbee, Linda Gray, and Linda Ronstadt.
Lindsay/Lindsey—English: From the isle of linden trees
This was originally a boy's name, but it caught on as a girl's name at the end of the 1970s. TV's "Bionic Woman," Lindsay Wagner, may have had an influence on this trend.
Linetta/Linette—Celtic: Graceful
Lanet, Linet, Lineta, Linnet, Lyneta, Lynetta, Lynette
Linnea/Lynnea—Swedish: The national flower
Liron—Hebrew: The song is mine
Lisa—Hebrew: Dedicated to God
Leesa, Leeza, Lisetta, Lisette, Lissa, Liza, Lizetta, Lizette, Lyssa

Livana—Hebrew: White

Livia—See: Olive

Livona—Hebrew: Spice
Livonia, Livonna, Livonne

Liza—See: Lisa

Lois—Greek: Battle maiden, renowned in battle

Lola—Spanish: Sorrowful one; English: Strong one
Lolita

Lolita—Spanish: Sorrows
Vladmir Nabokov's 1958 novel of the above name, and the subsequent film version (1962) made Lolita a well-known name. It's now a way of describing a sexy young girl: "She's a regular Lolita!"

Lorelei—German: Alluring
Loralee, Loralei, Lorelee, Lorilee, Lorilei, Lura, Luralee, Luraleen, Luralene, Luraline, Luralyne

Loretta—See: Laura

Lorice—Latin: Slender vine

Lorna/Lorne—English: Lost love
This name was created by R. D. Blackmore in the 1860s for his novel Lorna Doone.

Lorraine—German: Famous in battle; Place name: Former province of eastern France, then Germany (1871), and France again (1919)
Laraine, Laurraine, Lorain, Loraine, Lorayne, Lorrayn, Lorrayne
This province was the hometown of Joan of Arc. The saint is also referred to as "Joan of Lorraine."

Lottie/Lotty—See: Charlotte

Lotus—Greek: Dreamlike, lotus flower

Louella/Louelle—English: Elf, sprite
Loella, Loelle, Lou, Lu, Luella, Luelle, Lula, Lulu

Louisa/Louise—German: Noted woman of war
Eloisa, Eloise, Loisa, Loise, Louisetta, Louisette

Luana/Luane—German: Graceful woman of battle
Louanna, Louanne, Luanna, Luanne

Luba—Slavic: Lover

Lucille—See: Lucy

Lucinda—Latin: Bringer of light
Cinda, Cindee, Cindey, Cindi, Cindie, Cindy, Lucindee, Lucindia, Lucindy

Lucretia—Latin: Riches, treasure
There was a first lady named Lucretia, and she was married to President James Garfield.

Lucy—Latin: Light bearer
Lucee, Lucia, Lucie, Lucilla, Lucille, Lucine
"I Love Lucy"! Who doesn't? It is said that every minute of every day an "I Love Lucy" episode airs somewhere in the world.

Ludmilla—Slavic: Loved by the people

Lulu—See: Louella

Luna—Latin: Moon
Lunet, Lunetta, Lunette

Lurleen/Lurlene—German: Alluring
Lurel, Luretta, Lurette, Lurleena, Lurline, Lurlyna

Lydia—Greek: Cultured, voluptuous; Place name: A country in Asia Minor
Lidia, Lidya, Lyd, Lyddi, Lyddie, Lydie
The country of Lydia was the first place to have had a system of coinage.

Lynn/Lynne—English: Waterfall
Linn, Linnelle, Lynelle, Lynette

Lyris—Greek: Lyrical
Lyra

Lysandra—Greek: Liberator of men

M

Mabel/Mable—Latin: Lovable
Mab, Mabe, Mabela, Mabella, Mabelle, Maybel, Maybella, Maybelle

Madelina/Madeline—Greek: Tower of strength
Mada, Madalena, Madalyn, Maddi, Maddie, Maddy, Madelaine, Madeleine, Madelena, Madelene, Madella, Madelle, Madelon, Madelyn, Magda, Magdalena, Magdalene, Maud, Maude

Madge—See: Margaret

Madonna—Latin: My lady
Once it was a name spoken with reverence, but now people have a whole new attitude toward the name, due to the overwhelming success of the superstar born Madonna Louise Ciccone.

Maeve—Celtic: Joy; Gaelic: Delicate, fragile

Magda—See: Madelina/Madeline

Maggie—See: Margaret

Magnolia—French: A tree with large pink blossoms
The tree was named for French botanist Pierre Magnol.

Mahalia—Hebrew: Tenderness
Mahala, Mehala, Mehalia

Maida—German: Maiden
Mady, Maidel, Maidena, Maidene, Maidie, Mayda

Maisie—See: Margaret

Majesta—Latin: Majestic

Mala—See: Marlene

Malka—Hebrew: Queen
Malkeh, Malki, Malkit

Mallory—French: Wild duck, "mailed one" (referring to a suit
of mail worn by knights); Latin: To beat with a hammer
*In most older name books, this name is listed for boys. It
became a popular girl's name in the 1980s, probably
because of Justine Bateman's character, Mallory Keaton,
on "Family Ties."*

Malu—Hawaiian: Peacefulness

Mame—See: Mary

Manda/Mandy—See: Amanda

Mangena—Hebrew: Melody

Manuela— Spanish: God is with us
Manuelia, Manuelle, Manuely

Mara—See: Mary

Maranda/Miranda—Latin: Admirable

Marcella—Latin: Fierce, warlike
Marcela, Marcelle, Marcellina, Marcelline, Marchita, Marcia,
Marcie, Marcy, Marcyann, Marcyanna, Markie, Markita,
Marquita, Marsha, Martia

Marcia/Marsha—See: Marcella

Margaret—Greek: Pearl
Madge, Magee, Maggie, Maggy, Maisie, Margalo, Mar-
garita, Marge, Margery, Margey, Margie, Margit, Margita,
Margitta, Margitte, Margo, Margot, Margrit, Margritta,
Margritte, Marguerita, Marguerite, Margy, Marji, Marjie,
Marjo, Marjorie, Marjory, Marketa, Meg, Megan, Meggie,
Meghan, Meta, Peg, Pegeen, Peggie, Peggy
Margaret Mitchell, author of the best-seller Gone with the

Wind, *influenced the naming of babies not only with her story's characters but with her own, more conservative name.*

Margery—See: Margaret

Margo—See: Margaret

Marguerite—See: Margaret

Maria/Marie—See: Mary

Marian/Marianne—See: Mary

Maribel/Maribelle—Hebrew: Beautiful but bitter

Marice—German: Marsh flower

Marigold—English: Orange and yellow flower

Marilyn—See: Mary

In theatrical circles, often this name is paired with last names that begin with the same letter; e.g., Marilyn Miller, Marilyn Maxwell, Marilyn Monroe, and Marilyn Michaels.

Marina—Latin: Sea maiden

Maris—Latin: From the sea

Marisa, Marissa, Marisse, Marrisa, Marris, Marysa, Merisa, Merissa, Merys

Marjorie—See: Margaret

Markie—See: Marcella

Marla/Marlo—See: Mary

Marlo Thomas as "That Girl" (1966–71) was responsible for bringing attention to this name.

Marlene—Hebrew: The exalted

Mala, Malena, Malina, Marlee, Marleen, Marlena, Marlina, Marline, Marlyne

Marlene Dietrich was born Maria Magdalene Dietrich. She combined the first part of her first name (Mar) and the last part of her middle name (lene) and came up with a name (Marlene) that proved very lucky for her.

Marmara—Greek: Radiant

Marnina—Hebrew: Cause of joy

Marni

Marsha—See: Marcella

Martha—Aramaic: Lady, mistress

Marta, Martela, Martele, Marthe, Martie, Martita, Marty

We all know that Martha Dandridge Custis married George Washington and became the first first lady of the United States. But did you know that another Martha—Martha

Wayles Skelton—was also married to one of our early presidents? This Martha was the wife of Thomas Jefferson.

Martina—Latin: Warrior of Mars
Considering the meaning of this name, it's no wonder that Martina Navratilova is a tennis player who's out of this world.

Marva—Hebrew: Sage (the fragrant herb)

Marvel—Latin: Full of wonder
Marvella, Marvelle

Mary—Hebrew: Wished-for child, star of the sea
Maire, Mairi, Mame, Mamie, Manon, Manya, Mara, Maralin, Maraline, Mari, Maria, Mariam, Marian, Marianna, Marica, Marice, Marie, Mariel, Mariella, Marielle, Marietta, Mariette, Marilla, Marilyn, Marion, Mariska, Marite, Marla, Marlie, Marlin, Marlo, Marya, Maryann, Maryanna, Maryanne, Marye, Marylyn, Mayme, Miriam, Mitzi, Mollie, Molly
With the number of famous songs and poems featuring the name, we agree with George M. Cohan: "Mary's a Grand Old Name"!

Maryann/Maryanna/Maryanne—See: Mary

Mathilda/Mathilde—German: Powerful one
Matilda, Matilde, Matti, Mattie, Matty, Tilda, Tildie

Maud/Maude—See: Madelina/Madeline

Maureen—French: Dark skinned
Maura, Maure, Maurene, Maurine, Maurise, Maurita, Mauritzia, Moreen, Morena, Moryne

Mavis—French: Songbird

Maxine—Latin: Greatest one
Max, Maxi, Maxie, Maxy

May—Latin: Great
Mae, Mai, Maia, Maya, Maye

Meda—Latin: Healer
Medea, Medora

Meg—See: Margaret

Megan/Meghan—See: Margaret

Melanie/Melany—Greek: Dressed in dark clothes
Lani, Lanie, Lannie, Lanny, Malania, Mel, Mela, Melli, Mellie, Melly
Melanie Hamilton, a character in Gone with the Wind, *made the name popular both in 1934, when the novel was*

published, and in 1939, when the film was released. Olivia de Havilland played the part of Melanie.

Melantha—Greek: Dark flower

Melba—Celtic: From the mill stream

Melina—Greek: Canary yellow

Melinda—Greek: Gentle
Malinda, Malynda, Melynda, Melyndy, Mindee, Mindi, Mindie, Mindy

Melissa—Greek: Honeybee
Malissa, Melecent, Melessa
Singer Melissa Manchester and Melissa Gilbert, the star of "Little House on the Prairie," have made this an appealing name.

Melodie/Melody—Greek: Song

Melosa—Spanish: Sweet, gentle

Mercedes—Spanish: Merciful
Merci, Mercie, Mercy

Meredith/Meredyth—Welsh: Protector from the sea
Meridyth, Merridith, Merridyth, Merritha

Merla/Merle—French: Blackbird
Merl, Merlie, Merly, Meryl, Meryle, Myrla, Myrlena, Myrlene

Merry—English: Amiable, festive, pleasant, jolly
Meri, Merrey, Merrie, Merrielle, Merrilee, Merrill

Meryl—See: Merla/Merle
Two-time Academy Award winner Meryl Streep is largely responsible for the popularity of this name in the past decade.

Meta—Latin: Ambition

Mia—Italian: Belonging to me

Michaela—Hebrew: Who is like the Lord?
Micaela, Micaele, Michael, Michaele, Michaelina, Michaeline, Michalah, Michel, Michelina, Micheline, Michelle, Micki, Mickie, Micky, Midge, Miguela, Miguelina, Migueline, Miguelita, Mikaela, Mikaele, Mike, Mikie

Michelle—See: Michaela

Mignon—French: Dainty, graceful, delicate
Mignona, Mignone, Mignonetta, Mignonette

Mila—Czechoslovakian: Loved by the people

Mildred—English: Kind counselor
Mil, Mildreda, Mildrid, Milley, Milli, Millie, Milly

Milena—German: Mild

Millicent—German: Strength
Melicent, Melisanda, Melisande, Milicenta, Milicente

Mimi—Italian: My, my! (Also, a pet name for Miriam, Marie, and other "M" names)
Opera lovers know that Mimi is the heroine of Puccini's masterpiece, La Bohème.

Mina—See: Gemina

Mindy—See: Melinda

Minerva—Greek: Wisdom
Min, Minetta, Minette, Minnie, Minny

Minna—German: Tender affection

Minnie—See: Minerva

Mira—Latin: Wonderful
Mirella, Mirelle, Myra, Myril, Myrilla

Mirabella/Mirabelle—Latin: Of spectacular beauty
Mirabel, Mirabela

Miriam—See: Mary

Misty—English: Clouded vision

Mitzi—See: Mary

Miyoko –Japanese: Generation's beautiful child

Modesty—Latin: Humble, modest
Modesta, Modestia, Modestina, Modestine, Modestyna, Modestyne

Moira—Irish: Great woman
Moirae, Mora, Moyra

Mollie/Molly—See: Mary

Mona—Greek: Solitary

Monica—Latin: Advice giver
Moniqua, Monique

Morgan—Welsh: Woman of the sea

Moriah—Hebrew: God is my teacher
Mariah, Moria

Muriel/Murielle—Greek: Fragrant one

Murphy—Celtic: Sea warrior
Ever since the TV sitcom "Murphy Brown" caught on, girls have taken over this once mostly male name.

Musetta—Latin: A little music

Myra—French: Quiet song; Latin: Scented oil

Myrna—Irish: Polite, tender, beloved
Merna, Mirna, Morna

Myrtle—Greek: Victorious crown; Latin: Name of a flower
Myrta, Myrtell, Myrti, Myrtice, Myrtie, Myrtis

N

Nadia—Slavic: Hope
Nada, Nadeen, Nadie, Nadine, Nady, Nadya
Romanian gymnast Nadia Comaneci put this name on the map when she won our hearts in the 1976 Olympics.

Naiad/Naida—Greek: Water nymph
Nayad, Nyad
TV commentator Diana Nyad made a name for herself as a world-class swimmer. Last names too can be portents of things to come.

Nalani—Hawaiian: Calmness of the skies

Nancy—Hebrew: Grace
Nan, Nana, Nance, Nancee, Nanci, Nancie, Nanette, Nani, Nanica, Nanine, Nanna, Nannie, Nanny

Nanette—See: Nancy

Naomi—Hebrew: Pleasant, charming

Nara—Japanese: Oak (symbol of stability)

Natalie—Latin: Child of Christmas
Nat, Nata, Natala, Natalia, Natalina, Natalita, Natasha, Nathalia, Nathalie, Natty, Talie, Tasha

Natasha—See: Natalie

Nathania—Hebrew: Gift of God
Natania, Nataniela, Natanielle, Nathaniella

Navit—Hebrew: Beautiful

Naysa—Hebrew: Miracle of God

Nealy/Neely—Irish: Champion

Neda/Nedda—Slavic: Born on Sunday

Nelda—English: Of the elder tree

Nell—Greek: Light
Nellee, Nelli, Nellie, Nelly

Neoma—Greek: New moon

Nerine—Greek: Nymph of the sea
Nerice, Nerissa, Nerita

Nessa—See: Agnes, Vanessa

Netta/Nettie/Netty—See: Antonia

Neva—Spanish: Snowy

Nicola/Nicole—Greek: The people's victory

Cola, Nicaela, Nichola, Nichole, Nickie, Nicol, Nicolette, Nicolina, Nike, Nikee, Nikki, Nikola, Nikole, Nikoleen, Nikolene

Nina—Spanish: Girl
Nena, Ninetta, Ninette, Ninon
The Niña was one of Christopher Columbus's three ships; ships are almost always "female."

Nissa—Danish/Swedish: Friendly elf
Nisan, Nisse, Nissen, Nissie, Nissy, Nyssa

Nita—Native American (Choctaw): Bear

Noel—French: To be born
Noella, Noelle, Noellyn

Noelani—Hawaiian: Beautiful girl from heaven

Noga—Hebrew: Morning light
Nolcha

Nola—Latin: Noble woman; Gaelic: White shoulder

Nona—Latin: The ninth
Nonie, Nonna
Originally reserved for the ninth child of the family, no wonder this name is not a very common one!

Nora/Norah—See: Eleanor, Honora

Noreen—See: Norma

Nori—Japanese: Doctrine

Norma—Latin: As a rule, pattern
Noreen, Noreena, Norena, Norene, Norine
Speaking of patterns, fashion designer Norma Kamali has her name and her career all sewed up!

Numa—Arabic: Beautiful

Nydia—Latin: Safe refuge
Neda, Nedda

Nysa—Greek: Beginning

O

Obelia—Greek: Pillar of strength

Octavia/Octavie—Latin: The eighth
Octava, Octavine, Tavia, Tavie, Tavy
In ancient Roman families, if the eighth child was a girl, she most likely would have been given this name.

Odelia/Odelie—Hebrew: I will praise God

Odela, Odele, Odelet, Odelette, Odelinda, Odella, Odelle, Odile, Odillia, Othelia

Odessa—Greek: Long journey

Odetta/Odette—French: Love of one's home; German: Wealth
In the ballet Swan Lake, *Odette is the good swan and Odile is the evil swan. Both parts are often danced by the same ballerina.*

Okalani—Hawaiian: From heaven

Olathe—Native American: Beautiful

Oleander—American English: An evergreen with red or white blossoms
Oliana

Olga—Russian: Holy
Olia, Olienka

Olive—Latin: Olive tree
Livia, Livie, Livvie, Livvy, Livy, Olivette, Olivia, Ollie, Olva
Olive trees have been known to live up to two thousand years. The olive branch—as in "The dove returned to the ark with an olive branch in its beak" (Gen. 8:11)—has long been a symbol of peace.

Olivia—See: Olive

Olympia/Olympie—Greek: Heavenly, of Olympus (the mountain home of the gods)
Olympia Dukakis, the Moonstruck *mother of Cher, won an Oscar for her performance.*

Ona—Lithuanian: Graceful one
Oona, Una

Ondine—Latin: Of the water
Ondina, Undine

Oona—See: Ona

Opal—Hindi: Jewel
Opalina, Opaline
The opal, which is said to have a magic rainbow within its depths, is thought to be created from water and crystalline rock formations.

Ophelia—Greek: Immortality, wisdom, to help
Ofelia, Ofellia, Offie, Ofilia, Orphellia, Orphie, Orphillia, Phelia

Ora—Hebrew: Light
  Orah, Oralee, Orit, Orlee, Orlice, Orly
Orabel—French: Of golden beauty
  Orabella, Orabelle, Oribel
Oralia/Oralie—Latin: Eloquent speaker
Oriana—Celtic: Of white skin, fair
  Oriane, Oriel, Oriella, Orielle
Oriole—Latin: Fair haired
Orlena/Orlene—Latin: Golden
Orna—Latin: Decorate
Orpah—Hebrew: Fawn; German: Fatherland
  Ophrah, Oprah
  *It is said that TV star Oprah Winfrey's name was supposed
  to be Orpah, but her mother misspelled it. Oprah's name
  spelled backward, Harpo, is the name of Oprah's produc-
  tion company.*
Otillia—Greek: Fortunate maid of battle
  Otilla, Otillie, Otilly, Tilla, Tillie, Tilly

P

Padmani—Sri Lankan: Flower
Page/Paige—English: Young; Greek: Child
  Paget, Pagette, Payge
Paka—Swahili: Pussycat
Palma—Latin: Palm tree
  The leaves of this tree resemble the palm of one's hand.
Paloma—Spanish: Dove
  Palometa, Palomita
  *Jewelry designer Paloma Picasso has a perfume named
  Paloma.*
Pamela—Greek: Loving, kind
  Pam, Pamelia, Pamelina, Pamella, Pammi, Pammie, Pammy
Pandora—Greek: All-gifted
  Pan, Pandi, Pandie, Pandy
Pansy—French: A velvety, somewhat unusual-looking flower
Patience—French: Enduring
Patricia—Latin: Of the nobility, wellborn, patrician
  Pat, Patria, Patrica, Patrice, Patrizia, Patsy, Patti, Pattie,
  Patty, Tricia, Trish, Trisha, Trishia
Patsy/Patti/Patty—See: Patricia

Paula—Latin: Small

Paola, Paoleta, Paolina, Paoline, Paule, Pauletta, Paulette, Pauley, Pauli, Paulie, Paulina, Pauline, Paulita, Pauly, Pavla, Polly, Pollyanna

Pauletta/Paulette—See: Paula

Paulina/Pauline—See: Paula

Pazia—Hebrew: Golden girl

Paz, Paza, Pazice

Pearl—Latin: Ham (for the hamlike shape of the sea mussel)

Pearla, Pearle, Pearlie, Pearlina, Pearline, Pearly, Perla, Perle, Perlie, Perly

Pultizer Prize–winning, American-born author Pearl S. Buck spent her early years in China, and her books reflect her firsthand knowledge of that country.

Peg/Peggy—See: Margaret

Penda—Swahili: Love

Penelope—Greek: Weaver

Penni, Pennie, Penny

In Homer's Odyssey, *Penelope was the wealthy wife of Ulysses who put off her suitors by promising to marry one of them only* after *she finished weaving her tapestry. To prevent that from happening, she would weave all day and, at night, unravel the work she had completed. Ten years later, it paid off when her husband, previously believed dead, returned from his wanderings.*

Penina/Peninah—Hebrew: Pearl

Penny—See: Penelope

Peony—Greek: Giver of praise; English: Name of a flower

Perdita—Latin: Lost

This is the name of the young heroine in Shakespeare's Winter's Tale.

Persephone—Greek: Prosperous

Peri, Perri, Perrie, Perry

Petra—Latin: Rock

Peta, Petrea, Petrina, Petrine, Petrissa, Petronia, Petronie, Pier, Pierette

Petula—Latin: Seeker, saucy

Petulia, Petulie, Tula

Petunia—Native American (Tupi—a South American tribe): Sweet flower

Phaedra—Greek: Shining one

Phaedre, Phaidra, Phaidre, Phedra, Phedre

Phebe/Phoebe—Greek: Bright, shining

Philana—Greek: Friend of humankind

Phillippa—Greek: Lover of horses
Felipa, Felipe, Felippa, Felippe, Philippina, Philippine, Philli, Phillipe, Philly, Pippa, Pippi

Philomena—Greek: Loving harmony
Filomena, Filomene, Philomene, Philomine

Phyllis—Greek: Green bough
Phil, Philicia, Philis, Phillida, Phillis, Philly, Phylicia, Phyllys

Pia—Italian: Devout

Pier/Pierette—See: Petra

Pilar—Spanish: Supportive, responsible

Pippa—See: Phillippa

Pocahontas—Native American: Playful
Pocahontas was a nickname given to Indian Princess Matoaka. When she married John Rolfe and moved to England, she became Rebecca Rolfe.

Polly—See: Paula

Pollyanna—See: Paula

Pomona—Latin: Fruitful, fertile

Poppy—Latin: A bright red flower

Portia—Latin: Offering
Portia was the bright young heroine in Shakespeare's Merchant of Venice *who outwits Shylock and saves her husband's life by disguising herself as a lawyer.*

Prima—Latin: Firstborn

Primrose—Latin: First rose

Priscilla—Latin: From ancient times
Cilla, Pris, Prissie, Prissy

Providence—Latin: Divine direction
Dancer Nicole Fosse's middle name is Providence, because that's the way her parents, Gwen Verdon and Bob Fosse, felt about their little "miracle child."

Prudence—Latin: Discretion
Pru, Prudi, Prudie, Prudy, Prue

Prunella—French: Plum colored

Pythia—Greek: Prophet
Thia

Q

Queen—English: Royalty
Queenee, Queenie, Queeny
Quella—English: Pacify
Quenby—Swedish: Womanly
Querida—Spanish: Beloved
Quintina—Latin: Fifth Child
Quiric—Greek: Sunday's child
Quirita—Latin: Citizen

R

Rachel—Hebrew: Ewe, female sheep
Rachael, Rachele, Rachelle, Rachie, Rae, Rahel, Rahil,
Raitch, Rakel, Raquel, Raquelle, Ray, Rochel, Rochelle
*First lady Rachel Donelson Robards was married to
Andrew Jackson, America's first Democratic president.*
Radmilla—Slavic: Worker for the people
Rae/Ray—See: Rachel
Raina/Rayna—See: Regina
Raissa—French: Thinker
Raizel—Yiddish: Rose
Ramona—Spanish: Protectress
Ramonda, Ramunda, Raymona
*This name has enjoyed success as a song, a film, a series of
children's books, and more.*
Randi—English: Invincible
Randa, Randee, Randie, Randy
Rani—Hindi: Queen
Rana, Ranee, Rania
Ranita—Hebrew: Joy
Ranice, Ranit
Raphaela—Hebrew: Healed by God
Rafaela, Rafaella, Raphaella, Raphaelle
Raquel—See: Rachel
Rasheda/Rashida—Swahili: Righteous
Raven—English: Blackbird
Rayna/Reyna—Hebrew: Pure, clean
Razilee/Razili—Hebrew: My secret

Reba—See: Rebecca

Rebecca—Hebrew: To bind
Becca, Becka, Becki, Beckie, Becky, Reba, Rebeca, Rebeka, Rebekah
"To bind" is an appropriate meaning when you consider how many books use this name for their heroines: Sir Walter Scott's Ivanhoe, Rebecca of Sunnybrook Farm, and Daphne du Maurier's Rebecca, to name just a few. When the latter was made into a film in Spain, Joan Fontaine, who starred in the film, wore a cardigan in some scenes. The Spaniards picked up on that and began calling a cardigan a "Rebecca."

Regan—See: Regina

Regina—Latin: Queen
Raina, Rayna, Reagan, Rega, Regan, Reggi, Reggie, Reggy, Reina, Reine
Regina was the leading character in Lillian Hellman's play, The Little Foxes. In the first film version of it, Bette Davis turned in a memorable performance as the ruthless Regina.

Reiko—Japanese: Gratitude

Remy—French: From Rheims (or Reims)
Although Rheims is a town in central France that's known for its champagne, Rémy Martin is a cognac made in Cognac, which is in eastern France.

Rena/Rina—Hebrew: Song
Renni, Rennie, Renny

Renata—Latin: Reborn
Reanae, Rene, Renee, Renie

Rene/Renee—See: Renata

Reva—Latin: Renewed strength

Rhea—Greek: Stream

Rhoda—Greek: A rose
Rho, Rhode, Rhodia, Rhodocella, Rhodocelle, Rhodora, Rhody
This name became well known because of Valerie Harper's character, Rhoda Morgenstern, on "The Mary Tyler Moore Show."

Rhonda/Ronda—Welsh: Grand, strong river
Can you hear this name without singing: "Help me, Rhonda. Help, help me, Rhonda"?

Ricarda—English: Powerful ruler
Rica, Ricki, Rickie, Ricky, Rikki
Ricki/Rickie/Ricky/Rikki—See: Erica, Frederica, Ricarda
Rima—Spanish: Rhyme, poetry
Rima is the name of the nature-child heroine in Green Mansions. *As a memorial to its author, W. H. Hudson, a statue of Rima was erected in London's Kensington Gardens.*
Risa/Rise—Latin: Laughter
Rita—See: Margaret
Riva—French: Shore
Reeva, Rivalee, Rivi, Rivkah, Rivy
Roberta—English: Bright fame
Robbi, Robbie, Robby, Roberti, Robertie, Roberty, Robin, Robina, Robyn, Ruperta
Robin/Robyn—See: Roberta
Rochelle—See: Rachel
Rohana—Hindi: Sandalwood
Rolanda—German: Famous, notable
Rolli, Rollie, Rolly
Romelda—Latin: Glorious battle maiden
Milda, Romi, Romilda, Romy
Rona—Hebrew: My joy, my song; Place name: Island in the Hebrides off Scotland
Ronena, Roni, Ronit
Ronni/Ronnie/Ronny—See: Rowena, Veronica/Veronika
Rori/Rorie/Rory—See: Aurora
Rosalee/Rosalia/Rosalie—Latin: Feast of roses
Rosalind—Spanish: Lovely rose
Ros, Rosalin, Rosalina, Rosalinda, Rosaline, Rosallyn, Rosalyn, Rosalynd, Rosalynda, Rosa Lynn, Roslyn, Roz, Rozalin, Rozalind, Rozallyn, Rozzy
Rosamond—Greek: Noted guardian
Rosamund, Rosamunda, Rosemond, Rosemonda, Rosemund, Rosemunda
Rosanna/Rosanne—Hebrew: Graceful rose
Ranna, Roanna, Roanne, Roseann, Roseanna, Roseanne
This name is enjoying popularity now with the help of actress/comedienne Roseanne, singer Roseanne Cash, and actress Rosanna Arquette.
Rose—Greek: Rose

Rosa, Rosetta, Rosette, Rosie, Rosita, Rosy, Roze, Rozelle, Rozina

Rosemary—Latin: Fragrant herb, dew of the sea
Rosamaria, Rosamarie, Rosemaria, Rosemarie

Rowena—English: Well-known friend
Rena, Ronni, Ronnie, Ronny, Ro, Row, Rowe

Roxane—Persian: Brilliant one
Roxana, Roxanna, Roxanne, Roxene, Roxi, Roxie, Roxy
If you want to hear "Roxane" pronounced with the passion of a poet and the heart of a romantic, rent the video of the 1950 film Cyrano de Bergerac, *starring Jose Ferrer.*

Roz—See: Rosalind

Ruby—French: A deep red gem
Rubetta, Rubi, Rubia, Rubie, Rubina

Rudella/Rudelle—German: Famous one

Rue—German: Famous; English: Aromatic plant that was once called herb-of-grace
The "famous" meaning is appropriate for namesake Rue McClanahan, one of the stars of the hit TV sitcom, "Golden Girls."

Rula—Latin: Ruler

Rumer—English: Gypsy

Ruri—Japanese: Emerald
Ruriko

Ruth—Hebrew: Beauty, compassion
Rue, Ruthia, Ruthie, Ruthy

Ryba—Czechoslovakian: Fish

S

Sabina—Latin: Of the Sabines (an ancient Italian tribe)
Sabea, Sabena, Sabia, Sabine, Savina, Savine

Sabra—Hebrew: Thorny cactus, to rest

Sabrina—Latin: From the border
Sabreena, Sabrinna, Sabryna, Zabrina
If you like this name, see the wonderfully romantic 1954 film Sabrina, *starring Audrey Hepburn. You'll end up loving the name.*

Sacha/Sasha—Russian: Helper and defender of humankind

Sachiko—Japanese: Joy
Sachi

Sadie—Hebrew: Princess
   Sada, Sadella, Sadelle, Sadye, Syd, Sydel, Sydelle
Sakara—Native American: Sweet
Salena/Salina—Latin: Salt
Sally—See: Sara/Sarah
Salome—Hebrew: Woman of perfection, peace
Samantha—Aramaic: She who listens
   Sam, Sammi, Sammie, Sammy
   From 1967 to 1972, and now in syndication, Samantha, played by Elizabeth Montgomery, practiced witchcraft with a twitch of her nose on the sitcom "Bewitched."
Samara—Hebrew: Ruled by God
Sandra—See: Alexandra, Cassandra
Sara/Sarah—Hebrew: Princess
   Sal, Sallie, Sally, Sarena, Sari, Sarice, Sarika, Sarina, Sarine, Sarit, Sarita, Sarra, Sarrah, Shara, Zara, Zarah
Saxon—Latin: Large stone
   Saxi, Saxie, Sasunn
Scarlett—English: A rich red color
   Scarlett O'Hara from Gone with the Wind *is probably the most famous name in contemporary American literature. And yet, we don't know anyone named Scarlett. Do you?*
Sean—Hebrew: The Lord is favored
   Shawn, Shawna
Season—Latin: Time of sowing
   Not only are the seasons—autumn, winter, spring, and summer—used as names, but so is the category. Soap opera fans may know of Season Hubley, who played Angelique on "All My Children."
Seema—Greek: Symbol
Seena—German: Of the senate
Selena—Greek: Moon
   Selene, Selina, Selyna, Selyne
Selma/Zelma—Norse: Divinely protected
Seraphina—Hebrew: Ardent one, angel
   Sera, Serafina, Serafine, Seraphine
Serena/Serene—Latin: Calm, tranquil
   Serenity
Shaine—Hebrew: Beautiful
   Shaina, Shane, Shanie, Shayna, Shayne, Shifra

Shannon—Celtic: Slow waters; Gaelic: Old, ancient
   Shana, Shandy, Shani, Shanna, Shanon
Shari—See: Sharon
Sharman—English: Receiving or giving a fair share
Sharon—Hebrew: Princess
   Shara, Sharae, Sharai, Shari, Sharine, Sharona, Sharron,
   Shary, Sherri, Sherrie, Sherry
Shawn—See: Sean
Sheba—Hebrew: From Sheba (a southern Arabian region)
Sheena—Hebrew: God's gracious gift
   Sheenah, Sheina, Shena, Shiona
Sheila—Celtic: Musical
   Seela, Sela, Selia, Sheela, Sheelagh, Sheelah, Sheilagh,
   Shela, Shelagh
Shelby—English: Sheltered town
Shelley/Shelly—English: Island of shells
Sherri/Sherry—See: Cher, Sharon
Shira—Hebrew: Song
   Shirah, Shiri
Shirley—English: From the bright meadow
   Sherl, Sherleen, Sherlene, Sherline, Shirl, Shirlee, Shirleen,
   Shirlene, Shirline
   *Shirley Temple was an adorable child actress in the 1930s
   and became, as Shirley Temple Black, a U.S. ambassador in
   the 1970s. Throughout the thirties and into the forties, the
   whole country went crazy about this curly-haired kid and
   the name Shirley quickly became a popular one.*
Shoshana—Hebrew: Flowering lily
   Shoshan, Shoshi
Sibyl/Sybil—Greek: Prophetess
   Cybil, Cybill, Cybilla, Sebila, Sevilla, Sibbie, Sibby, Sibel,
   Sibelle, Sibilla, Sybila, Sybille, Sybyl, Sybylla, Sybylle
Sidonia—Phoenician: Enchantress
   Sid, Sidney, Sidonie, Syd, Sydney, Sydonia, Sydonie
Sigourney—French: Daring king
Sigrid—Norse: Beautiful victory
Silver—English: A precious metal
Sima—Aramaic: Treasure
Simone—Hebrew: One who hears
   Simona, Simonetta, Simonette

Siobhan—Irish: The Lord is gracious
Shavon, Shavonne, Shivaughn

Sirena—Greek: Seductive singer

Skyler—Norse: Projectile; Dutch: Scholar
Schuyler, Schyler, Sky, Skye, Skylar

Solana—Spanish: Sunshine

Solange—French: Sun angel

Solita—Latin: Alone, solitary

Sondra—See: Alexandra, Cassandra

Sonia—Greek: Wisdom
Sonja, Sonni, Sonnie, Sonny, Sonya, Sunni, Sunnie, Sunny, Sunya

Sophia/Sophie—Greek: Wisdom
Sofia, Sofie, Sophronia, Sophy, Zofia, Zofie, Zosia
Sophie Tucker was from the old school of singers with heart. Her real name was Sophia; her nickname, "the Last of the Red-Hot Mamas." Some would say the nickname also fits actress Sophia Loren.

Sparkle—English: Glisten

Spring—Nature name: From the springtime

Stacy—See: Anastasia, Eustacia

Star—English: Celestial body
Starette, Starla, Starr, Starry

Stella—See: Estelle

Stephanie—Greek: Crowned
Stefa, Steffi, Steffia, Steffie, Steffy, Stepha, Stephana, Stephani, Stephania, Stephi, Stephie, Stevana, Stevena, Stevie

Stockard—English: From the yard of tree stumps

Sue—See: Susan

Suki—Japanese: Beloved

Sumi—Japanese: Clear, refined

Summer—Nature name: From the summertime

Sunny—See: Sonia

Susan—Hebrew: Lily flower
Sana, Sanna, Sonel, Sue, Sukey, Sukie, Susana, Susanna, Susannah, Susanne, Susette, Susi, Susie, Susu, Susy, Suzanna, Suzanne, Suzetta, Suzette, Suzi, Suzie, Suzy, Zsa Zsa
Susan B. Anthony, leader of the women's suffrage movement, and also known as "America's First Libber," has

feminists naming their children in her honor. (In case you're wondering, her middle initial stands for Brownell.)

Susanna/Susanne—See: Susan

Suzu—Japanese: Little bell, long lived, round

Svetla—Czechoslovakian: Light
Svetlana

Sydelle—See: Sadie

Sydney—See: Sidonia

Sylvia—Latin: From the forest
Silva, Silvi, Silvia, Silvie, Silvy, Sylvie

Syna—Greek: Together

T

Tabitha—Aramaic: Gazelle
Tab, Tabba, Tabbi, Tabbie, Tabby
Tabitha is the third-generation nose-twitcher on the hit TV series "Bewitched."

Tacita—Latin: Silent
Tace, Taci, Tacye

Taffy—Welsh: Beloved

Tai/Thai—American English: A person from Thailand
U.S. Olympic figure skater Tai Babilonia broke the ice by introducing this name to the world.

Talia—Hebrew: Heaven's dew, lamb
Tal, Tali, Talli, Thalia

Talitha—Aramaic: Maiden; Hebrew: Child
Taletha, Talla, Talli, Tallie, Tally

Tallulah—Native American (Choctaw): Running water
Lula, Tal, Tallou, Talloulah, Talula

Tamah—Hebrew: Innocent, honest
Tama, Tammi, Tammie, Tammy, Thamah

Tamara—Hebrew: Palm tree
Tama, Tamar, Tamarah, Tammi, Tammie, Tammy

Tammy—See: Tamah, Tamara
In the late 1950s and the early 1960s, the name was associated with a series of "Tammy" movies in which the title character was a wholesome and irresistible country girl. But then, in the 1980s, the name became associated with Tammy Faye Bakker, the former wife of televangelist Jim Bakker.

Tani—Japanese: Valley

Tania/Tanya—Russian: Fairy queen

Tansy—Greek: Immortality
Tandie, Tansee, Tansey, Tansie, Tanzey

Tara—Irish: Tower
Tarah, Taryn

Tasha—See: Natalie

Tate—English: Cheerful
Tatiana, Tattie, Tatty, Tatum

Tatiana—See: Tate, Titania

Tatum—See: Tate
Actress Tatum O'Neal brought this name to the attention of the American moviegoing public.

Taylor—English: Tailor
Famous novelist Taylor Caldwell would probably like to know that this is becoming a name of the nineties: Garth Brooks named his daughter Taylor, and it also was the name of a spunky and sophisticated young woman on "All My Children." (Well, isn't that where many name trends start?)

Temperance—Latin: Moderation

Tempest—French: Storm
Tempestt Bledsoe was one of the young actresses on "The Cosby Show."

Teresa—See: Theresa

Terri/Terry—See: Theresa

Tess/Tessa—See: Theresa
Writers seem to favor this name: Tess McGill, portrayed by Melanie Griffith, is the main character in Working Girl; Tess of the D'Urbervilles *by Thomas Hardy was made into a film called* Tess, *which starred Nastassja Kinski; Dick Tracy's girlfriend in Chester Gould's comic strip is Tess Trueheart; and the list goes on. . . .*

Thalassa—Greek: Sea

Thea—Greek: Goddess
Theasa

Thelma—Greek: Nursling, will
Telma
Thelma & Louise—*need we say more?*

Theodora—Greek: God's gift
Fedora, Tedda, Teddi, Teddie, Teddy, Tedra, Teodora, Theda, Theo, Theodosia

Theora—Greek: Thinker

Thera—Greek: Untamed

Theresa—Greek: Reaper
Tera, Teresa, Terese, Teresina, Teresine, Teresita, Teri, Terie, Terri, Terrie, Terry, Tess, Tessa, Tessi, Tessie, Tessy, Therese, Tresa, Tressa

Thirza—Hebrew: Pleasant
Thyrza, Tirza

Thomasina—Greek: Small twin
Sina, Thomasa, Thomasin, Thomasine, Tomasa, Tomasina, Tomasine, Tommi, Tommie, Tommy, Tommyna

Thora—Norse: Thunder
Thordia, Thordis

Thyra—Greek: Shield bearer

Tiffany—Latin: Appearance of the Divine
Tiffanee, Tiffi, Tiffiani, Tiffie, Tiffy, Tyfany, Tyffany
In the Middle Ages, this was a popular name, especially for children born on January 6, the Epiphany (the day the Christ child was first seen by the Magi). The name seemed to disappear for many years, then flourished as the name of an exclusive jewelry store on Fifth Avenue in New York City. In the 1970s, Tiffany resurfaced as a popular name for baby girls.

Tillie/Tilly—See: Otillia

Timothea—Greek: Honor to God
Timma, Timmi, Timmie, Timmy, Timo

Tina—See: Christina/Christine, Ernestine, Valentine

Titania—Greek: Great one
Tatiana
This is the name of the fairy queen in Shakespeare's Mid-summer Night's Dream.

Tivona—Hebrew: Lover of nature

Toby—Hebrew: God is good
Toba, Tobey, Tobi, Tobie, Tova, Tovah, Tovey

Toni/Tonia/Tonie/Tony/Tonya—See: Antonia

Topaz—Greek: A gemstone

Tora—Japanese: Tiger

Tori—Japanese: Bird
Torey, Tory

Tosia—Polish: Priceless

Tova/Tovah—See: Toby

Tracy—Latin: Brave one
Trace, Tracee, Tracey, Traci, Tracie, Tracye, Trasy
Treva—Celtic: Prudent
Tricia—See: Patricia
Trilby—Italian: Sings with trills
Trina—See: Catherine
Trisha—See: Patricia
Trista—Latin: Melancholy
Trixie—See: Beatrice
Trudy—See: Gertrude
Tuesday—English: Born on Tuesday
Actress Susan Ker Weld changed her name to Tuesday, even though she was born on a Friday.
Tulia—Latin: Of the family; Place name: Town in Texas
Tuli, Tulie, Tulley, Tulli, Tullia, Tully
Twila/Twyla—English: A method of weaving
Instead of using wool, famed choreographer Twyla Tharp uses dancers to weave her living tapestries.

U

Udele—German: Prosperous, rich
Uda
Ula—Celtic: Sea jewel
Ulani—Hawaiian: Lighthearted
Ulema/Ulima—Arabic: Wise
Ulrica—German: Ruler of all
Rica, Rikki, Rikky, Ulrika
Ultima—Latin: The greatest, the end, final
This is the name of a successful line of cosmetics.
Uma—Hebrew: Nation
Umeko—Japanese: Plum-blossom child
Una—See: Ona
Undina/Undine—Latin: A wave
Unity—English: Oneness
Urania—Greek: Heaven
Urbana—Latin: Courteous, belonging to the city
Uriana—Greek: The unknown
Ursula—Latin: Female bear
Ulla, Ursa, Ursala, Ursela, Ursola, Ursule, Ursulina
Uta—German: Fortunate maid of battle

As both an actress and an acting teacher, Uta Hagen is one of the most prestigious figures in New York theater circles.

V

Vala—German: Chosen one
Valda—German: Battle heroine
Valentine—Latin: Strong, healthy, valorous
  Tina, Val, Vale, Valeda, Valencia, Valentia, Valentina, Valli, Vallie, Vally, Valora, Valore
  Name your daughter for this saint and she'll always be your Valentine. (Also, think of the great selection of greeting cards you can choose from!)
Valerie—French: Strong
  Valera, Valeree, Valeri, Valeria, Valery, Valory
Valeska—Slavic: Glorious ruler
Vana/Vanna—English: High (Also see: Vanessa)
Vanda—Slavic: Wanderer
Vanessa—Greek: Butterfly
  Nessa, Nessi, Nessie, Nessy, Phanessa, Van, Vana, Vanna, Vanni, Vannie, Vanny
Vania/Vanya—Hebrew: God's gift
Vanora/Vanore—Celtic: White wave
Vardis—Hebrew: Rose
  Varda, Vardia, Vardice, Vardina, Vardyce
Varina/Varine—Slavic: Stranger
Veda—Hindi: Sacred knowledge
Veerani—Sri Lankan: Perseverance
Vegena—Hawaiian: Maidenly
Velda—German: Wisdom
  Veleda
Velika—Slavic: Great one
Velma—German: Resolute guardian
Velvet—Latin: A smooth, luxurious fabric
Venus—Latin: Goddess of love
  Venda, Veneta, Venetia, Venita
Vera—Latin: True, faithful
  Veradis, Veral, Vere, Verena, Verene, Verina, Verine, Verity, Verla
Verbena—Latin: Sacred plant
Verda—Latin: Young, fresh

Verna/Verne—Latin: Springlike
Vernette, Vernice, Vernine, Vernis, Vernita, Vernona

Veronica—Latin: True likeness
Ronnee, Ronni, Ronnie, Ronny, Veronike, Veronique, Veronka, Vonnee, Vonni, Vonnie, Vonny

Actress Veronica Lake was known in the 1940s for a hairdo that covered one eye, thus earning her the nickname "the Peekaboo Girl."

Vesta—Latin: Guardian of the sacred fire

Vevila—Irish: Melodious voice

Vicki/Vicky—See: Victoria

Victoria—Latin: Victorious one
Tori, Toria, Torri, Torrie, Torry, Vic, Vicki, Vickie, Vicky, Victorine, Vikki, Vitoria, Vittoria

Queen Victoria's sixty-four-year reign is the longest in English history. Because she was so loved by her people, many parents named their offspring in her honor.

Vida—See: Davida

Vilma—Russian: Protector
Valma

Vincentia—Latin: Conqueror
Vincenta, Vincenza, Vincie

Vinna—Spanish: From the vine
Vinni, Vinnia, Vinnie, Vinny

Violet—Latin: A violet flower
Vi, Viola, Violaine, Violanie, Violenta, Violeta, Violetta, Violette, Vyolet, Vyolette

Virginia—Latin: Maidenly, pure
Ginni, Ginnie, Ginny, Girgi, Girgie, Girgy, Jinnia, Vergi, Vergie, Vergy

Virginia Dare was the first child of English parents to be born in the U.S. It happened in 1587 on Roanoke Island. This first natural-born citizen was named both for the state of Virginia and in honor of Elizabeth, "the Virgin Queen."

Vita—Latin: Life

Viveca—Scandinavian: Alive, lively
Viva, Viveka

Vivian—Latin: Vital, full of life
Viv, Viviana, Vivianne, Vivie, Vivien, Vivienne, Vivy, Vivyan, Vivyanne

Voleta—Greek: Veiled one
Vrida—Spanish: Green

W

Walda—German: Ruler
Wallis—English: From Wales
  Wallace, Walli, Wallie, Wally
  This name was made famous by Wallis Warfield Simpson, the twice-divorced American whose friendship with England's King Edward VIII led to his abdication and their marriage.
Wanda—German: Wanderer
  Wandi, Wandie, Wandis, Wandy
Waneta/Wanetta—Native American: Charger
Wendy—English: Fair
  Wendee, Wendi, Wendie
  This name's fame goes back to 1904 when J. M. Barrie's Peter Pan was published. Today, we associate the name with a fast-food chain!
Whitney—English: From clear water
  Whitnee, Whitni, Whitnie, Whitny
  This name has been at the top of the charts for young girls since singer Whitney Houston first appeared on the music charts.
Wilda—English: Untamed
Wilhelmina—German: Resolute guardian
  Vilhemina, Vilhemine, Vilma, Wilameena, Wileen, Wilhelmine, Willa, Willee, Willella, Willetta, Willette, Willi, Willie, Willy, Wilma, Wilmena, Wilmett, Wilona, Wilone, Wylma
Willa—See: Wilhelmina, Willabelle
Willabelle—German: Chosen one
  Willa, Willabel, Willabella, Willee, Willi, Willie, Willy
Wilma—See: Wilhelmina
Winda—Swahili: Hunter
Winema—Native American: Woman chief
Winifred—German: Friend of peace; Welsh: White wave
  Freddi, Freddie, Freddy, Fredi, Win, Winri, Winnie, Winny, Wynn
Winona—Native American (Sioux): Firstborn daughter; Place name: Town in Minnesota

Wenona, Wenonah, Winnie, Winonah, Wynnona, Wynona
*Actress Winona Ryder (née Winona Laura Horowitz) was
born in Winona, Minnesota.*

Winter—Nature name: From the wintertime
Wyanet—Native American: Beautiful
Wynne—Celtic: Fair
Wyn, Wyna, Wynetta, Wynette

X

Xanthe—Greek: Golden haired
Xantah
Xaviera—Arabic: Brilliant
Xaverie
Xena—Greek: The welcomed
Xene, Xenia, Ximena, Zena, Zenia
Ximena—Hebrew: He heard
Xylia—Greek: Wood dweller

Y

Yaffa/Yaffah—Hebrew: Lovely
Yamuna—Hindi: Sacred river
Yarmilla—Slavic: Merchant
Yasmine—See: Jasmine
Yedda—English: Singer
Yetta—German: To give (Also see: Henrietta)
Ynez—See: Agnes
Yoko—Japanese: Positive child, good
*Yoko Ono, widow of Beatle John Lennon, has made this
name known worldwide.*
Yolanda—French: Violet flower
Iolanda, Iolande, Iolantha, Iolanthe, Yolande, Yolane,
Yolantha, Yolanthe
Yonina—Hebrew: Dove
Yona, Yonah, Yoni, Yoninah, Yonit, Yonita
Yorki—Japanese: Trustworthy
Yovela—Hebrew: Rejoicing

Yvette—See: Yvonne
Yvonne—French: Archer; Greek: Yew wood
Evette, Evonna, Evonne, Ivonne, Vonni, Vonnie, Vonny,
Yevette, Yvette

Z

Zabrina—See: Sabrina
Zada/Zaida—Arabic: Lucky one
Zahara—Swahili: Flower
Zahra—Arabic: White
Zandra—See: Alexandra
Zara/Zarah—See: Sara/Sarah
Zaza—Arabic: Flowery; Hebrew: Movement
Zehava—Hebrew: Golden
Zehavi, Zehavit
Zelda—See: Griselda
Zelenka—Czechoslovakian: Little innocent one
Zelia—Greek: Zealous
Zella/Zelly—See: Giselle
Zelma—See: Selma
Zena—See: Xena/Xene, Zenobia
Zenevera/Zenavere/Zenevieve—See: Guenevere/Guinevere
Zenobia—Greek: Given life by Zeus
Zena, Zenaida, Zenaide, Zenda, Zendia, Zizi
Zephyra—Greek: West wind
Zepha, Zephra, Zephrys, Zyra
Zeva—Greek: Sword; Hebrew: Wolf
Zevida—Hebrew: Gift
Zevuda
Zia—Hebrew: To tremble; Place name: Town in New Mexico
Zila—Hebrew: Shadow
Zilla, Zillah
Zinia/Zinnia—English: A brilliant flower
*The flower zinnia was named for German botanist Johann
Gottfried Zinn.*
Zippora—Hebrew: Little bird, sparrow
Zippi, Zippie, Zipporah, Zippy
Zita—Spanish: Little rose
Ziva—Hebrew: Brilliance, brightness
Zizi—Hungarian: Dedicated to God

Zoe—Greek: Life
Zoa, Zoela, Zoeta, Zoia, Zolida, Zolita
Zofia/Zofie—See: Sophia/Sophie
Zohra—See: Isadora/Isidora
Zora—Slavic: Dawn
Zorah, Zorana, Zorane, Zorina, Zorine, Zyra
Zsa Zsa—See: Susan
Colorful show-business personality Zsa Zsa Gabor is best known for her many marriages, her run-in with the Los Angeles Police, and her unusual first name.
Zulema—Arabic: Peace
Sulema

A-to-Z
Boys' Names

A

Aaron—Hebrew: Enlightened one, to sing, to shine, mountain
Aaran, Aaren, Aeron, Aharon, Aron, Haroun
Abbot/Abbott—Aramaic: Father
Ab, Abad, Abba, Abbe, Abbey, Abbie, Abby, Abott
Abdul/Abdullah—Arabic: Servant of the Lord, generous and powerful son of Allah
Abe—See: Abraham
Abelard—German: Highborn; English: Keeper of the abbey's larder
Abby, Abel, Abell, Able, Aleard
Abner—Hebrew: Father of light
Abner Doubleday was nicknamed "the Father of Baseball" because he invented the game. NOT! Baseball was actually created in England and originally called "rounders." In fact, Jane Austen refers to baseball in a novel written at the end of the 1700s.
Abraham—Hebrew: Father of the multitudes
Abe, Abie, Abira, Abrahan, Abram, Abramo, Abramus, Aram, Avram, Avrom, Bram, Ibaheem, Ibrahim
Abraham Lincoln, sixteenth president of the U.S., had many nicknames. The first that comes to mind is "Honest Abe," which some historians say Lincoln earned as a judge and referee at cockfights.
Ace—Latin: Unity, topnotch, first-rate
There are lots of positive associations with this name: It's the top card in a deck of cards; in racket games, a serve that one's opponent cannot return; a person who is an expert in his/her field; and, in the phrase "an ace in the hole," a hidden advantage.
Achilles—Greek: Without lips
Achill, Achille, Achilleus
The hero of Homer's Iliad *had a small but mortal weakness.*

He was invulnerable in all places except in the heel of his foot.

Acim—Hebrew: The Lord will judge
Achim, Akim

Adam—Hebrew: Man, human being, son of the red earth
Adamo, Adams, Adan, Adao, Addam, Addams, Addis, Addison, Addy, Ade, Adham, Edam
According to biblical lore, Adam was, of course, the first man. And in case you've always wondered how the Adam's apple got its name, one theory says that it's a vestige of Adam's first sin—a piece of the forbidden fruit, which lodged in his throat.

Addison—See: Adam

Adlai/Adley—Hebrew: Refuge of God; Arabic: To act justly
Adlai Ewing Stevenson was Grover Cleveland's vice president. Adlai Ewing Stevenson II was a statesman, diplomat, ambassador, and presidential candidate who was nicknamed "Egghead" because of his great intellect. And Adlai Ewing Stevenson III was a U.S. senator.

Adler—German: Eagle

Adley—Arabic: The just

Adolph—German: Noble wolf
Adolf, Adolphus, Dolf, Dolph, Dolphus

Adonis—Greek: Masculine beauty

Adrian—Latin: Dark one
Adriance, Adriano, Adrien, Hadrian, Hadrien

Aherne—Celtic: Lord of the horses
Ahearn, Ahearne, Ahern, Hearn, Hearne

Ahmad/Ahmed—Arabic: Most praised

Aidan—Gaelic: Fire
Actor Aidan Quinn has brought this name to the attention of TV viewers and film fans.

Ainsley—Gaelic: He himself; English: My meadow or land
Ain, Ainslie, Ayn

Akira—Japanese: Bright boy

Al—Nickname for names starting with "Al"

Aladdin—Arabic: Height of religion
Laddie, Laddy

Alan/Allan—Celtic: Handsome
Ailin, Alain, Alano, Alen, Allen, Alleyn, Allyn

Alaric—German: Ruler of all
  Alar, Alarick, Aleric, Alric, Alrick, Aric, Arick

Alastair—Greek: Avenging one
  Alasdair, Alaster, Alastor, Alistair

Albert—German: Nobly bright
  Adalbert, Adelbert, Ailbert, Alber, Alberto, Albie, Alby,
  Athelbert, Edelbert, Elbert

Alden— English: Old learned friend
  Aldin, Aldwin, Aldwyn, Alwin, Elden, Eldin, Eldwin,
  Eldwyn

Aldous—English: From the old house
  Aldis, Aldo, Aldus, Eldis, Eldous
  *Author Aldous Leonard Huxley, who gained fame for his
  satirical novels and short stories, is best known for* Brave
  New World.

Aldrich—English: Wise ruler
  Aldric, Aldridge, Allric, Alrick, Eldrich, Eldridge

Alec/Alex—See: Alexander
  *Sir Alec Guinness, a fine actor, is not the only talented thes-
  pian with this first name. Alec Baldwin is also right up there
  on the marquee, with his name above the title.*

Alexander—Greek: Protector of humankind
  Alec, Alejandro, Alejo, Aleksander, Alessandro, Alex,
  Alexandre, Alexio, Alexis, Alexius, Alic, Alisander, Alister,
  Alix, Alsandair

Alfie—See: Alfred

Alfred—English: Good counselor and judge
  Aelfred, Ailfred, Alf, Alfie, Alfredo, Alfy
  *English poet laureate Alfred Lord Tennyson was the
  spokesperson for the Victorian age. Alfred E. Neuman is
  the mascot for* Mad *magazine.*

Alger—German: Noble spearman

Algernon—French: With a mustache

Ali—Arabic: The greatest, a form of Allah (the title of the
  supreme being in the Muslim faith)

Allard—English: Determined, noble

Allen—See: Alan/Allan

Alonso/Alonzo—See: Alphonse/Alphonso

Aloysius—See: Lewis

Alphonse/Alphonso—German: Ready for battle

Alfons, Alon, Alonso, Alonzo, Alphie, Fons, Fonsie, Fonz, Fonzie, Lon, Lonnie, Lonny

Alva/Alvah—Hebrew: Exalted one

American inventor Thomas Alva Edison is one of a few noted Americans whose middle name is well known.

Alvin—German: Old friend

Alban, Albin, Aloin, Aluin, Aluino, Alvan, Alvie, Alvy, Alwin, Alwyn

Alvis—Norse: All-wise

Country-and-western singer Buck Owens was born Alvis Edgar Owens.

Amadeus—Latin: Love of God

Amadea, Amadeo, Amadis, Amado, Amias

The film Amadeus, *about the* wunderkind *composer Wolfgang Amadeus Mozart, taught us not only about his life, but how to pronounce his middle name.*

Amandus—Latin: Worthy of love

Amand, Amando

Ambros/Ambrose—Greek: Divine, immortal

Ambie, Ambrogio, Ambroise, Ambrosio, Ambrosius, Ambrotos, Ambrozio, Amby, Brose

Amiel—Hebrew: Lord of my people

Amin—Hindi: Faithful, loyal

Amen, Ammon, Amnon, Amon

Amos—Hebrew: Borne by God

Anatol/Anatole—Greek: Rising sun

Anatolio, Toli, Tolio

Andre—See: Andrew

Andre Agassi, the 1996 Olympic gold medal winner, is sure to influence the name choice of expectant tennis fans.

Andrew—Greek: Strong, manly

Anders, Andie, Andre, Andrea, Andreas, Andres, Andrie, Andry, Andy

Seventh U.S. president Andrew Jackson was called "Old Hickory" by his soldiers in the War of 1812 because he was said to be as tough as hickory.

Andy—See: Andrew

Angelo—Greek: Angel

Ange, Angel, Angell, Angelos, Angie, Angy, Engel

Angel (Thomas) Cordero, Jr., won the Kentucky Derby twice and is one of the highest-earning jockeys of all time.

Angus—Celtic: Chosen one, unique strength

Anselm/Anselme—German: With divine protection
Anse, Ansel, Anselmi, Anselmo, Ansthelm, Elmo

Anson—English: Son of a nobleman
Anse, Hanson
Fans of "Happy Days" know Anson Williams as Warren "Potsie" Weber.

Anthony—Latin: Priceless, inestimable beyond praise
Antoin, Antoine, Anton, Antone, Antoni, Antonin, Antonio, Antonius, Antony, Toni, Tonio, Tony
Actor Anthony Hopkins won an Academy Award for his memorable performance in The Silence of the Lambs.

Anwar—Arabic: Shafts of light
Anwar Sadat was the Egyptian leader noted for promoting peace with Israel.

Apollo—Greek: Powerful

Archer—See: Archibald

Archibald—English: Very bold
Arch, Archer, Archibaldo, Archibold, Archie, Archy

Arden—French: Fiery, flashing
Ardie, Ardin, Ardy

Argus—Greek: Vigilant

Argyle—Celtic: From the land of the Irish

Ari—See: Aries, Aristotle

Aric—See: Alaric

Aries—Latin: Ram, first sign of the zodiac

Aristotle—Greek: Best of thinkers
Ari, Aristo
Aristotle (384–322 B.C.) is known as "the Pope of Philosophy." Aristotle Socrates Onassis (1906–75) is known as Jacqueline Kennedy's second husband and as "the Golden Greek" who parlayed his hourly earnings of twenty-five cents into millions before he was thirty.

Arlo—See: Harlow

Armand—German: Army man
Arman, Armando, Armin

Arnold—German: Strong as an eagle
Arn, Arnaldo, Arnaud, Arne, Arney, Arnie, Arno, Arnoldo, Arno, Arnot, Arny
As a bodybuilder, Arnold Schwarzenegger sure lived up to the meaning of this name. He was three-time winner of the

Mr. Universe title and seven-time winner of the Mr. Olympia title.

Arthur—Welsh: Noble, high
Art, Artair, Arte, Arth, Artie, Artur, Arturo, Artus, Arty, Aurthur

Arvad/Arvid—English: Friend
Arv, Arvin, Arvy

Asa—Hebrew: Healer, physician

Asher—Hebrew: Happy one

Ashley—English: From the ash-tree meadow
Ashlin, Ashly
Americans know this name from the Gone with the Wind *character Ashley Wilkes, played in the film by English actor Leslie Howard. Recently Ashley has been enjoying great popularity as both a boy's and a girl's name.*

Aubrey—German: Powerful, elf ruler
Alberik, Auberon, Aubry, Aulberich, Avery

August/Auguste—Latin: The exalted, the sacred
Agosto, Aguistin, Agustin, Augie, Augustin, Augustine, Augusto, Augustus, Augy, Austen, Austin

Austen/Austin—See: August/Auguste

Averell—English: Born in April
Ave, Averil, Averill

Avery—See: Aubrey

Avi—Hebrew: My Father (implying God)

Axel—German: Divine reward
Aksel, Ax, Axe, Axtel, Axtell
Axel Foley is the Beverly Hills Cop *portrayed by Eddie Murphy.*

Azrael—Hebrew: The Lord is my help
Azar, Azrail, Azreel, Azriel

B

Bailey—Latin: Trusted public servant
Bailie, Baillie, Bailly, Baily, Bayley

Baldwin—German: Bold friend
Baldovino, Balduin, Baudoin, Baudouin

Balin—Hindi: Mighty soldier

Ballard—German: Bold, strong

Bancroft—English: From the bean field
Bannie, Banny
Barclay—English: From the birch-tree meadow
Barc, Berk, Berkeley, Berkie, Berkley, Berky
Barnabas—Hebrew: Son of prophecy
Barna, Barnaba, Barnabe, Barnaby, Barnebas, Barney,
Barnie, Barny
*The name and its derivatives lend themselves to popular TV
characters: Barnabas (played by Jonathan Frid), the sym-
pathetic vampire in the soap opera "Dark Shadows";
Barnaby Jones (played by Buddy Ebsen), the private inves-
tigator in the series of the same name; Barney Miller
(played by Hal Linden), a police captain in a sitcom of the
same name; Barney Rubble (Mel Blanc's voice), Fred's
neighbor in "The Flintstones"; and Barney Fife (played by
Don Knotts), an inept deputy sheriff on "The Andy Griffith
Show."*
Barnett—English: Nobleman
Barnet, Barney, Barnie, Barny
Barney—See: Barnabas, Barnett
Barret/Barrett—German: Bearlike strength
Barry—Celtic: Pointed, spearlike
Bart—See: Bartholomew, Barton
*Bart Simpson. If we need to explain who he is, chances are
you won't want to know.*
Bartholomew—Hebrew: Son of a farmer
Bart, Bartel, Barth, Barthel, Barthelemy, Barthol, Bartho-
lomeus, Bartlet, Bartlett, Bartley, Bartol, Bartolome, Bar-
tolomeo, Bartolos, Bat, Bortolo
Barton—English: From the barley farm
Bart
Baruch—Hebrew: Blessed
Basil—Greek: Royal
Bas, Basile, Basilio, Basilius, Vasilis, Vassily
Baxter—English: Baker
Bayard—English: With reddish brown hair
Beau—See: Beaumont, Beauregard
Beaumont—French: From a beautiful mountain
Beau, Bo
Beauregard—French: Beautiful view
Beau

Beck—English: A brook

Ben—Hebrew: Son (Also: Nickname for names starting with "Ben")

Benedict—Latin: Blessed
Bendix, Benedetto, Benedick, Benedicto, Benedike, Benedikt, Benedix, Benet, Benito, Bennet, Bennett, Benoit, Bento, Benzel

Benjamin—Hebrew: Favorite son
Benjie, Benjy, Bennie, Benny, Binyamin
Benjamin Franklin was a revolutionary, statesman, author, publisher, scientist, inventor, philanthropist, and philosopher. Yet even with Franklin's many talents, it took a young guy named Benjamin Braddock (played by Dustin Hoffman), who was fresh out of college in the 1967 film The Graduate, *to make the name popular.*

Bennet/Bennett—See: Benedict

Benson—Hebrew: Son of Benjamin
Robert Guillaume played Benson DuBois, the governor's butler, in the TV sitcom "Benson."

Bentley—English: From the meadows

Benton—English: Moor-dweller
Most of the boys' names listed here were family names that are now being used as first names. Benton, as in Thomas Hart Benton, is a perfect example. Benton served as senator from Missouri for thirty years. He initiated the issuance of gold coins. In fact, he was so identified with gold coins that they were referred to as "Benton's Mint Drops."

Berkeley/Berkley—See: Barclay

Bernard—German: Brave as a bear
Barnard, Bearnard, Bern, Bernaldo, Bernardo, Bernarr, Bernhard, Bernie, Berny

Bert/Burt—English: Bright; See Burton (Also, a nickname for names starting or ending with "Bert")
Burt Reynolds was born Burton Leon Reynolds, Jr. When he and Bert Convy formed a company together, they called it Burt & Bert Productions.

Berthold—German: Brilliant ruler
Berthoud, Bertie, Bertold, Bertolde, Bertoldi, Berty

Bertram—English: Bright raven
Bartram, Bartrand, Bertran, Bertrand, Bertrando, Burtrand

Bertrand Russell was a British philosopher, essayist, mathematician, and active opponent of the arms race.

Bevan—Celtic: Young archer
Bev, Beven, Bevin

Bill/Billy—See: William
Nicknames such as these are big in show biz and used by Bill Cosby, Bill Bixby, Bill Murray, Billy Dee Williams, Billy Crystal, Billy Joel, and Billy Ray Cyrus, to name just a few.

Bingham—German: From the stone hamlet
Bing, Bingam

Birch—English: At the birch tree

Birney—English: Dweller on the brook island
Birn, Burney, Burny

Bjorn—Swedish and Norse: Bearlike
Swedish-born Bjorn Borg, a five-time winner at Wimbledon, is responsible for introducing this name to Americans.

Blaine—Gaelic: Thin one
Blainey, Blane, Blayn, Blayne

Blair—Gaelic: From the field

Blake—English: Fair haired, fair complected
Blake Edwards, director, producer, screenwriter, actor, and husband of Julie Andrews, was born William Blake McEdwards.

Blaze—German: Torch, firebrand
Biagio, Blaise, Blas, Blase, Blasien, Blasius, Blayze

Bo—See: Beaumont, Bogart

Boaz—Hebrew: Swift, strong

Bob/Bobbie/Bobby—See: Robert
If you thought Bill and Billy were popular show-biz nicknames, take a look at this: Bob Newhart, Bob Barker, Bob Saget, Buffalo Bob Smith, Bob Vila, Bob Hope, Bob Eubanks, Bob Denver, Bob Einstein, Bob Keeshan, Bob Costas, Bob Goulet, Bob Dylan, Bobby Vinton. This could take up the rest of the book, so we'd better cut the list short. Bobby Short.

Bogart—Danish: Archer
Bo, Bogie, Bogy

Bolton—English: Of the manor farm
Bolt

Bond—English: One who tills the soil

Boone—French: A blessing

Booth/Boothe—English: Hut

Borden—English: From the boar's valley

Boris—Slavic: Warrior
Actor Boris Karloff, the star of the 1931 film Frankenstein, *was born William Henry Pratt.*

Boyd—Irish: Fair haired
Bow, Bowen, Bowie, Boyde, Boyden

Brad—Nickname for names starting with "Brad"

Braden—English: From the wide valley
Brade, Bradie

Bradford—English: From the wide river crossing

Bradley—English: From the broad meadow
Brad, Bradleigh, Bradly, Bradney

Brady—Irish: Spirited one

Bram—See: Abraham

Brandon—English: Swordlike
Bran, Brand, Brandt, Brant, Branton

Brendan—Irish: Little raven
Bren, Brend, Brenden, Brendin, Brendon, Brennan, Brennen, Brennon

Brent—English: Tall, erect

Bret/Brett—Celtic: Native of Brittany
Brit, Britt
Bret Harte, teacher, gold seeker, and journalist, wrote novels and humorous poems of the early West.

Brewster—German: Brewer

Brian—Irish: Strong, formidable
Briano, Briant, Brien, Brion, Bryan, Bryant, Bryon

Brice/Bryce—Celtic: Swift moving, ambitious

Brigham—English: Dweller at the bridge
Mormon leader Brigham Young encouraged and practiced polygamy. Nicknamed "the Lion of the Lord," he is said to have had twenty-seven wives and forty-seven children. Now he is one who could have used this book!

Brock—English: A badger
Brock Peters, one of the leading black film actors of the sixties and seventies, was born Brock Fisher.

Broderick—English: From the broad ridge

Brodie/Brody—Irish: Ditch

Bronson—English: Son of the dark-skinned one
Bron, Bronnie, Bronny, Bruns

Brooke—English: Dweller at the brook
  Brook, Brooks
Bruce—French: From the brushwood
  Broose, Brucie, Brucy
  With the popularity of Bruce Willis and "the Boss," Bruce
  Springsteen, this name has taken on a more macho associa-
  tion than it had during the Johnny Carson "Tonight Show"
  era.
Bruno—Italian: Brown-haired one
Bryan/Bryant—See: Brian
Buck—English: Male deer
  Buckie, Bucky
  Buck Owens, country-and-western singer and host of "Hee
  Haw," was born Alvis Edgar Owens.
Bud—German: To puff up
  Budd, Buddie, Buddy
Burgess—German: Townsman; English: Citizen
Burke—French: From the fortress
  Berk, Berke, Bourke, Burk, Burkett
Burl—English: Wine servant
  Byrl, Byrle
  Actor and folk singer Burl Ives was born (believe it or not)
  Icle Ivanhoe.
Burr—Swedish: Youth
Burton—English: Bright fame
  Burt
Byram—Aramaic: Celebration
Byrd—English: Birdlike
Byron—English: From the country estate

C

Caesar—Latin: Hirsute (hairy)
  Casar, Cesar, Cesare, Cesario, Kaiser
  Legend has it that Julius Caesar was born "from the incised
  womb of his mother" and named for the Latin words for
  the process (caesus—the past participle of caedere, *to*
  cut). That's why we now refer to that birth method as
  "Caesarean."
Cahil—Turkish: Young, innocent
Cain—Hebrew: Possession

Cal—Nickname for names starting with "Cal"

Caleb/Kaleb—Hebrew: Dog, impetuous and bold, faithful

Caley—Gaelic: Lithe
   Cale, Calie, Cally

Calhoun—Celtic: Warrior

Calvin—Latin: Bald one
   Calve, Calvert, Calvino, Calvy
   The thirtieth president of the U.S. was born John Calvin Coolidge. He was nicknamed "Silent Cal" because he was a man of few words. Maybe that's why he dropped the "John." That way, when asked his name, it was one less word to say.

Camden—Gaelic: Dweller in the winding valley

Cameron—Celtic: Crooked nose

Campbell—French: From a bright field

Canute—Latin: White haired
   Cnut, Knut, Knute

Carey/Cary—Welsh: Dweller near the castle
   Archibald Alexander Leach changed his name to Cary Grant.

Carl—See: Charles (Also, a nickname for names starting with "Carl")

Carlin—Gaelic: Little champion

Carlisle/Carlyle—English: From the loyal stronghold

Carlos—See: Charles

Carlton—English: Farmer's settlement
   Carl, Carleton, Carlie, Carly, Charl, Charley, Charlie, Charlton

Carmine—Latin: Song

Carney/Carny—Gaelic: Victorious warrior, winner

Carol/Carroll—See: Charles
   Carroll O'Connor was the big-time bigot Archie Bunker in the ten-season hit sitcom "All in the Family."

Carr—Norse: From the marshland

Carson—Welsh: Son of a marsh-dweller

Carter—English: Cart driver, maker of carts

Carver—English: One who carves
   Carv, Carvey, Carvy

Casey—Irish: Watchful one

Casimir—Slavic: A command for peace
   Cas, Cass, Kashmir, Kasimir, Kazimir

Casper—Persian: Holder of treasure; Place name: A town in Wyoming
Caspar, Gaspar, Gasper
Caspar or Gaspar is one of the three wise men (Magi) from the East who journeyed to Bethlehem to present the baby Jesus with gifts.

Cassidy—Irish: Ingenious one

Cassius—Latin: Vain
Cash, Cass, Cassie, Cassy, Caz
The full name of J. C. Penney, founder of the national chain store of the same name, is James Cash Penney. How is that for parents' intuition!

Cato—Latin: Wise one
Cate, Caton

Cavanaugh—Celtic: Handsome

Cecil/Cecile—Latin: Dim sighted
Cece, Cecilio, Cecilius, Cecyl, Kilian

Cedric—English: Chieftain
Cedric is the father of Rowena, the heroine in Sir Walter Scott's Ivanhoe.

Chad—Celtic: Defender; Place name: A landlocked country in north-central Africa
The country gets its name from Lake Chad, on the western border with Niger and Nigeria.

Chaim—Hebrew: Life
Hy, Hyman, Hymie

Chandler—French: Candlemaker

Channing—Latin: Singer

Chapman—English: Tradesman
Chap, Chappie, Chappy

Charles—German: Strong, manly
Carel, Carl, Carlino, Carlo, Carlos, Carol, Carolo, Carrol, Carroll, Caryl, Charley, Charlie, Charly, Chas, Chaz, Chick, Chickie, Chuck, Chucky, Karel, Karl
This is a name for all mediums: songs ("Charlie, My Boy," "Clap Hands, Here Comes Charlie"), TV series ("Charles in Charge," "Charlie's Angels"), plays (Charley's Aunt), comic-strip characters (Charlie Brown), and films (Charlie Chan, Charley Varrick). Plus, it's a name for a lot of super-achievers—Dickens, Lindbergh, Chaplin, de Gaulle, Darwin, Revson—and for royalty—French Kings I–X; Hungarian

Kings I–IV; Spanish Kings I–V; Swedish Kings IX–XII; Neapolitan Kings I–III; Portuguese King I; English, Scottish, and Irish Kings I–II; and England's current Prince of Wales, Charles Philip Arthur George Windsor.

Charlton—See: Carleton/Carlton

Chase—French: Hunter

Chauncey—English: Church official
Chance, Chancellor, Chancey, Chaunce

Chen—Chinese: Vast, great

Chester—Latin: From the walled camp
Ches, Cheston, Chet
This was a popular politician's name in the middle 1800s. There was Chester Alan Arthur, who was our twenty-first president, and U.S. senator Chester Ashley, from Arkansas. By insisting that the name of his state be pronounced "Arkansas," not "Ar-ken-saw," Ashley made a name for himself. He would only answer roll calls when addressed as "the senator from Ar-kansas."

Chico—See: Francis

Christian—Greek: Follower of Christ
Chris, Christen, Christiano, Christin, Cris, Cristiene, Kris, Kriss, Kristian, Kristos

Christopher—Greek: Christ bearer
Chris, Christo, Christoffer, Christoforo, Christoph, Christophe, Christophorus, Christovao, Cristoforo, Cristogal, Kit, Kristo, Kristofor, Kristoforo
Thanks to Cristoforo Colombo, American history proper began on October 12, 1492, when the Genoan sailor landed on the sandy shore of San Salvador.

Chuck—See: Charles

Cicero—Italian: Sightseeing guide; Latin: Chickpea
Ciceron, Ciro, Cyrano, Cyro

Clarence—Latin: Illustrious one
Clair, Clare

Clark/Clarke—English: Learned one
Clark Gable, born William Clark Gable, was known as "the King of Hollywood."

Claud/Claude—Latin: Lame one
Claudio, Claudius, Claus

Clayborn/Clayborne—English: Born of the earth
Claiborn, Clay

Clayton—English: From the clay town

Clement—Latin: Merciful, kind
Clem, Clemence, Clemens, Clemente, Clementius, Clemmi, Clemmie, Clemmons, Clemmy, Clim, Klemens

> *"'Twas the night before Christmas,"*
> *And whether rich or poor,*
> *We all know this poem,*
> *Thanks to Clement Clarke Moore.*

Cleveland—English: Cliff land; Place name: A city in Ohio
Cleve

Clifford—English: Dweller at the ford near the cliff
Cliff, Cliffie, Cliffy

Clifton—English: Farm by the cliff

Clinton—English: Hill town
Clint
Clint Eastwood, born Clinton Eastwood, Jr., is an actor, director, and producer.

Clive/Clyve—English: From the cliff
Clive Davis, world-renowned music impresario, and president and founder of Arista Records, is responsible for launching the careers of Barry Manilow, Lisa Stansfield, Aretha Franklin, Dionne Warwick, and Whitney Houston.

Clovis—German: Of holy fame

Clyde—Welsh: Heard from afar

Cody—Irish: Helpful; English: Pillow
Kathie Lee Gifford (costar of "Live with Regis & Kathie Lee") and husband Frank Gifford have a son named Cody. Since she reports on his progress almost daily on national TV, Kathie Lee is responsible for the fast-growing popularity of this name.

Colbert—English: Outstanding seafarer
Calvert, Cole, Colvert, Culbert

Colby—English: From a coal town

Coleman/Colman—English: Charcoal burner
Cole, Colum, Columbo, Columbus

Colin—Gaelic: Child
Colan, Collin

Collier—English: Miner
Colier, Colis, Collie, Colly, Collyer, Colyer

Conan—Celtic: Intelligent
Conal, Conant, Conlan, Connal, Kynan

This name was associated with Sir Arthur Conan Doyle, the creator of Sherlock Holmes. But that has changed since the release of the sword-and-sorcery films Conan the Barbarian *(1982) and* Conan the Destroyer *(1984) and appearance of Conan O'Brien.*

Connor—Celtic: Wise aid
   Connaire, Connie, Conny
Conrad—German: Wise counselor
   Conrade, Conrado, Cort, Curt, Konrad, Kort, Kurt
   Conrad Hilton was the founder of the major international hotel chain.
Conroy—Irish: Wise man
Constantin/Constantine—Latin: Firm, constant
   Constant, Constantino, Constantinus, Konstantin, Konstantine
Conway—Celtic: Wise way
Cooper—English: Barrel maker
   Coop
Corbet/Corbett—French: Raven
   Corbie, Corbin, Corby
Cordel/Cordell—French: Small rope
   Cord, Cordie, Cordy
Core/Cory—English: Chosen one
   Corey, Correy, Corry, Currey, Curry
Cornelius—Latin: Battle born
   Cornel, Cornelio, Cornell, Cornellus
Cosmo—Greek: Order, harmony, universe
   Cosimo, Cosmos, Kosmo, Kosmos
Courtland—English: Dweller in the court
   Cort, Court, Courtenay, Courtnay, Courtney
Craig—Scottish: From the stony hill
Creighton—English: From the town near the creek, rocky spot
   Crei, Creight, Crichton
Crispin—Latin: Curly haired
   Crepin, Cres, Crespin, Crisp, Crispino, Crispo, Crispus
Crosby—English: Dweller near the town crossing
   Crosbey, Crosbie
Cullen—Irish: Handsome one
   Cull, Cullan, Cullie, Cullin, Cully
Curran—Irish: Champion, hero

Curr, Currey, Currie, Curry
Curtis—French: Courteous one
Curcio, Curt, Curtiss
Curtis Sliwa is the courageous founder of the Guardian Angels.
Cyrano—Greek: From Cyrene (Also see: Cicero)
Of course you know of Cyrano de Bergerac, the fictional character created by Edmond Rostand. But do you know there was a French author, playwright, soldier, and adventurer with the same name, who lived from 1619 to 1655? The one thing the two Cyranos had in common was a very long nose.
Cyril—Greek: Lord
Ciril, Cirille, Cirillo, Ciro, Cy, Cyr, Cyrill, Cyrille, Cyrillus, Cyro, Kyril, Kyrillos
Cyrus—Persian: Sun
Ciro, Cy, Cyro, Kyros

D

Dakota/Dakotah—Native American (Sioux): Friend
Dalbert—German: From a bright place
Dal
Dale—German: Valley dweller
The surname of Dale Carnegie, author of the self-help classic How to Win Friends and Influence People, *was originally "Carnegey." He changed the spelling when he was about to lecture at—you guessed it—Carnegie Hall.*
Dallas—Celtic: Skilled; Place name: A city in Texas
Dalton—English: From the valley
Daly—English: Counselor
Damon—Greek: Constant one
Damas, Damian, Damiano, Damien
Damon Runyon, who was born Alfred Damon Runyon, was a journalist and short-story writer who gave us Guys and Dolls.
Dan/Dannie/Danny—See: Daniel
Dana—Norse: From Denmark
Daen, Dain, Dane, Dayn, Dene
Daniel—Hebrew: God is my judge
Dan, Daniell, Dannel, Dannie, Danny

This popular name, in all its forms, has always been big in show biz: Consider Danny DeVito, Dan Duryea, Dan Daily, Danny Thomas, Danny Aiello, Danny Kaye, Daniel Day-Lewis, Dan Rowan, and Daniel J. Travanti, for starters.

Dante—Latin: Enduring one
Darte, Duran, Durand, Durant, Durante

Darby—Celtic: Free man

Darcy/Darsy—Irish: Dark looking
Darcel, Darcey, Darsey

Darius—Greek: Wealthy
Dare, Darie, Dario
This was the name of some ancient Persian rulers.

Darnel/Darnell—French: From the hidden place

Darrel/Darryl—English: Beloved
Darrell, Darrilo, Darrol, Daryl, Derrell, Derryl, Deryl
As a boy's name, it's more popular than you might think. It was popular even before the TV sitcom "Newhart," with brothers First Darryl and Second Darryl. There were movie mogul Darryl F. Zanuck, baseball player Darryl Strawberry, and singer/songwriter Daryl Hall (John Oates's partner), all of whom were given the name at birth.

Darren/Darrin—See: Dorian

Darwin—German: Daring friend; English: Dear friend
Darwyn, Darwynn, Derwin, Derwynn

David—Hebrew: Beloved, adored
Dack, Dak, Dake, Dave, Davey, Davidde, Davide, Davie, Davy, Dawood, Dawson, Dawud, Devi, Devid, Tavid
This name must be very beloved, or else it wouldn't have appeared on the top-ten names list for boys in the U.S. for the past forty years.

Dean—Latin: Religious official; English: Valley
Dino
Two U.S. secretaries of state—Dean Acheson and Dean Rusk—had this first name.

Dedrick—English: Gifted ruler
Dedric, Diedrick, Dietrich

Delano—French: Healthy dark man, nighttime
Del, Delane, Delaney
Franklin Delano Roosevelt, our thirty-second president, weighed ten pounds at birth.

Delbert—English: Bright as day

Dell—See: Wendel/Wendell

Delmer—Latin: From the sea
Delmar, Delmore

Demetrius—Greek: Lover of the earth
Demeter, Demetre, Demetri, Demetris, Demmy, Dimitri,
Dimitrios

Dempsey—Celtic: Proud one

Denby—Norse: From the Danish land
Danby, Danbey, Denbey

Denis/Dennis—Greek: Lover of fine wine
Dennet, Dennett, Dennie, Denny, Densil, Denzel, Denzil,
Dion, Dione, Dionisio, Dionysus
*One day in 1951, the wife of cartoonist Hank Ketcham said
to her husband, "Our son Dennis is a menace." And that's
how an idea came into being. That year, Hank Ketcham sold
"Dennis the Menace" to the Post-Hall syndicate, and the
rest is cartoon history.*
*Academy Award–winning actor Denzel Washington was in
the film* Mo' Better Blues, *in which he played trumpeter
Bleek Gilliam.*

Derek—See: Derrick

Dermot/Dermott—Irish: Free from envy

Derrick—German: Ruler, leader
Darrick, Dereck, Derek, Derk, Derreck, Derrek, Dirk, Dirke,
Dyrk, Dyrke

Derry—Irish: Reddish haired

Derwin—English: Beloved friend

Desmond—Celtic: Man of the world
Des, Dess, Desmund

Deverell—Welsh: From the riverbank

Devin/Devine—Celtic: Poet
Devon, Devyn

Devlin—Irish: Brave one
Devland, Devlen, Devlyn

Dewey—Welsh: Treasured one

DeWitt—Flemish: Fair, blond
Dewitt, Dwight, Witt
*Dwight D. Eisenhower, our thirty-fourth president, was
born David Dwight Eisenhower. His parents called him
Dwight, so he changed his first two names around just
before attending West Point.*

Dexter—Latin: Right-handed one

Dick—See: Dickson, Richard

Dickson—English: Son of the powerful ruler
Dick, Dixon

Diego—See: James

Digby—Norse: By the dike water

Dirk—See: Derrick

Dolf/Dolph—See: Adolph, Rudolph

Dominic/Dominick—Latin: Of the Lord
Dom, Domenic, Domico, Domingo, Domingus, Nick

Don/Donnie/Donny—See: Donald

Donald—Irish: Prince of the universe
Don, Donal, Donalt, Donley, Donnally, Donnell, Donnie, Donny

Donato—Latin: Given

Donovan—Irish: Dark warrior
The singer Donovan brought attention to this name in the 1960s, when his "Mellow Yellow" topped the charts.

Dooley—Greek: Dark hero

Dorian—Greek: Gift
Dare, Darey, Darren, Darrin, Doran, Dore, Dorey, Dorie, Doron, Dory
Bandleader/musician Herb Alpert has a son named Dore. The name was created by the first two notes of the musical scale—"do" and "re."

Doron—Hebrew: Gift of the Lord

Dotson—English: Son of Dorothy

Douglas/Douglass—Scottish: From the dark stream
Doogie, Doug, Dougie, Dougy, Dug, Dugald
Before the nineteenth century, Douglas was as much a girl's name as it was a boy's. But in 1915, when the swashbuckling silent-film star Douglas Fairbanks came upon the scene, he gave the name a macho identity, as did his son, Douglas Fairbanks, Jr. New attention is now being paid to the name—or the nickname—because of the teenage doctor in the sitcom "Doogie Howser, M.D."

Dov—Hebrew: Bear

Doyle—Irish: Dark stranger

Drake—German: Male swan

Drew—Welsh: Wise

Drury—German: Sweetheart

Dudley—English: From the meadow
Dudley did Moore for this name than anyone.

Dugan—English: To be worthy

Duke—Latin: Leader

Duncan—Gaelic: Dark-skinned warrior

Dunham—Celtic: Dark man

Dunstan—English: From the brown-stone fortress

Durward/Durwood—English: Gatekeeper

Dustin—English: Valiant one
*Sources say that Dustin Hoffman's mother was a movie fan
and named her son after Dustin Farnum, the silent-screen
cowboy star. Now mothers are naming their sons after the
Academy Award–winning movie star Dustin Hoffman!*

Dwayne—Celtic: From the dunes
Duane, Dwaine

Dwight—See: DeWitt

Dylan—Welsh: From the sea
Dillon, Dyllan, Dyllon
*Acclaimed poet Dylan Thomas sold his first poem at the age
of twelve. However, the way the story goes, Dylan didn't
actually write the poem; he took it from a local newspaper.
Talk about taking . . . Superstar songwriter and performer
Bob Dylan, born Robert Allen Zimmerman, took his stage
name from his idol, Dylan Thomas.*
*Dylan was one of the most popular fictional TV characters.
He was played by Luke Perry on "Beverly Hills 90210."*

E

Earl—English: Nobleman
Earle, Earlie, Early, Erie, Erle, Erly, Errol, Erroll, Jarle
*Every Perry Mason fan knows the Erle version of this name
because of author Erle Stanley Gardner, as does every
crossword-puzzle fan.*

Earvin—See: Irvin

Ebenezer—Hebrew: Stone of help
Eban, Eben
*This name makes one think of "A Christmas Carol," a
dickens of a story with a lead character named Ebenezer
Scrooge.*

Ed/Eddie/Eddy—Nicknames for names starting with "Ed"

Edan—Celtic: Fire

Eden—Hebrew: Place of delight

Edgar—English: Protector of property, happy warrior
Eadgar, Edgard, Edgardo, Ned, Neddie, Neddy
Edgar Allan Poe, poet, critic, and short-story writer, is considered the father of the modern detective story. In his honor the Mystery Writers of America named their annual award "the Edgar."

Edison—English: Son of Edward
Eddison, Edson

Edmond/Edmund—English: Prosperous protector
Eamon, Edmondo, Edmont, Edmundo, Ned, Neddie, Neddy

Edric—English: Rich king

Edsel—English: From the rich man's estate

Edward—English: Prosperous protector
Edik, Edouard, Eduard, Eduardo, Edvard, Ned, Neddie, Neddy, Ted, Teddie, Teddy
During World War I, Edward V. Rickenbacker was America's leading fighter pilot, and Edward became a hero's name. During World War II Rickenbacker volunteered to carry out missions for the War Department. When his B-17 went down in the Pacific Ocean, the whole country prayed for his safe return. After twenty-three days on a raft, he and seven other men were rescued. Once again, the name Edward became popular.

Edwin—English: Prosperous friend
Edlin, Eduiono, Evino
Edwin "Buzz" Aldrin and Neil Armstrong, the first men to walk on the moon, left behind the plaque that stated: "Here men from the planet Earth first set foot upon the moon July, 1969 A.D. We came in peace for all mankind."

Efrem—See: Ephraim/Ephriam

Egan/Egon—English: All-powerful

Egbert/Egberto—English: Bright as a sword

Egor—See: George

Eldon—English: From the holy hill
Elden, Eldin, Eldyn
Eldin, the housepainter/artist on the TV sitcom "Murphy Brown," was such a likeable character that this "bet-you-

never-knew-anyone-with-this-name-before" name is starting to catch on.

Eli/Ely—Hebrew: On high

Elias—See: Elijah

Elihu—See: Elijah

Elihu Yale, for whom Yale University is named, is thought to be the first American millionaire. He made his money in black pepper, which, obviously, is nothing to sneeze at.

Elijah—Hebrew: The Lord is my God
Eli, Elia, Elias, Elie, Eliel, Elihu, Eliot, Ellie, Elliot, Elliott, Ellis, Elly, Ely

Eliot—See: Elijah

Eliot Ness, a federal law officer, took nine federal agents after the Capone mob at the end of the 1920s to the early 1930s. Because the agents couldn't be bought, the underworld called them "the Untouchables."

Elisha—Hebrew: The Lord is salvation

Ellery—German: One who lives near the elder tree
Ellary, Ellerey

Ellery Queen, author of the famous detective novels and stories, was really two people—cousins, in fact: Frederic Dannay and Manfred B. Lee. When they started their collaboration, they chose Ellery because it was the name of a friend at school, and Queen simply because it sounded good with Ellery. The rest is literary history!

Elliot/Elliott—See: Elijah

Ellis—See: Elijah

Ellison English: Son of Ellis

Elmer—English: Of famed dignity
Aylmar, Aylmer, Elmar, Ulmer

Elmo—Greek: Amiable

Elroy—Latin: Royal

Elton—English: From the old estate

Reginald Kenneth Dwight, a fan of saxophonist Elton Dean and singer John Baldry, changed his name to Elton John— and added Hercules as a middle name, to give him the strength to succeed. It worked!

Elvis—Norse: All-wise

The birth certificate says Elvis Aron Presley, but the tombstone at Graceland says Elvis Aaron Presley.

Elvis Costello, the British rock singer, was born Declan Patrick McManus.

Elwin/Elwyn—English: Friend to the elves
Elvin

Emanuel/Emmanuel—Hebrew: God is always with us
Emmanuele, Immanuel, Immanuele, Mannie, Manny, Manuel

Emerson—German: Son of the industrious leader

Emery—German: Industrious leader
Almerick, Amerigo, Amory, Emeri, Emeric, Emmery, Emory

Emile—German: Industrious; Latin: Eager to please
Amal, Emelen, Emil, Emilian, Emilio, Emilius, Emlen, Emlyn

Emmett—English: Hard worker
Emmet, Emmit, Emmitt, Emmot, Emmott
Emmett Ashford was the first black baseball umpire in the majors. In April of 1966, he started for the American League, and he worked his first World Series in 1970.
Emmett Kelly, world-renowned clown, was named by his Irish immigrant father in honor of Irish patriot Robert Emmett.

Engelbert—German: Bright as an angel
Englebert, Ingelbert, Inglebert
The singer Engelbert Humperdinck, christened Arnold George Dorsey at birth, borrowed his professional name from the composer of the opera Hansel and Gretel.

Enoch—Hebrew: Dedicated

Enos—Hebrew: Mortal man

Ephraim/Ephriam—Hebrew: Very fruitful
Effie, Effy, Efrem, Ephrem, Ephrim

Erasmus—Greek: Lovable
Erasmios, Erasmo, Erastus, Rasmos, Rasmus

Eric/Erick—Norse: Eternal ruler
Arek, Arick, Erich, Erik

Ernest—English: Earnest
Ernesto, Ernestus, Ernie, Ernst, Erny
Ernest Hemingway was the journalist, novelist, and short-story writer. Ernie Davis was the first black man to win football's coveted Heisman Trophy. At the time—in 1961—he was a halfback playing for Syracuse University.

Erroll—See: Earl/Earle

Erskine—Scottish: From the high cliff

Ervin/Erwin—Czechoslovakian: Friend of the sea

Esmond/Esmund—English: Gracious protector

Este/Estes—Italian: From the east

Ethan—Hebrew: Strong, firm

Eugene—Greek: Noble, wellborn
Eugenio, Eugenios, Eugenius, Gene
Four-time Pulitzer Prize–winner Eugene O'Neill is considered one of America's greatest playwrights.

Eustace—Latin: Stable, tranquil
Eustache, Eustasius, Eustazio, Eustis

Evan—Welsh: Wellborn one
Bowen, Evin, Ewan, Ewen, Owain, Owen, Yvain, Ywaine
The best-selling novelist (The Blackboard Jungle), *screenwriter, and TV writer who was born Salvatore Lombino changed his name to Evan Hunter right after graduating from New York City's Hunter College.*

Evelyn—Hebrew: Life
This name is quite popular in England as a male name (for example, author Evelyn Waugh); in America, it's more popular as a female name.

Everett—English: Mighty as a boar
Eber, Everard, Evered, Everet, Everhard, Everit, Everitt, Evraud, Evre, Ewardo, Ewart, Rhett
Everett Dirksen, the late great senator from Illinois, was not given a middle name at birth. Almost a year after Everett's birth, when William McKinley was elected president, Dirksen's dad decided to give his son the middle name of McKinley.

Ewing—English: Legal friend

Ezekiel—Hebrew: Strength of God
Ezechiel, Ezequiel, Zeke

Ezra—Hebrew: Helper
Esdras, Esra, Ezrah

F

Fabian—Latin: Prosperous farmer, bean grower
Fabe, Faber, Fabiano, Fabien, Fabio, Fabius, Fabyan

Fabron—Latin: Mechanic
Fabra, Fabriano, Fabrizio, Fabroni

Farley—English: From the far meadow
Fairleigh, Farleigh, Farlie, Farly

Farrel/Farrell—Irish: Valorous, heroic
Ferrel, Ferrell

Fedor—Russian: Gift of God

Felix—Latin: Fortunate
Felice, Felicio, Felike, Felizio
As long as there are TV reruns, there will be Felix Unger, the neat one *on "The Odd Couple."*

Fenton—English: Marshland dweller

Ferdinand—German: Peacemaker
Ferd, Ferdie, Ferdinando, Ferdy, Fergus, Fernando, Hernan, Hernando

Fergus—Celtic: Very choice man

Ferris/Farris—Irish: Choice one
The name has been immortalized on film in Ferris Bueller's Day Off, *with Matthew Broderick in the title role.*

Fidel—Latin: Faithful
Fidele, Fidelio

Fielding—English: From the field
Field, Fielder

Filbert—English: Brilliant
Filberte, Filberti, Filberto, Philbert, Philberto

Finlay—Irish: Fair-haired fighter
Findlay, Findley, Finley, Finn, Finnie, Finnley, Finny

Fisk/Fiske—English: Fish

Fitzgerald—English: Son of the spear-mighty
Can we ever hear this name without thinking of JFK?

Fitzpatrick—English: Son of a nobleman

Flavian—Latin: Fair, blond

Fleming—English: Man from the lowlands

Fletcher—French: Arrow maker

Flint/Flynt—English: Stream

Florian—Latin: To flourish
Fiorello, Flo, Florence, Florents, Florentz, Florenz, Florian, Florrie, Florry

Floyd—See: Lloyd

Fonda—Latin: Deep one

Forbes—Irish: Wealthy owner of the fields

Ford—German: River crossing

Forest—German: One who lives in the woods
Forrest, Forrester, Forrie, Forry, Forster, Foss, Foster

Francis—Latin: Free man
Chico, Fran, France, Francesco, Franchot, Francisco, Franciskus, François, Frank, Frankie, Franky, Frannie, Franny, Frans, Franz, Franze
While this is not a popular name today, there are three famous Americans with the name who come to mind: Francis Scott Key, Francis Albert Sinatra, and Francis Ford Coppola.

Frank—See: Francis, Franklin
Frank Baum, born Lyman Frank Baum, is the wizard who created the classic "Oz" stories. He also wrote under the pen names Schuyler Stanton, Floyd Akers, and Dith Van Dyne.

Franklin—Latin: Freeholder (of land)
Francklin, Francklyn, Frank, Frankie, Franklyn, Franky

Fraser—English: Curly haired
Frase, Frasier, Fraze, Frazer, Frazier
The hit TV sitcom "Cheers," and its spin-off, "Frasier," has actor Kelsey Grammer playing the part of Dr. Frasier Crane. Both Kelsey and Frasier are fast becoming popular names.

Frayne—English: Stranger
Fray, Frey, Freyne

Fred—See: Alfred, Frederic
Fred Austerlitz sounds like a name for a storm trooper, not a song-and-dance man. Fred thought so, too, and changed his name to Fred Astaire.

Frederic—German: Peace king
Fred, Freddie, Freddy, Fredek, Frederich, Frederick, Frederico, Fredericus, Frederigo, Frederik, Fredi, Fredo, Fredric, Friedrich, Fritz

Fritz—See: Frederic

Fuller—English: Clothing presser

Fulton—English: People's estate; Scottish: Leafy town

G

Gabriel—Hebrew: Devoted to God
Gab, Gabbie, Gabby, Gabe, Gabie, Gabrelli, Gabriele, Gabriello, Gaby, Gavril
Gadiel—Hebrew: God is my fortune
Gad, Gadi, Gadman
Gage—French: A pledge
Galen—Gaelic: Bright one, intelligent one
Gael, Gaelan, Gaelen, Gail, Gale, Galeno, Gayle
Gallagher—Celtic: Eager helper
Galton—English: One who lives on rented land
Galvin—Irish: Sparrow
Galvan, Galven
Gamble—Norse: Old
Gannon—Irish: Fair complected
Gardener—English: One who tends the garden
Gar, Gardie, Gardiner, Gardner, Gardy
Gareth—Welsh: Gentle
Gar, Garth, Gerth
Garett/Garrett—English: Mighty spear
Garrard, Garrott
Garfield—English: Triangular field
Cartoonist Jim Davis catapulted his feline cartoon character, Garfield, to the top of many best-seller lists.
Garland/Garlande—English: From the battleground
Garlen
Garner—English: To gather, to store
Garnet/Garnett—A dark red jewel
Garnyd
Garrick/Garrich—German: Mighty ruler with a spear
Garth—See: Gareth
The current popularity of this name comes from the success of country singer Garth Brooks.
Garvey—German: Spear bearer
Garvin/Garwin—German: Friend in strife
Garwood—English: From the fir-tree forest
Gary—English: Spear holder
Gare, Garey, Gari, Garry
Cartoonist Garry Trudeau got the name of his "Doonesbury"

comic strip by combining "Doone"—slang at Yale for "a good-natured fool"—and "sbury"—the second part of Pillsbury, his college roommate's last name.

Gaspar—Spanish: Master of treasure

Caspar, Casper, Gaspard, Gaspardo, Gaspare, Gasper, Jaspar, Jasper

Gaston/Gascon—French: From the Gascony region of France, hospitable

Gavin—German: Battle hawk

Gavan, Gaven, Gawain, Gawen

Actor Gavin MacLeod, well known for his role as the captain on "The Love Boat," was born Allan George William. He changed his name to Gavin simply because he liked it, and took the name MacLeod as a tribute to his college acting teacher.

Gavrie—Russian: Man of God

Gabril, Ganya

Gaylord—English: Lively one

Gaillard, Gallaird, Gaye, Gayelord, Gayler, Gaylor

Gaynor—Irish: Son of a fair-haired man

Gainer, Gaines, Gainor, Gayne, Gayner, Gaynes

Gearey/Geary—English: Adaptable to change

Gene—See: Eugene

Geoffrey/Geoffry—See: Jeffrey

George—Greek: Farmer

Egor, Georas, Geordie, Georg, Georges, Georgi, Georgios, Georgy, Giorgio, Goran, Jorg, Jorge

When Nathan Birnbaum first started in vaudeville, his acts were so bad that he had to keep changing his name in order to be hired again. Some of the names he used were Captain Betts, Jed Jackson, Buddy Links, Willie Delight, Harry Pierce, Jimmy Malone, and Willy Williams. When he finally got an act that he felt good about, he decided to stick with the name George Burns.

Gerald—German: Mighty spearman

Garald, Garalt, Garcia, Garold, Gearalt, Gearard, Geralde, Geraldo, Gerold, Gerrie, Gerry, Girald, Giralt, Giraud, Jerald, Jerold, Jerrald, Jerry

Gerald Ford's name at birth was Leslie Lynch King, Jr. His mother got divorced and remarried Gerald Rudolff Ford, whose name the future president adopted (changing Rudolff to Rudolph).

Gerard—English: Brave with a spear
Garrard, Garrat, Garrett, Gerrard

Gershom—Hebrew: Exiled
Gersh, Gersham

Gibor—Hebrew: Strong

Gideon—Hebrew: Great warrior

Gifford—German: Magnificent gift
Giff, Gifferd

Gil—Nickname for names starting with "Gil"

Gilbert—German: Bright pledge
Gibbie, Gibby, Gil, Gilberto, Gilburt, Gilibeirt, Gill, Gillie, Gilly, Gilpin, Guilbert, Wilbert, Wilbur, Wilburt

Gilchrist—Irish: Servant of Christ

Giles—Greek: Shield bearer
Egide, Egidio, Egidius, Gide, Gidi, Gilles, Gyles, Gylles, Jilly

Gilroy—Irish: King's servant

Glen/Glenn—Irish: From the valley
Glennie, Glenny, Glyn, Glynn, Glyynie, Glynny

Godard/Goddard—German: Firm nature
Godart, Goddart, Gotthard, Gotthart

Godfrey—See: Jeffrey

Godwin—English: Friend of God
Godewyn, Godine, Goodwin

Goliath—Hebrew: Giant

Gordon—English: From the cornered hill
Gordan, Gorden, Gordie, Gordy

Gore—English: Spear
Best-selling author Gore Vidal was named for his grand-father, Senator Thomas Pryor Gore of Oklahoma.

Gower—Welsh: Pure man of virtue

Grady—Irish: Illustrious, noble

Graham—German: From the gray home
Graeham, Graeme, Grahame
Genius inventor Alexander Graham Bell was one of the founders of National Geographic. *He once wrote an article for the magazine under the pen name of* H.A. Largelamb, *an anagram of A. Graham Bell.*

Granger—English: Farmer
Grange
Grant—Latin: Great
Noted artist Grant Wood, famous for his painting American Gothic, *said that all of his good ideas came to him while he was milking a cow.*
Granvill/Granville—French: From the big town
Grayson—English: Son of a judge
Gregory—Greek: Vigilant
Greg, Gregg, Greggie, Greggy, Gregoire, Gregoor, Gregor, Gregorio, Gregorius, Grischa
Tony Award–winner Gregory Hines was born on St. Valentine's Day. He certainly can act and dance his way into anyone's heart!
Gresham—English: From the grazing land
Griffin—Latin: Half eagle and half lion
Griff, Griffe, Griffie, Griffith, Griffy, Gryphon
Griffin Dunne, actor and producer, is bringing attention to a name that has been (until now) more common as a surname than a first name.
Griswold—German: From the gray forest
Grover—English: From a grove of trees
This may come as a surprise, but President Grover Cleveland's real name was Stephen Grover Cleveland, after Stephen Grover, a minister in his family's church.
Gunther—German: Bold one
Gun, Gunnar, Gunnor, Gunter, Gunthar
Gurion—Hebrew: Great strength
Gustav—Swedish: Noble staff bearer
Gus, Gussie, Gussy, Gustaf, Gustave, Gustavius, Gustavo
Guthrie—German: Army warrior
Guy—French: Guide
Guido, Guyon
Gwynn—Welsh: Fair, blond one
Guin, Gwin, Gwinn, Gwyn

H

Hackett—German: Little woodsman
Hacket, Hackit, Hackitt

Haddan—English: From the heather-filled land
Hadan, Haden, Hadon, Hadden, Haddon, Hadleigh, Hadley
Hadrian—Latin: From Adria (an Italian city in the north)
Hadrian was a Roman emperor who had the famous Hadrian Wall built in Britain in about 121 A.D. It's one of the largest Roman remains preserved by the British government.
Hakeem—Arabic: Wise
Hakim
Hale—English: Hero, from the hall
Haele, Haley
Halil—Turkish: Intimate friend
Hall—English: From the manor
Halsey—English: Greeting, salutation
Halstead, Halsted
Hamal—Arabic: Gentle lamb
Hamilton—English: Fortified castle
Hamel, Hamelton, Hamil
Hamish—See: Jacob
Hamlet—German: Little home
The best-known Hamlet is Shakespeare's Prince of Denmark, who is thought to be (or not to be) English literature's first truly modern character.
Hamlin/Hamlyn—French: Little home-lover
Hank—See: Henry
Hank Aaron, the Baseball Hall of Famer, broke Babe Ruth's home-run record in 1974, when he hit his 715th home run while playing for the Atlanta Braves.
Hanley—English: From the high meadow
Hanly, Henley, Henly
Hans—See: John
It's a good thing that Hans Christian Andersen was a great children's storyteller. As he was dyslexic, it was difficult for him to read.
Hanson—Scandinavian: Son of Hans
Hansen, Hanssen, Hansson
Haram—Hebrew: Mountaineer
Harden—English: To make bold
Harde, Hardie, Harding, Hardy
Harel—Hebrew: God's mountain

Harlan—English: From the battle land
Harland, Harlen, Harley, Harlin, Harlyn
Harlow—English: From the battle hill
Arle, Arlo
Harold—Norse: Army commander
Hal, Haldon, Harald, Haraldo, Harral, Harry, Herald, Herold, Herrick, Herry
Harold Washington made history on April 12, 1983, when he was sworn in as the first black mayor of Chicago.
Harper—English: Harp player
Harp, Harpo
Harrison—Son of Harry
Harris
Actor Harrison Ford made a big name for himself as Han Solo in Star Wars *and became a major international star after playing the title role in the "Indiana Jones" films.*
Harry—See: Harold
As a young boy, magician Ehrich Weiss changed his name to Harry Houdini. The first name came either from his nickname, "Ehrie," or from Harry Kellar, America's most popular magician at the time. After reading about Jean Eugene Robert-Houdin, France's greatest magician, the young boy added an "i" to the second half of the last name and took the name Houdini.
Hartley—English: From the deer pasture
Hart, Harte, Hartleigh, Hartly, Hartman
Harvey—German: Warrior; Celtic: Eager for battle
Harv, Hervé, Hervey
Hasan/Hassan—Arabic: Handsome
Haskel/Haskell—Hebrew: Understanding
Haslet/Haslett—English: From the land of hazel trees
Haz, Hazlet, Hazlett
Hasting—German: Swift one
Hastings, Hasty
Havelock/Havelocke—Norse: Contest at sea
Haven—English: Place of refuge
Hagan, Hagen, Hazen
Hawley—English: From the hedged meadow
Hayes—English: From the hedged place
Hayden, Haydon, Hayward, Haywood, Heywood
Heathcliff—English: From the heath by the cliff

Cliff, Heath, Heathcliffe
Heathcliff is the passionate hero of Emily Brontë's
Wuthering Heights. But who, in this day and age, would use
the name? Well, the lead character on the hit TV series "The
Cosby Show" (1984–92) was Dr. Heathcliff Huxtable,
played by Bill Cosby.

Hector—Greek: Steadfast
Ettore
In the Iliad, Hector is the oldest son of Priam and Hecuba,
and he possesses these human virtues: compassion, affec-
tion, loyalty, piety, and devotion to his parents.

Helmut—French: Warrior

Henry—German: Ruler of an estate
Enrico, Enrique, Enzio, Hank, Heindrick, Heinie, Heinrich,
Heinrik, Heintz, Hendrick, Hendrik, Henny, Henri, Henrik
Producer, director, and actor Henry Winkler created one of
the most charismatic characters in the history of television:
Arthur "the Fonz" Fonzarelli on "Happy Days."

Herbert—German: Brilliant soldier
Erberto, Harbert, Hebert, Heberto, Herb, Herberte, Herbie,
Herby, Hilbert
President Herbert Hoover's wife, Lou Henry, called her
husband Bert. When you think about it, it makes sense,
because he was "her Bert" (Herbert).

Hercules—Greek: Gift of glory
Ercole, Heracles, Herc, Hercule
Agatha Christie's fictional detective is Hercule Poirot.

Herman—German: Noble warrior
Armand, Armando, Armin, Arminio, Armond, Armyn,
Ermanno, Ermin, Harman, Harmon, Herm, Hermann,
Hermie, Hermon, Hermy

Hermes—Greek: Lordly
This son of Zeus is known as Mercury to the Romans and is
noted for his inventiveness.

Hernando—See: Ferdinand

Herrick—See: Harold

Herschel—Hebrew: Deer
Hersch, Hersh, Hershel, Hirsch, Hirschel
Herschel Walker is the first football player to turn pro
before his college eligibility expired.

Hewett/Hewitt—French: Small and intelligent one

Hilary/Hillary—Latin: Merry, cheerful
Alair, Hilar, Hilare, Hilario, Hilarius, Hilery, Hill, Hillery, Hillie, Hilly

Hillel—Hebrew: Greatly praised

Hilton—English: From the hill estate

Hiram—Hebrew: Most noble one
Hi, Hirah, Hy, Hyram

Hobson—English: Goodly, beautiful

Hogan—Irish: Youth

Holden—English: From the hollow in the valley
Holbrook, Holbrooke
As popular as J. D. Salinger's classic novel Catcher in the Rye *was, and continues to be, the name of the book's hero, Holden Caulfield, has not caught on.*

Hollis—English: From the holly-tree grove

Holt—English: From the forest

Homer—Greek: A pledge
Homere, Homero, Homerus, Omero
Homer is the author of the classic epics the Iliad *and the* Odyssey.

Horace—Latin: Timekeeper
Horacio, Horatio, Horatius, Orazio

Horatio—See: Horace

Horten/Horton—English: From the gray estate

Hosea—Hebrew: Salvation

Houghton—German: From the manor on high

Houston—English: Hill town; Place name: A city in Texas that was named for soldier and statesman Sam Houston

Howard—English: Guardian
Hovard, Howe, Howey, Howie
Knock, knock. Who's there? Howard. Howard who? Howard you like to have the money earned by "the Bashful Billionaire," industrialist and recluse Howard Hughes?

Howland—English: From the hill
Howell

Hubert—German: Alert, chipper
Eubie, Hobard, Hobart, Hube, Hubey, Hubie
Hubert H. Humphrey, former U.S. senator and vice president, was nicknamed "Pinky" in high school because his skin sunburned easily.

Hudson—English: Son of the hooded one

Hugh—English: Intelligent
Hew, Hewe, Huey, Huggin, Hughes, Hughie, Hugo, Hugues, Hutch, Hutchin, Ugo
TV personality Hugh (Malcolm) Downs lives up to the meaning of his first name. This all-around sportsman is an airplane pilot, the author of more than a half dozen books and an orchestral suite, and a science and astronomy buff.

Hume—German: Home lover

Humphrey—German: Peace-loving protector
Humfrey, Humfrid, Humfried, Humfry, Humph, Humphrie, Humphry, Hunfredo, Onfredo, Onfroi
Who can hear this name without thinking of Humphrey Bogart, the actor with the tough-guy screen image?

Hunter—English: Hunter
Hunt, Huntington, Huntly

Hurd—English: Strong minded, hard

Hussein—Arabic: Small and handsome one
Husain, Husein, Hussain

Huxley—English: Huckster

Hyatt—English: From the high gate

Hyman—See: Chaim

I

Iago—See: Jacob

Ian—See: John
Ian (Lancaster) Fleming was a journalist and the author of thirteen thrillers, in which the hero is James Bond (Agent 007).

Ibsen—German: Archer's son

Ichabod—Hebrew: Glory has departed
Ichabod Crane is the naive and shy schoolmaster in Washington Irving's "Legend of Sleepy Hollow."

Ignatius—Latin: Fiery, determined
Iggie, Iggy, Ignace, Ignacio, Ignacius, Ignats, Ignaz, Ignazio, Inigo

Igor—Norse: Hero

Ingamar—Norse: Famous son
Ingar, Ingemar, Inger, Ingmar

Innis—Irish: From the island
Inis, Innes, Inness, Inniss

Ira—Hebrew: Watchful, vigilant

Irving—English: Friend of the sea

Earvin, Erv, Ervin, Erwin, Irv, Irvin, Irvine, Irwin

Jewish songwriter Irving Berlin (born Israel Baline) wrote "White Christmas" and "Easter Parade," songs celebrating two of the most important Christian holidays. Earvin "Magic" Johnson performed his magic on the basketball court for the L.A. Lakers and was part of the U.S. "Dream Team" in the 1992 Olympics. Irvin C. Mollison was the first black federal judge in the U.S.

Irwin—See: Irving

Isaac—Hebrew: Laughter

Ike, Ikey, Ikie, Isaak, Isacco, Itzaak, Itzak, Izaak, Yitzaak, Yitzak

Writer Isaac Asimov was known for variety (writing in areas as diverse as science fiction and limericks) and volume (creating more than four hundred books). Because of his clear and articulate writing style, he was called "the Great Explainer."

Isaiah—Hebrew: God is my helper

Ishmael—Hebrew: The Lord will hear

The famous first line in Herman Melville's Moby Dick *is "Call me Ishmael." The name in this fictional story was inspired by the biblical Ishmael, "the dweller in the wilderness."*

Isidor/Isidore—Greek: Gift

Esidor, Isadore, Isidoro, Isodoro, Izzie, Izzy

Israel—Hebrew: The Lord's warrior

Israelos, Srully, Yisrael, Ysrael

Playwright Israel Horowitz once had four Off-Broadway hits in four months. He's written more than thirty-five plays, which have been translated into more than twenty languages, and on any given night more than twenty of these plays are performed throughout the world.

Itzak—See: Isaac, Yitzhak

Itzak Perlman has been hailed as one of the world's greatest classical violinists. The violin he plays is a Stradivarius from the year 1714.

Ivan—See: John

Ivan Lendl, world tennis champion from Czechoslovakia, pronounces his name E-vahn´.

Ivar—Norse: Archer
Ifor, Ive, Iver, Ives, Ivon, Ivor, Yves, Yvor, Yvors

J

Jack—See: Jacob, John
Born John Uhler Lemmon III, actor Jack Lemmon once used a stage name at Harvard, billing himself as Timothy Orange (obviously he likes citrus names).

Jackson—See: Jacob, John

Jacob—Hebrew: Supplanter
Cob, Cobie, Coby, Giacobo, Giacomo, Giacopo, Hamish, Iacovo, Iago, Jack, Jackie, Jackson, Jacky, Jacobo, Jacques, Jacquet, Jaime, Jake, Jakie, Jakob, Jakov, Jakub, James, Jamesie, Jamesy, Jamey, Jamie, Jasch, Jay, Jayme, Jamie, Jim, Jimmie, Jimmy, Jimson, Jock, Seamus, Shamus

Jael—Hebrew: Mountain goat, symbol of the zodiac sign Capricorn.

Jake—See: Jacob

James—See: Jacob
Five U.S. presidents were named James: Buchanan, Garfield, Madison, Polk, and Carter.
The world-famous fictional Secret Agent 007 was named by his creator Ian Fleming after the author of a book that always graced Fleming's coffee table: Birds of the West Indies *by ornithologist James Bond.*

Jamil—Arabic: Handsome

Jan—See: John

Japhet—Hebrew: Enlargement
Japheth, Yaphet, Yaphett

Jared—See: Jordan

Jarl—Norse: Nobleman
Jarley

Jaron—Hebrew: To sing

Jarrett—English: Spear-brave
Jaret, Jarrot, Jarrott

Jarvis—English: Driver; German: Sharp as a spear
Jarvey, Jervey, Jervis

Jason—Greek: Healer
Mention Jason Priestly of "Beverly Hills 90210" to most young teenage girls today, and watch their reaction.

Jaspar/Jasper—See: Gaspar/Gasper

Jay—See: Jacob

Jean—See: John

Jedediah/Jedidiah—Hebrew: Beloved by the Lord
Jed, Jedah, Jedd, Jeddie, Jeddy

Jedrek—Polish: Strong, manly

Jefferson—English: Son of Jeffrey
Jeff, Jeffer, Jefferies, Jeffers, Jeffie, Jeffy

Jeffrey—French: Divinely peaceful
Geoff, Geoffrey, Geoffry, Gofrey, Goffredo, Gottfried, Jeff,
Jeffery, Jeffie, Jeffy
*Two contemporary leading men in films use the short form
of this name: Jeff Bridges and Jeff Goldblum.*

Jeremiah—Hebrew: Exalted of the Lord
Geremia, Jer, Jereme, Jeremias, Jeremy, Jerrie

Jeremy—See: Jeremiah
*Jeremy Irons, born in England, is the Academy Award–
winning actor known for playing haunted, upper-class types.*

Jermaine—German: From Germany

Jermyn—Hebrew: One from Germany
Germaine, Germano, Jarman, Jermaine, Jerman

Jerome—Latin: Sacred name
Gerome, Geronimo, Gerrie, Gerry, Hierom, Hieronymus,
Jere, Jereme, Jeromo, Jeronimo, Jerrome
Reclusive writer J. D. Salinger, author of Catcher in the
Rye, *was born Jerome David Salinger.*

Jerrell—English: Strong, open-minded
Jerel, Jerrel, Jerryl, Jeryl

Jerry—See: Gerald (Also, a nickname for names starting with
"Ger" and "Jer")

Jerzy—Polish: Farmer

Jesse—Hebrew: Preeminence
Jess, Jessie, Jessy
*Olympic superstar Jesse Owens got his name because of a
simple misunderstanding. He was born James Cleveland
Owens and had always been called J.C. But when he went to
a Cleveland, Ohio, grammar school and told the teacher his
nickname, she thought he said Jesse. That's what she wrote
down, that's what he was soon called, and that's how the
world knows this great athlete.*

Jethro—Hebrew: Wealth, abundance

Jilly—See: Giles

Jim/Jimmie/Jimmy—See: Jacob
Jim Palmer, the only American League pitcher to win the Cy Young Award three times, was elected to the Baseball Hall of Fame in his first year of eligibility (1990). And he looks good in Jockey underwear, too!

Joab—Hebrew: Praise the Lord

Joachim—Hebrew: The Lord will judge
Achim, Akim, Joaquin, Joaquino, Kim

Job—Hebrew: Afflicted one

Jody—Latin: Playful
Jody Powell, President Carter's press secretary, was born Joseph Lester Powell, Jr. He was nicknamed Jody after the young boy in the book The Yearling, *by Marjorie Kinnan.*

Joe—See: Joseph

Joel—Hebrew: The Lord is God
Ioel, Yoel

Johann/Johannes—See: John
Johann Sebastian Bach produced many musical compositions—and almost as many children: seven with his first wife and thirteen with wife number two.

John—Hebrew: God is gracious
Eoin, Gian, Gianni, Giannini, Giovanni, Hanan, Hans, Hansel, Hanson, Iain, Ian, Ioannes, Ivan, Jack, Jackie, Jackson, Jacky, Jan, Janos, Jean, Jehan, Jen, Jens, Jock, Jocko, Johan, Johann, Johannes, Johnnie, Johnny, Johnson, Jon, Jonnie, Jonny, Jonson, Juan, Juanito, Sean, Seann, Shamus, Shane, Shawn, Yvan, Zane
This name is one of America's classic names for boys. There have been four presidents with the name: John Quincy Adams, John Adams, John Tyler, and John Fitzgerald Kennedy.

Jonah—Hebrew: Dove
Jona, Jonas
Jonas Salk's 1954 polio vaccine was the medical breakthrough of the decade.

Jonathan/Jonathon—Hebrew: Gift of the Lord
Johnathan, Johnathon, Johnny, Jon, Jonnie, Jonny

Joram—Hebrew: The Lord is exalted
Jorie, Jory

Jordan—Hebrew: Descending

Jared, Jaret, Jerad, Jordie, Jordy, Jori, Joris, Jory, Jourdain, Jourdan

Jorge—See: George

Jory—See: Major

Jose—See: Joseph

Joseph—Hebrew: He shall add
Che, Guiseppe, Iosep, Ioseph, Joe, Joey, Jose, Josef, Josephe, Josephus, Joska, Josko, Jozef, Pepe, Pepito, Yoseph, Yussuf
Russian dictator Joseph Stalin was born Joseph Vissari-onovich Djugashvili. He took the name Stalin, the Russian word for "steel," to signify his strength and grit.

Joshua—Hebrew: God of salvation
Josh, Joshuah

Josiah—Hebrew: May the Lord heal and protect

Judah—Hebrew: Praised one
Jud, Juda, Judas, Judd, Jude, Judson, Yehuda, Yehudah, Yehudi

Jules—See: Julius

Julian—See: Julius

Julius—Greek: Hairy-faced youthful one
Giuliano, Giulio, Giulius, Jule, Jules, Julian, Julie, Julien, Julio, Julion, Julot
Julius Winfield Erving II, now retired, was one of basket-ball's most beloved players. His nickname started in high school as "the Doctor," and when he went pro, the nick-name was changed to Dr. J.

Junius—Latin; Born in June
Junias, Junior, Unot

Jurl/Juris—Latvian: Farmer

Justin—Latin: Just, upright
Giustino, Giusto, Just, Justino, Justis, Justo, Justus, Justyn

K

Kadar/Kedar—Arabic: Powerful

Kadin—Arabic: Friend, companion

Kahlil—Arabic: Friend
Kalil, Khalil

Kaiser—See: Caesar

Kane—Hawaiian: God of men

Cane, Kain, Kaine, Kayne

Kaniel—Hebrew: Reed

Kareem—Arabic: Highborn, generous and powerful son of Allah

Born Lew Alcindor, this 7'3" basketball star changed his name to Kareem Abdul-Jabbar when he changed his religion from Catholic to the black orthodox Hanafi sect.

Karl—See: Charles

When Karl Malden became an actor, he changed his name from Mladen Sekulovich just so it would fit on theater marquees. Notice that his new last name is a variation of his original first name.

Keane—English: Sharp, bold

Kean, Keanan, Keen, Keenan, Keene

Keefe—Irish: Handsome, gentle, lovable

Keegan—Irish: Small and determined

Keenan—Irish: Very old and small

Keen, Keenen, Kienan, Kienen

Keir—Gaelic: Dark skinned

Actor Keir Dullea played the part of David Bowman in the film 2001: A Space Odyssey.

Keith—Welsh: From the forest

Kelley/Kelly—Irish: Warrior

Kelsey—Norse: Dweller by the water

Kelcey, Kelson, Kelton

Ken/Kenn/Kennie/Kenny—Nicknames for names starting with "Ken"

Kendall—English: From the bright valley

Kendal, Kendel, Kendell

Kendrick—English: Princely ruler

Kenric, Kenrick

Kenley—English: Dweller from the king's meadows

Kennard—English: Strong

Kennedy—English: Royal ruler

Kenneth—Gaelic: Handsome, fair

Ken, Kennet, Kenny

Kent—English: From the king's estate

Kenton

Kenward—English: Brave soldier

Conward, Kenway

Kenyon—Irish: White haired, blond

Kerem—Turkish: Nobility, kindness

Kermit—Gaelic: Free man
With the creation of Jim Henson's Muppets, the name Kermit has become synonymous with a frog.

Kern—Celtic: Mysterious
Kearne, Kearney, Kearny

Kerr—Celtic: Dark one
Keir, Keiran, Kerrie, Kerrin, Kerry, Kier, Kieran, Kiernan

Kerwin/Kerwyn—Irish: Little black one

Kevin—Irish: Gentle
Kevan, Keven, Kevon, Kevyn
This is a popular name for leading men in films and TV: Costner, Kline, and Dobson, to name just a few.

Kim—See: Joachim, Kimball

Kimball—English: Royal warrior
Kemble, Kim, Kimbell, Kimble, Kimmie, Kimmy
Fictional character Kimball O'Hara (no relation to Scarlett) is better known as Kim, in Rudyard Kipling's novel of the same name.

King—English: Ruling monarch

Kingsley—English: From the king's meadow
Kingsleigh, Kingston

Kinsey—English: Prince of victory

Kipp—English: From the pointed hill
Kip, Kippie, Kippy

Kirby/Kerby—Norse: From the church village

Kirk—Norse: Dweller by the church
Kirke, Kirkland, Kirkley, Kirwood
Born Issur Danielovitch, actor Kirk Douglas gave himself this not-too-common first name. When it came to naming his four sons, though, he kept it simple: Michael, Joel, Peter, and Eric.

Kit—See: Christopher
Kit Carson was an American frontiersman and guide in the West during the middle 1800s.

Kito—Swahili: Jewel

Kivi/Kiva—Hebrew: Protected

Knute—See: Canute
Knute Rockne, the famous Notre Dame football coach, was nicknamed by the press "the Great Man."

Konrad—See: Conrad

Konstantin—Latin: Steadfast, firm, constant
Constantin, Konstant, Konstanz, Kostas
Kornel—Latin: Hornlike
Kristian—Greek: Annointed Christian
Kris
Kristopher—Greek: Carrier of Christ
Kris, Kristofer, Kristoffer, Kristophor
Kris Kristofferson is probably the only Rhodes Scholar to use his Oxford education to become a country-music writer.
Kurt—See: Conrad
Kwamen—Akan, Ghana (African): Born on Saturday
Kyle—Celtic: Cattle-grazing hill

L

Lachlan—Gaelic: From the water, belligerent
Ladd—English: Boy, servant
Lad, Laddie, Laddy
Lael—Hebrew: He is God's
Lafayette—French: Faith
Laird—Scottish: Proprietor of land
Lal—Hindi: Beloved
Lalo—Latin: To sing a lullaby
This musical name belongs to one of television's most successful composers, Lalo Schifrin. One of his memorable musical contributions is the pulsating, jazz-oriented theme for "Mission Impossible."
Lamar—Latin: From the sea; German: Land-famous
Lambert—German: Bright land
Lamberto, Landbert
Lamont—Norse: Lawyer; Spanish and French: The mountain
Lamond, Lammond
Lance—Latin: One who serves, light spear
Lancelot, Lancing, Lansing, Launce, Launcelot
Landers—French: From the grassy lawn
Landis, Landman, Landon, Landry, Langdon, Langston, Lannie, Lanny
Lane—English: Path
Laney, Lanie, Layne, Laynie
Langley—English: Long meadow
Langston—English: Tall man's town

Novelist, composer, playwright, and poet Langston Hughes was discovered by poet Vachel Lindsay. They met when Langston was working as a busboy in a Washington, D.C., hotel restaurant and left some poems by Vachel's plate.

Lanny—See: Landers

Larkin—See: Lawrence

Larry—See: Lawrence

This popular name belongs to an interviewer (Larry King), a basketball player (Larry Bird), a novelist (Larry McMurtry), a boxer (Larry Holmes), a TV star (Larry Hagman), and one of the Three Stooges.

Lars—See: Lawrence

Laszlo—Hungarian: Famous ruler

Latham—Norse: From the barn
Lathe, Lathrop

Latimer—English: Teacher, interpreter

Laughton/Lawton—English: Man of refinement

Lauren—See: Lawrence

Lavi—Hebrew: Lion

Lawford—English: From the ford at the hill

Lawler—Gaelic: Soft-spoken

Lawrence—Latin: Laurel crowned
Larkin, Larrie, Larry, Lars, Larson, Lauran, Lauren, Laurence, Laurens, Laurent, Laurentius, Laurie, Lauritz, Lawrance, Lawrie, Lawron, Lawry, Lawson, Loran, Loren, Lorenz, Lorenzo, Lorin, Lorne, Lorrie, Lorry, Lowrance
T. E. (Thomas Edward) Lawrence, British adventurer, soldier, and scholar, was also known as Lawrence of Arabia.

Lazarus—Hebrew: God will help
Eleazar, Lazar, Lazare, Lazaro, Lazer, Lazlo

Leal—English: Loyal friend

Leander—Greek: Lionlike
Leandre, Leandro

Lear—German: Of the meadow

Lee—Nickname for names starting with or containing the sound of "Lee"
Lido Anthony Iacocca, called Lee for short, is the corporate superman responsible for turning Chrysler around.

Leif/Lief—Norse: Beloved
Leif Eriksson, Norwegian navigator, discovered Vinland, which is now thought to have been coastal North America.

When he returned to Norway, he was honored with the name Leif the Lucky.

Leighton—English: From the meadow farm
Layton, Leigh

Leland—English: From the meadowland

Lemuel—Hebrew: Consecrated to the Lord
Lem, Lemmie, Lemmy

Lennon—Gaelic: Little cape

Lenny—See: Leonard

Leo—Latin: Lion

Leon—Latin: Lionlike
Leone, Lion, Lionel, Lionello, Lyonel

Leonard—French: Strong, brave as a lion
Len, Lenard, Lennard, Lennie, Lenny, Leonard, Leonardo, Leonardus, Leonerd, Lienard

Leopold—German: Patriotic, brave for the people
Leopoldo, Leupold

Leor—Hebrew: Light is mine

Leroi/Leroy—French: The king

Les—See: Leslie

Leslie—Gaelic: From the gray fortress
Les, Leslee, Lesley, Lezley
This name was thought of as an American girl's name and an English boy's name. Now, with the success of the "Naked Gun" films, actor Leslie Nielsen has made the name more acceptable for boys in this country.

Lester—English: From the shining lamp; Latin: camp, protected area

Levi—Hebrew: Harmonious, uniting
Leavitt, Lev, Levic, Levy
Levi Strauss went west in 1849 in the California gold rush. A friend who was mining for gold complained that his pants weren't durable enough. Levi sewed together a more durable pair from tent canvas. They were the first "Levi's"—and the start of a major industry worth more than gold for Levi Strauss.

Lew/Lewis—See: Louis
The real name of Lewis Carroll, the creator of Alice in Wonderland, *is Charles Lutwidge Dodgson. It is said that he got his pen name by translating his given names into Latin (Carolus Ludovicus), then reversing them and translating*

them back into English-sounding names. It might have been easier just to keep his original name.

Liam—See: William

Lincoln—English: Place by the pool
Linc, Link

Lindall—English: From the linden tree
Lin, Lind, Lindal, Lindberg, Lindbergh, Lindel, Lindell, Lindsay, Linsey, Lyndsay

Lindsay—See: Lindall

Linus—Greek: Flaxen haired

Lionel—See: Leon
Lionel (Leo) Hampton is king of the vibes (vibraphone). Because "the Hamp" (one of his nicknames) found a spiritual home in Israel, he earned another nickname, "the Great Rabbi of Jazz."

Llewellyn—Welsh: Lionlike
Lew, Llewellen, Llewelyn

Lloyd—Welsh: Gray haired, sacred
Floyd, Floydie, Lloydie

Locke—English: From the enclosed place

Lodge—French: Campground

Logan—Gaelic: From the little hollow

Lombard—Latin: Long bearded
Lombarda, Lombardi, Lombardo

Lon/Lonnie/Lonny—See: Alphonse

Lord—English: Guardian of the manor

Lorimer—Latin: Harness maker
Lorimar, Lorrie, Lorrimer, Lorry

Lorin—See: Lawrence

Lorne—See: Lawrence
"Saturday Night Live" fans know the name Lorne Michaels, the executive producer who helped formulate the show.

Lou—See: Louis

Louis—German: Famous warrior
Aloysius, Lew, Lewes, Lewie, Lewis, Lou, Louey, Louie, Ludvig, Ludwig, Luigi, Luis
Louis Armstrong, the great jazz trumpeter and singer, was called Satchelmouth by a London journalist. Eventually it was shortened to Satchmo. When Armstrong was asked if he objected to that nickname, his answer was a widemouthed grin.

Lowell—French: Little wolf
Lovel, Lovell, Lowe, Lowel

Loyal—French: Faithful, true
Loy

Lucius—Latin: Bringer of light
Luca, Lucas, Lucca, Luce, Lucian, Luciano, Lucias, Lucien, Lucio, Luck, Lucky, Lukas, Lukash, Luke

Ludlow—English: From the prince's hill

Ludwig—See: Louis

Luke—See: Lucius
Luke Perry was the teenage hearthrob star of the hit TV series "Beverly Hills 90210."

Lundi/Lundy—French: Born on Monday

Luther—German: Renowned warrior
Lotario, Lothar, Lothario, Lowther
We have botanist Luther Burbank to thank for the Shasta daisy and the Burbank rose. It's no wonder he has been called "the Plant Inventor" and "an Architect of Nature."

Lyle—French: From the island
Lisle, Lyall, Lyell, Lysle
The very successful and somewhat controversial publisher Lyle Stuart has been affectionately referred to as "the Bad Boy of American Publishing."

Lyman—English: Man from the valley

Lyn/Lynn—English: From the waterfall
Football player Lynn Swann said that with a name like Lynn, he had to become a football player!

Lyndon—English: Dweller at the linden-tree hill
Lindan, Linden, Lindon, Lindy, Lyndy
President Lyndon Baines Johnson was referred to as LBJ. His wife, Claudia Alta Taylor, was called Lady Bird, which gave her the same initials. The president liked the idea of that so much that he and his wife named their daughters Luci Baines and Lynda Bird, and one of their dogs Little Beagle.

Lysander—Greek: Liberator

M

Mac/Mack—Irish/Scotch/Gaelic: Son of (Also, nicknames for names starting with "Mac" and "Max")

Macdonald—Gaelic: Son of Donald
*Macdonald Carey was one of America's most enduring
actors. From the silver screen, he went to TV as part of the
original cast of the soap opera "Days of Our Lives." That
was in 1965. He played the part of Dr. Tom Horton for close
to thirty years.*

Mace—Latin: Aromatic spice; English: Club
Macey, Macy

Mackenzie—Irish: Son of the leader

Macklin—Gaelic: Son of Flann

Maclean/McLean—Gaelic: Son of Leander

Madison—English: Good
Maddie, Maddison, Maddy, Madisson

Madoc—Welsh: Fortunate
Maddie, Maddoc, Maddock, Maddy, Maduc

Magnus/Manus—Latin: Great one

Mahir—Hebrew: Expert, industrious

Mahon—Celtic: Strong one
Mahoney

Maitland—English: From the meadowland

Major—Latin: Greater
Jorie, Jory, Maje, Majer, Mayer, Mayor

Malachai—Hebrew: My angel
Malachi, Malachy

Malcolm—Arabic: Dove
*Malcolm X, whose birth name was Malcolm Little, was a
black civil-rights leader and founder of the Organization of
Afro-American Unity.*

Malik—Islamic: Master

Malin—English: Little warrior
Mallin, Mallon, Malon

Mallory/Malory—German: Army counselor

Mandel/Mandell—German: Almond

Manfred—English: Man of peace
Manfredo, Manfrid, Manfried

Mannie/Manny—See: Emanuel/Emmanuel (Also, a nickname for names staring with "Man")

Manning—English: Son of the hero

Manuel—See: Emanuel/Emmanuel

Marcel—Latin: Little warrior
Marcellin, Marcellino, Marcello, Marcellus

Marcus—See: Mark

Marcus seems to be a name for healers of all types. There was the seven-year hit TV series "Marcus Welby, M.D.," and there was Roman philosopher Marcus Cicero, who recommended eating cabbage after drinking wine to prevent and/or cure a hangover.

Mario—See: Mark

Mario Lanza, considered one of the world's greatest operatic tenors, was born Alfred Arnold Cocozza.

Mark—Latin: Warlike

Marc, Marcel, March, Marco, Marcos, Marcus, Mario, Marion, Marius, Marjoe, Marko, Markos, Markus

Samuel Langhorne Clemens was a Mississippi steamboat pilot. When he began writing for a Nevada newspaper, he took the name Mark Twain, a nautical term that means "two fathoms deep."

Marlon—French: Little falcon

Marlen, Marlin

Marlowe—English: From the hill by the lake

Marlo, Marlow

Marshall—French: Keeper of the horses

Marsh, Marshal

Marston—English: From the place by the lake

Martin—Latin: Warlike

Mart, Martain, Marten, Martie, Martino, Marton, Marty, Mertin, Merton

Martin Luther King, Jr., the youngest person to win the Nobel Peace Prize, was baptized Michael Luther King, Jr. Six years later, his father, Rev. Michael Luther King, Sr., changed the Michael to Martin, for both himself and his son, in honor of the Reformation leader Martin Luther.

Marvel/Marvell—Latin: Miracle

Marvin—English: Famous friend

Marv, Marve, Marvyn, Marwin, Merv, Merven, Mervin, Mervyn, Morv, Morven

When award-winning composer Marvin Hamlisch was a young boy, his nickname was "Fingers" because he was always practicing the piano.

Mason—French: Stoneworker

Matt/Mattie/Matty—See: Matthew

Matthew—Hebrew: Gift of the Lord

Mata, Mateo, Mathia, Mathias, Mathieu, Mathius, Matias, Matio, Matt, Matteo, Matthaeus, Matthaus, Matthes, Mattheus, Matthias, Matthieu, Mattie, Matty

Matu—Native American: Brave

Maurice—Latin: Dark skinned

Maur, Mauricio, Maurie, Maurise, Mauruey, Maurite, Mauritis, Maurizio, Mauro, Maurus, Maury, Morice, Morie, Moritz, Moriz, Morrice, Morrie, Morris, Morritz, Morry, Mory

Artist Maurice Sendak is nicknamed "the Picasso of Children's Books."

Max—See: Maximillian, Maxwell

Maximillian—Latin: Greatest

Massimiliano, Massimo, Max, Maxie, Maxim, Maxime, Maximilliano, Maximilianus, Maximo, Maximus, Maxy

Maxwell—English: From the great well

Max, Maxey, Maxie, Maxy

Mayer/Myer—Latin: Great

Maynard—English: Mighty, brave

Mayne, Menard

Mayo—English: Kinsman

Mead/Meade—German: From the meadow

Medwin—English: Powerful friend

Meir/Meiri—Hebrew: One who shines

Melbourne—English: From the mill stream

Mel, Melborne, Melburn, Melden, Meldon, Mil, Milbourne, Milburn

Melville—English: Village near the mill

Mal, Malville, Mel

Melvin—Irish: Polished chief

Mal, Malvern, Malvin, Mel, Melvyn

Mel Brooks's name was Melvin Kaminsky. He said that he changed his name when he got a job as a drummer in the Catskills, because his real name wouldn't fit on the drums. So he used Mel, and Brooks came from his mother's maiden name, Brookman.

Menachem/Menahem—Hebrew: Comforter

Mendel, Mendeley, Mendie, Mendy

Mercer—Latin: Merchant; French: Dealer in textiles

Meredith—Celtic: Guardian from the sea

Meredeth, Merideth

Merle—French: Blackbird

Merlin—Welsh: Sea fort
Marlin, Merl

Merrick—English: Ruler of the sea

Merrill—French: Famous; English: Body of water
Merle, Merrel, Merrell, Merril, Meryl, Meryll

Merrit/Merritt—Latin: Valuable

Merton—English: From the town by the sea
Mertin, Merty

Merv/Mervin/Mervyn—See: Marvin
Merv (Mervyn) Griffin was the popular TV host who started "theme" talk shows.

Merwin/Merwyn—See: Marvin

Meyer—German: Head servant
Mayer, Myer

Michael—Hebrew: Like unto the Lord
Mica, Micah, Micha, Michal, Micheil, Michel, Michele, Michon, Mickel, Mickey, Mickie, Micky, Miguel, Miguelito, Mikael, Mike, Mikel, Mikey, Mikhael, Mikhail, Mikkie, Mikky, Mischa, Mishael, Mitch, Mitchel, Mitchell
For the past two decades this has been the most popular boys' name. Many celebrities with this name were born with it: Michael J. Fox, Michael Douglas, Michael Jackson, and Mikhail Baryshnikov.

Miles—Latin: Soldier; Greek: Merciful
Milan, Milo, Myles, Mylo
We all know that Miles Standish, one of the Mayflower settlers, sent John Alden in his place to propose to Priscilla Mullins. But do you know that Miles was captain of the Pilgrims' military forces?

Millard—German: From the mill
Mill, Millais, Millay, Miller, Milman, Milne
Millard Fillmore, the thirteenth U.S. president, was born in a log cabin in New York State.

Milton—English: From the mill town
Milt, Miltie, Milty

Miner/Minor—Latin: Miner

Mitch/Mitchell—See: Michael

Mohammad/Mohammed—See: Muhammad

Mohan—Hindi: Delighted

Monroe—Irish: From the red marsh

Monro, Munro, Munroe

Montagu/Montague—French: From the pointed hill

Montgomery—French: From the rich man's hill castle
Monte, Monty
When Monty Hall, host of TV's "Let's Make a Deal," first started in show biz, he made a deal with his Toronto, Canada, radio-station manager to change his name from Monte Halparin.

Mordecai/Mordechai—Hebrew: Taught of God

Morgan—Celtic: One who lives near the sea

Morley—English: Meadow on the moor
Canadian-born Morley Safer is an investigative reporter on "60 Minutes."

Morris—See: Maurice

Morse—English: Son of the dark-complected one

Mortimer—French: From the quiet waters
Mort, Morty
Mortimer Benjamin Zuckerman is a self-made multimillionaire real-estate magnate and publisher.

Morton—English: Town near the sea
Mort, Morten, Mortin, Morty

Moses—Hebrew: A child saved from the water
Moe, Moise, Moises, Moishe, Mose, Mosheh, Moss, Moyes, Moys, Moyses, Mozes
Moses (Eugene) Malone, the first basketball player to sign a pro contract directly out of high school, became the youngest millionaire in sports history.

Mosi—Swahili: Firstborn

Muhammad—Arabic: Greatly praised
Mahmoud, Mahmud, Mohammad, Mohammed, Muhamet, Muhammed
Muhammad Ali, which is the Black Muslim name of one of the all-time greatest heavyweight prizefighters, was born Cassius Marcellus Clay, Jr. Ali's great-great-grandfather was a slave owned by Cassius Marcellus Clay, the American ambassador to Russia in the 1860s.

Mungo—Celtic: Lovable

Murdock—Gaelic: Wealthy sailor
Murdoch, Murtagh, Murtoch

Murphy—Irish: Sea warrior

Murray—Celtic: Sailor

Murrey, Murry
Murray Kaufman, better known as Murray the K, was the country's most popular disc jockey in the 1950s and 1960s.

Myron—Greek: Fragrant, sweet, perfumed

N

Nadim—Arabic: Friend

Namir—Hebrew: Swift as a leopard

Napoleon—Greek: New town
Napoleone, Nappie, Nappy

Nasser—Arabic: Victorious one

Nathan—Hebrew: God gave a gift
Nat, Nate, Nathon

Nathaniel—Hebrew: God has given
Nat, Natanael, Nataniel, Nate, Nathanael, Nathon, Natty, Nethanel
Singer Nathaniel Adams Coles had a group called the Nat Coles Trio. A manager renamed the group the King Cole Trio. Thereafter, the singer was known as Nat "King" Cole. He was the first black show host on national television.

Neal—Irish: Champion
Neale, Neall, Neel, Neil, Neill, Neils, Nels, Nial, Niall, Niel, Niels, Niles, Nils

Ned—See: Edgar, Edmond/Edmund

Nehemiah—Hebrew: Comforted by the Lord
Nahum, Nehamias, Nemiah, Nemian, Nemo

Neil—See: Neal
For men in show business, Neil seems to be the preferred spelling of the name—e.g., Neil Simon, Neil Diamond, Neil Sedaka.

Nelson—English: Son of Neal; son of a champion
Nealson, Nilson
South African activist Nelson Mandela has rekindled interest in this name, which nearly faded away since Nelson Eddy and Nelson Rockefeller were in the public eye.

Nero—Italian: Black one

Nestor—Greek: Wisdom of the aged

Neville—French: From the new town
Nevil, Nevile, Nevvy
History books taught us that Neville Chamberlain was

England's prime minister, but did you know that he also invented the game of snooker?

Nevin—Latin: Of the snow; English: Middle; Gaelic: Holy
Nevins, Niven, Nivens

Newall/Newell—Latin: Kernel, fruit seed, something new

Newton—English: From the new town

Nicholas—Greek: Victory of the people
Niccolo, Nichol, Nick, Nickie, Nickolaus, Nicky, Nico, Nicol, Nicola, Nicolai, Nicolao, Nicolas, Nicolaus, Nicolo, Niki, Nikita, Nikki, Niklas, Nikolai, Nikolas, Nikolaus, Nikolos

Nick/Nickie/Nicky—See: Nicholas

Nicodemus—Greek: Victory over the people

Nigel—Latin: Dark one; Gaelic: Champion

Nissan—Hebrew: Banner, emblem

Nissim—Hebrew: Miracles, signs

Noah—Hebrew: Rest, comfort
Noach, Noak

Noble—Latin: Well known, famous

Noel/Noël—French: Born at Christmas
Natal, Natale, Nowell

Nolan—Irish: Noble, famous
Noland, Nolen, Nolend, Nolin, Nollan
In keeping with one of the meanings of the name, Nolan Miller is one of Hollywood's most famous fashion designers.

Norbert—Norse: Brilliant hero

Norman—French: From the north
Norm, Normand, Normen, Normie, Normy
The name Norman has never made it to the top ten, but many of its bearers have reached the top of their fields: TV producer/director/writer Norman "All in the Family" Lear, film director Norman "Moonstruck" Jewison, actor Norman "Three's Company" Fell, novelist Norman Mailer, artist Norman Rockwell, clergyman Dr. Norman Vincent Peale, and military leader Norman Schwarzkopf.

Norris—French: Comes from the north
Norrie, Norry

Northrop—English: From the north farm
North, Northrup

Norton—English: From the northern town

Norville—French: From the north estate
Norval, Norvel, Norvell, Norvil, Norvill, Norvylle
Norvin—English: Friend from the north
Norvyn, Norwin
Norward—English: Northern guardian
Nova—Latin: New one
Noy—Hebrew: Beauty
Nugent—English: To shove
Nuncio—Italian: Messenger
Nuntius, Nunzio
Nuria—Hebrew: Fire of the Lord
Nye—English: Islander

O

Oakes—English: From the oak-tree grove
Oak, Oakie, Oakley, Oaky
Obadiah—Hebrew: God's servant
Oba, Obad, Obadias, Obed, Obediah, Obie, Oby
Oberon—French: Obedient
Oberon is king of the fairies and husband of Titania in Shakespeare's A Midsummer Night's Dream.
Obert—German: Wealthy and bright one
Octavius—Latin: Eighth-born child
Octave, Octavian, Octavus, Ottavio
Odell—Norse: Rich man
Ogden/Ogdon—English: From the oak valley
Ola—Hebrew: Eternity
Olaf—Norse: Ancestor
Olaff, Olav, Olave, Olavi, Olen, Olin, Olof, Olov
Oliver—Latin: Olive tree (a symbol of peace)
Oliveiro, Olivero, Olivier, Oliviero, Olivio, Ollie, Olly, Olvan
The name Oliver attracted attention in the seventies, when Oliver Barrett IV, Jenny's husband in Love Story, *appeared in both book and film form. The name attracted even more attention in the eighties, when Colonel Oliver North made headlines during what has come to be known as Iranscam.*
Omar—Arabic: Highest
Omer, Omri
Omar Sharif is one of the few actors born with the name

Michael who changed it. He went from Michael Shalhoub to Omar El Sharif in Egyptian films and Omar Sharif in English-language films.

Onan—Turkish: Prosperous

Oral—Latin: Speech
How appropriate that someone named Oral (Granville) Roberts is a preacher!

Oram—English: From the riverbank enclosure

Oran—Irish: Pale-complected one; Hebrew: Pine tree
Oren, Orin, Orren, Orrin

Orel—Latin: Listener
Every baseball fan knows about Orel Hershiser's records, titles, and awards.

Oren—See: Oran

Orestes—Greek: Mountaineer

Orien/Orion—Greek: Son of light

Orlan—English: From the pointed land
Orland, Orlando

Orman—English: Spearman

Orrick—English: Dweller at the old oak tree

Orson—Latin: Bearlike

Orville—French: From the golden city
Orval, Orvie, Orvy
Who says Orville is an unusual name? There are at least two of 'em: one of the two Wright brothers who flew the first motor-driven airplane; and the prince of popcorn himself, Orville Redenbacher.

Osbert—English: Divinely brilliant

Osborne—English: Divine warrior
Osborn, Osbourne, Oz, Ozzie, Ozzy

Oscar—Norse: Divine spearman
Oskar, Oskie, Osky, Ossie, Ossy
The Oscar is the film industry's most coveted award. Legend has it that it got its name when Margaret Herrick, the librarian at the Academy of Motion Picture Arts and Sciences, looked at the statuette and said that it looked like her uncle Oscar. Isn't that Wilde?

Osgood—English: Divine creator

Osmond—English: Divine protector
Osmont, Osmund, Osmunt

Oswald—English: Divinely powerful

Oswaldo, Oswell, Oswold, Oz, Ozzie, Ozzy

Otello/Othello—See: Otto

Othello, Shakespeare's protagonist, is a Moor in the military service of Venice and is married to Desdemona.

Otis—Greek: Keen of hearing

Otto—German: Rich

Odo, Otello, Othello, Otho

Ovid—Latin: Egg

Owen—See: Evan

Ozias—Hebrew: Strength of the Lord

Ozzie/Ozzy—See: Osborn/Osborne, Oswald

One of the perfect families during TV's Golden Age was the Nelsons, headed by Oswald "Ozzie" Nelson.

P

Pablo—See: Paul

Pablo Picasso's name at birth was Pablo Nepomuceno Crispiniano de la Santissima Trinidad Ruiz y Picasso. He initially signed his paintings with his first initial, and then his mother's and father's last names—P. Ruiz Picasso. He eventually dropped Ruiz, because it was a very common name, and stayed with his mother's more unusual name of Picasso.

Paco—Native American: Bold eagle

Paddy—See: Patrick

Paddy Chayefsky, the brilliant playwright and screenwriter, was originally named Sidney. When he was in the army and wanted to avoid K.P. duty one Sunday, he told his lieutenant that he had to go to mass. The lieutenant must have had a good sense of humor, for he nicknamed this Jewish soldier from the Bronx "Paddy," a classic Irish Catholic name. It stuck!

Page—French: Youthful attendant

Padge, Padget, Padgett, Paget, Paige

Palma/Palmer—English: Palm bearer

Paris—Place name: A city in France

This was the name of a prince of Troy who, according to Greek legend, abducted the beautiful Helen, thus causing the Trojan War.

Parker—English: Guardian of the park

Parnell—See: Peter

Parrish—English: From the churchyard
Parish, Parrie, Parrisch, Parry

Parvis—Latin: Of paradise

Pascal—Hebrew: Pertaining to Easter or Passover
Pace, Pasch, Paschal, Pascoli, Pasquale

Pat/Pattie/Patty—Nicknames for names starting with "Pat"

Patrick—Latin: Nobleman
Paddie, Paddy, Padraic, Padrick, Padruig, Pat, Patraic, Patric, Patricio, Patrize, Patrizio, Patrizius, Patsy, Patten, Pattie, Patty, Payton, Peyton
The popularity of actors Patrick Duffy and Patrick Swayze have done wonders for the popularity of this name.

Paul—Latin: Small
Pablo, Paley, Pall, Paoli, Paolino, Paolo, Paulie, Paulis, Paulot, Pauly, Paval, Pavel, Pavlo, Pavol, Pawl, Pawley, Poul
Here is a perfect example of how the meaning of a name didn't affect the person: Paul Bunyan. (Okay, so Paul Bunyan was a fictional character.) These real Pauls, no matter what their size, have all had big careers: Paul Anka, Paul Cezanne, Paul Gauguin, Paul Harvey, Paul McCartney, Paul Muni, Paul Newman, Paul Robeson, Paul Scofield, and Paul Williams.

Paxton—Latin: Town of peace
Pax, Paxon, Paxten, Paxtun, Payton

Penrod—German: Noted commander
Pen, Penn, Pennie, Penny

Pepin—German: One who seeks favors
Pepe, Pepi, Peppie, Peppy

Percival—French: Perceptive
Parsefal, Parsifal, Perce, Perceval, Percy

Percy—See: Percival
Percy Bysshe Shelley was one of the most radical of the English Romantic poets.

Perry—See: Peter

Perth—Celtic: Thornbush thicket

Peter—Greek: Stone
Panos, Parnell, Parry, Peadar, Pearce, Peder, Pedro, Peirce, Perkin, Pernel, Pero, Perrie, Perry, Petar, Pete, Petey, Petie,

Petri, Petros, Petruscha, Pierce, Piero, Pierre, Pierrot, Piers, Piet, Pieter, Pietro

There are so many famous men with the name Peter, or a variation of the name, that it was hard for us to single out one. So here's a select list, to give you an idea of how popular the name was, is, and will continue to be: Saint Peter, Peter Stuyvesant, Peter Cooper, Peter Pan, Peter Falk, Peter O'Toole, Peter Jennings, Peter Bogdanovich, Peter Benchley, Peter Arno, Peter Max, Pete Rose, Pete Seeger, Pete Hamill (the list is starting to peter out), Perry Como, Perry King, Pierce Brosnan, Pierre Salinger, Pierre August Renoir, Piers Anthony, Piet Mondrian, and Pieter Brueghel.

Peverell—French: Whistler
Peverel, Peveril

Phillip—Greek: Lover of horses
Feeleep, Felipe, Filip, Filippo, Flip, Phil, Philip, Phillie, Phillipe, Phillipo, Philly

Phil Donahue was the first national TV talk-show host to make the audience an integral part of the show.

Philo—Greek: Loving

Phineas—Greek: Mouth of brass; Egyptian: Dark skinned
Fineas, Finnie, Finny, Pincas, Pinchas, Pincus

Pinchas Zukerman, world-renowned violinist, violist, and conductor, is called "Pinky" by friends.

Phoenix—Greek: Purple

Pierce—See: Peter

Pierpont—Latin: From the stone bridge
Pier, Piers

Pierre—See: Peter

Pius—Latin: Devout, conscientious, kind

Placido—Spanish: Serene
Opera singer Placido Domingo, one of the world's foremost tenors, made this name familiar to Americans.

Plato—Greek: Broad shouldered

Platt—French: From the flat land

Pomeroy—French: From the apple orchard

Pontius—Latin: Fifth one
Ponce, Pontie, Ponty

Porter—Latin: Keeper of the gate

Prentice/Prentiss—English: Apprentice, learner

Prescot—English: From the priest's house
Prescot, Prestcot, Prestcott
Presley—English: Priest's meadow
Presleigh, Presly, Prestly
Because of Elvis Presley's enormous popularity, it is now not unusual for Presley to be used as a first name.
Preston—English: From the priest's town
Price/Pryce—English: Value
Primo—Italian: First child (if a son)
Primus
Prince—Latin: The first in rank
The performer formerly known as Prince, born Prince Rogers Nelson, is not just another pretty face. This talented musician who as of this writing wishes to be known as "The Artist," writes and arranges the music on his albums and also plays more than twenty musical instruments.
Procter/Proctor—Latin: Leader, manager
Pryor—Latin: Head of a monastery
Pyne—English: Pine tree

Q

Quain—French: Clever one
Quennel—French: Dweller at the little oak tree
Quenn, Quennell
Quentin—Latin: Fifth child (if a son)
Quent, Quenten, Quenton, Quint, Quintin, Quinton, Quintus
Quentin was the name of President Theodore Roosevelt's aviator son, who was nicknamed "Quentin the Eagle." Quinton is the name Burt Reynolds and Loni Anderson gave their son.
Quiller—English: Writer
Quill
Quimby/Quinby—Norse: From the woman's estate
Quincy—Latin: Fifth one; Place name: A town in Massachusetts
Quincy Jones, Jr., whose middle name is Delight, delights millions with his music.
Quinlan—Irish: Well shaped, athletic
Quinn—Celtic: Wise, intelligent

R

Radborne—English: Lives by the red brook
   Rad, Radbourn, Radburn, Raddic, Raddy, Radley
Radcliffe—English: From the red cliff
Rafael—See: Raphael
Rafe/Rafer—See: Raphael
Raferty/Rafferty—Irish: Rich, prosperous
Rafi—Arabic: Exalting
   Raffi, Raffy, Rafy
Raleigh—English: Dweller at the roe-deer meadow
   Rawley, Rawly
Ralph—English: Fearless adviser
   Raff, Ralf, Ralphie, Ralphy, Raoul, Rolf, Rolph
   *There are some names—and they're not always the most
   popular ones—that belong to many people from different
   walks of life. Ralph is one of those names. To give you an
   idea of what we mean, here are a bunch of Ralphs: Bunche,
   Nader, Abernathy, Waldo Emerson, Lauren, Metcalfe, Mac-
   chio, and the famous but fictional Ralph Kramden, whom
   Jackie Gleason played on "The Honeymooners."*
Ramon—See: Raymond
Ramsay/Ramsey—English: From the ram's island
   Ram, Ramsy
Rance—French: A kind of Belgian marble
Randall—See: Randolph
Randolph—English: Shield-wolf (implying a protective
   cover) Rand, Randal, Randall, Randell, Randie, Randle,
   Randolf, Randolfe, Randolphe, Randy
Randy—See: Randolph
   *This name seems to be catching on since country singer
   Randy Travis started winning all those Grammies.*
Ranen/Ranon—Hebrew: To be joyous, to sing
Ranger—French: Guardian of the forest
   Rainger, Range
Rankin—English: Little shield
Ransom—English: Son of a warrior
Raoul—See: Ralph
Raphael—Hebrew: God has healed
   Rafael, Rafaelle, Rafaello, Rafe, Rafer, Raff, Rephael

Ravi—Hindi: Sun

Ravid—Hebrew: Jewelry, ornament

Raviv—Hebrew: Rain, dew

Ray—French: Kingly (Also, a nickname for names starting with "Ray")

Singer Ray Charles's last name is Robinson, but he chose not to use it because he didn't want to be confused with the boxer Sugar Ray Robinson.

Rayburn—English: From the roe-deer brook

Raybourn, Reyburn

Rayfield—English: Stream in the field

Rayford—English: Ford over the stream

Raymond—English: Wise protector

Raimond, Raimondo, Raimund, Raimundo, Ramon, Ray, Raymondo, Raymund, Raymundo

Long before he played Perry Mason, Raymond Burr worked for the Oregon Forest Service and spent five months on his own because he was snowed in. In this case, his last name was extremely appropriate: Burr!

Raynor—German: Wisdom, advice

Ragnor, Rainer, Rainier, Ranier, Raynar, Rayner, Regnier

Reade—English: With red hair

Read, Reed, Reid

Redford—English: From the red-river crossing

Reese—Welsh: Ardent one

Ree, Reece, Rees, Reiss, Rhett, Rhys, Rice

Reeve/Reeves—English: Steward

Regan—German: Wise

Reagan, Reagen, Regen, Regin

Reginald—English: Powerful, mighty

Reg, Reggie, Reginard, Reginauld

Reginald Martinez Jackson, known to baseball fans and candy lovers as Reggie Jackson, led the New York Yankees to a World Series victory in 1977 and tied Babe Ruth's record for World Series single-game homers by hitting three of them in the sixth game.

Regis—Latin: Kingly, regal

Regis Philbin, living up to the meaning of his name, is one of the rulers of morning TV.

Remington—English: From the raven estate

Remy

Remington Steele, played by Pierce Brosnan, was the hand-some, cultured, and very charming detective on the TV series of the same name.

Remus—Latin: Changeling
Remi, Remo, Remy

Rene—See: Ronald

Renny—Gaelic: Small and powerful

Reuben—Hebrew: Behold a son
Reubin, Reuven, Rouvin, Rube, Ruben, Rubie, Rubin, Ruby

Reuel/Ruel—Hebrew: Friend of God

Rex—Latin: King

Reynard—French: Fox
Rainardo, Raynard, Raynardo, Regnard, Reinhard, Rein-hart, Renard, Renart, Renaud, Rey

Reynold/Reynolds—See: Ronald

Rhett—See: Everet/Everett, Reece/Reese

Rhodes—Greek: Place of the roses

Richard—German: Wealthy and powerful
Dick, Dickie, Dicky, Ric, Ricard, Ricardo, Riccardo, Ricci, Ricciardo, Ricco, Rich, Richart, Richie, Richy, Rick, Rickart, Rickert, Rickie, Ricky, Rico, Rikki, Ritchie, Ritchy
Because Richard and all its variations have been, and continue to be, quite popular, we could fill this chapter with Richard names. Here are just a few: Richard Chamberlain, Richard Burton, Richard Nixon, Richard the Lionhearted, Richard Dreyfuss, Richard Pryor, Richard Avedon, Richard Dawson, Rick Blaine (Humphrey Bogart's character in Casablanca), *Ricky Nelson, Ricardo Montalban, Dick Cavett, and Dick Clark.*

Richmond/Richmund—German: Powerful protector

Rick—See: Richard (Also, a nickname for names starting or ending with "Ric" or "Rick")

Rider/Ryder—English: Horseman

Ridgley—English: By the meadow's edge
Riddley, Ridge, Ridley, Ridly
The hardly ever heard name Ridley can be seen on movie credits: Ridley Scott is the director of Alien, Aliens II, Blade Runner, Black Rain, Thelma & Louise, *and more.*

Rigby—English: Ruler's valley

Riley—Irish: Valiant
Reilly, Ryley

Rimmon/Rimon—Hebrew: Pomegranate
Ring/Ringo—English: Ring
Once upon a time in England, there was a group named Rory Storm and the Hurricanes. Each of the musicians decided to find American cowboy names for themselves. And so drummer Richard Starkey became Ringo Starr, keeping that name when he joined the Beatles.
Riordan—Irish: Royal poet
Reardon, Reorden
Ripley—English: From the shouter's meadow
Ritter—German: Mounted warrior, knight
Ritt
Roald—German: Famous ruler
Roarke—Irish: Mighty
Roark, Rorke, Rourke, Ruark
Rob/Robbie/Robby—See: Robert (Also, nicknames for names starting with "Rob")
Robert—English: Bright fame
Bert, Berty, Bob, Bobbie, Bobby, Rob, Robb, Robbie, Robbin, Robbinson, Robby, Roberto, Robertson, Robin, Robinson, Rupert, Ruperto, Ruprecht
As with the name Richard, Robert and all its variations have been and continue to be quite popular. It is said that Robert De Niro, when growing up in New York City's Little Italy, was nicknamed "Bobby Milk" because he was so pale and thin.
Robin—See: Robert
Robinson—English: Son of Robert
Rochester—English: Rocky fortress
Rockwell—English: From the rocky spring
Rocco, Rock, Rockne, Rocky
Rocky—Nickname for names starting with "Roc" and "Rock"
There were world boxing titleholders Rocky Graziano and Rocky Marciano, but the most famous boxing Rocky of all was Sylvester Stallone's fictional Rocky ("Yo, Adrian!") Balboa.
Rod—Nickname for names starting with "Rod"
Roderick—German: Renowned ruler
Roddie, Roddy, Roderic, Roderich, Roderigo, Rodrick, Rodrigo, Rodrique, Rory, Rurik, Rury
Rodman—English: One who clears the land, farmer

Rodney—English: From the island clearing

Roger—German: Famous noble warrior

Rodge, Rodger, Rogerio, Rogers, Rugero, Ruggiero, Rutger

While Roger has never been on the top-ten lists, it has been fairly popular through the years. There's Roger Moore, Roger Maris, Roger Williams, Roger Ebert, Roger Mudd, Roger Stevens, Roger Bannister, Roger Corman, Roger Vadim, Roger Rabbit, the Jolly Roger . . . and Roger, over and out!

Roland—German: From the well-known island

Roeland, Rolando, Roldan, Rollan, Rolland, Rollie, Rollin, Rollo, Rolly, Rowland

Roland, one of Charlemagne's most famous and accomplished knights, is the legendary prototype of the loyal, courageous, self-sacrificing hero of chivalry.

Famous psychologist and author Rollo May was named after the Little Rollo character in Jacob Abbott's series of books. As a kid, he hated his name until he found out that there was a Norman leader named Rollo the Conqueror.

Rolf—See: Ralph

Roman—Latin: Citizen of Rome

Romain, Rome, Romeo, Romer, Romualdo, Romulus

Romeo—See: Roman

Romney—Welsh: Curving river

Ronald—English: Powerful, mighty

Ranald, Raynold, Reinald, Reinaldo, Reinaldos, Reinhold, Reinwald, Renaldo, Renato, Renaud, Renault, Rene, Reynold, Reynolds, Rinaldo, Ron, Ronaldo, Ronnie, Ronny

This name enjoys the spotlight because of both a former U.S. president and a clown: Ronald Reagan and Ronald McDonald.

Ronan—Celtic: A pledge

Ronel—Hebrew: Joy of God

Roone—English: Counsel

ABC-TV sports and news fans know this unusual name because of Roone (Pinckney) Arledge, Jr.

Rooney—Irish: Red haired

Roosevelt—Dutch: Field of roses

Rosey, Rosie

Roper—English: Rope maker

Rory—See: Roderick

Roscoe—Norse: From the deer forest
Scoey
*Roscoe Robinson brings honor to this name. In 1982, he was
promoted to four-star general in the army (becoming the
first African American to achieve that rank).*

Rosey/Rosie—See: Roosevelt

Ross—Gaelic: From the island
Rossi, Rossy
*Billionaire and 1996 presidential candidate Henry Ross
Perot prefers being billed as H. Ross Perot and is generally
referred to as Ross Perot.*

Roswald—German: Mighty steed
Roswell

Roth—German: Red haired

Rowen—Gaelic: Red haired
Rowan, Rowe

Roy—French: King
Roi, Ruy

Royal—French: Royal one

Royce—English: Son of the king

Ruben/Rubin—See: Reuben

Ruby—See: Reuben/Reubin

Rudolph—German: Famous and glorious wolf
Dolf, Dolph, Rodolfo, Rodoifus, Rodolph, Rodolphe,
Rudie, Rudolf, Rudolfe, Rudolfo, Rudulph, Rudy
*Just one song ("Rudolph the Red-Nosed Reindeer"), and a
name becomes associated with one of Santa's helpers; Just
one actor from Sweden (Dolph Lundgren), and a shortened
version of that same name becomes associated with a
muscle man.*

Rudy—See: Rudolph

Rudyard—English: From the red enclosure

Rufus—Latin: Red-haired one

Rupert—See: Robert

Ruskin—French: Red-haired one

Russ—See: Russell

Russell—French: Redheaded
Russ, Russel, Rustie, Rusty

Ryan/Ryen—Irish: Little king
Actor Ryan O'Neal was born Patrick Ryan O'Neal. He let

*go of Patrick so that people wouldn't confuse him with his
third cousin, actor Patrick O'Neal.*
Rylan/Ryland—English: Dweller at the rye land

S

Sabian/Sabin—Latin: Of the Sabines (an ancient Italian tribe)
Saint—Latin: Holy
   Sanche, Sanchez, Sancho, Santo
Sakima—Native American: King
Salim—Arabic: Good
Salvador/Salvadore—Italian: Savior
   Sal, Sallie, Sally, Salvatore, Sauveur
Sam—Hebrew: To hear (Also, a nickname for names starting
   with "Sam")
   *For a time, this name belonged to the geriatric generation.
   Now, there are lots of young boys called Sam, and perhaps
   the resurgence of this name may be partially due to the
   popularity of the leading character on "Cheers." Actor Ted
   Danson as Sam Malone, the tall, attractive bachelor bar-
   tender with an eye for the ladies, has been charming TV
   audiences since 1982.*
Samir—Arabic: Entertainer
Samson—Hebrew: Like the sun
   Sam, Sammie, Sammy, Sampson, Sansao, Sansom, San-
   some, Sansum, Shem, Shimson
Samuel—Hebrew: His name is God
   Sam, Samel, Sammie, Sammy, Samouel, Samuele, Shem,
   Shemuel
Sanborn—English: From the sandy brook
Sancho—See: Saint
   Sancho Panza is the fictional peasant squire in Cervantes's
   Don Quixote.
Sanders—English: Son of Alexander
   Sanderson, Sandor, Sandors, Saunders, Saunderson
Sandie/Sandy—Nickname for names starting with "San"
Sanford—English: From the sandy ford
Sargent—French: To serve
   Sarge, Sergant, Serge, Sergeant, Sergei, Sergent, Sergi,
   Sergio
Saul—Hebrew: Borrowed

Winner of the Nobel Prize in literature, novelist Saul Bellow has also written plays. In keeping with the meaning of his name, Saul says his characters are borrowed from real people, including his relatives.

Savill/Saville—French: From the estate of willow trees

Sawyer—English: One who works with a saw

Saxon—English: Swordsman
Sax, Saxen, Saxin

Sayers—Welsh: Carpenter
Sayer, Sayre, Sayres

Scanlon—Irish: Charmer
Scanlan, Scanlen

Schuyler—Dutch: To hide, to shield
Shuylar, Skuyler, Sky, Skylar, Skyler

Scoey—See: Roscoe, Scoville

Scott—English; Scotsman
Scot, Scotti, Scottie, Scotty
Scott Joplin is called "the King of the Ragtime Composers." His musical composition "The Entertainer," which was the theme of the film The Sting, *won an Academy Award more than fifty years after he died.*

Scoville—French: From the Scotchman's estate
Scoe, Scoey

Scribe—Latin: Writer
Scribner, Scrivener

Scully—Irish: Town crier

Sean—See: John
Sean Connery's real first name is Thomas.

Searle—German: Armed one
Searl, Serle

Sebastian—Latin: Honored above others
Bastian, Bastien, Seb, Sebastiano, Sebastiao, Sebastien

Selby—English: From the farmstead

Selden/Seldon—English: Rare, strange, valley of willows

Selig—German: Blessed one, happy one

Selwin/Selwyn—English: Blessed friend

Seth—Hebrew: Appointed one

Seton—English: From the place by the sea
Seaton, Seetin, Seeton

Seward—English: Victorious defender

Sewell—English: Wall near the sea

Sewal, Sewald, Sewall

Sexton—English: Church official

Seymour—French: From the sea moors
Seymore, Sy

Shafer—Aramaic: Good, beautiful

Shalom—See: Solomon
Journalist and short-story writer Shalom Aleichem, born Sholem Rabinowitz, has been nicknamed "the Yiddish Mark Twain." Fiddler on the Roof *is based on one of his stories.*

Shamus—See: Jacob

Shanahan—Irish: Wise one

Shandy—English: Rambunctious

Shane—See: John
Movie mavens agree that Shane *is one of the greatest Westerns ever made. Alan Ladd portrayed the title character in this 1953 classic.*

Shanley—Gaelic: Wise hero

Shannon/Shanon—Irish: Little wise one

Shaw—English: From the grove of trees

Shawn—See: John

Shea—Irish: Ingenious, majestic, courteous one

Sheehan—Irish: Little and peaceful

Sheffield—From the crooked field

Shelby—English: Sheltered town

Sheldon—English: Protected hill

Shelley/Shelly—English: Island of shells (Also, nicknames for names starting with "Shel")

Shephard/Shepherd—English: One who tends sheep
Shep, Shepard, Sheperd, Sheppard, Shepperd, Sheppie, Sheppy

Sheridan—Irish: Wild one

Sheriff—English: Lawman

Sherlock/Sherlocke—English: Fair- or white-haired one
Originally, Arthur Conan Doyle was going to name his fictional detective Sherrinford, but he thought the name was awkward-sounding, so he changed it to Sherlock. The name Holmes was inspired by author and physician Oliver Wendell Holmes.

Sherman—English: Sheep shearer

Sherwin/Sherwyn—English: Splendid friend

Sherwood—English: From the bright forest

Sidney—Phoenician: Enchanter
Sid, Sidon, Syd, Sydney
This seems to be a name for successful directors—Sidney Lumet, Sidney Poitier, and Sydney Pollack—who enchant moviegoers with their work.

Siegfried—German: Victorious peace
Siffre, Sigefredo, Sigfrid, Sigfroi, Sigvard

Sigmund—German: Victorious protector
Sig, Siggy, Sigimundo, Sigismond, Sigismund, Sigmond, Ziggy, Zigimond, Zigimund, Zigmon

Silas—See: Silvanus

Silvanus—Latin: Forest dweller
Silas, Silva, Silvain, Silvano, Sylvan

Simon—Hebrew: He who hears
Simeon, Simmie, Simmon, Simms, Simmy, Simone, Simpson, Symms, Symon, Ximenes

Sinclair—Latin: Clear sign
How many book reports were written on Nobel Prize–winner Sinclair Lewis's Babbit, Main Street, and Arrowsmith?

Skelly—Irish: Storyteller
Skelley, Skellie

Skipper—Dutch: Shipmaster
Skip, Skipp, Skippie, Skippy

Slade—English: From the valley

Sloan/Sloane—Irish: Warrior

Smith—English: Blacksmith
Smitty, Smyth

Sol—See: Solomon

Solomon—Hebrew: Peace
Salamon, Salman, Salmon, Salom, Salomo, Salomone, Shalom, Shelomoh, Shlomo, Sholom, Sol, Sollie, Solly, Solman, Zalman, Zalmen, Zalmon
If you look at a $10,000 bill, you'll see that Salmon P. Chase's name is on it. And rightfully so, considering that, as secretary of the treasury under President Lincoln, he established a national banking system and issued a legal-tender currency.

Somerset—English: Summer settlement
Somerset Maugham was known as a novelist, playwright, and short-story writer. But did you know he was also a medical doctor? He first wrote about his experience as a physician in a London slum and then decided to continue

*writing, abandoning his medical career. Also, Somerset was
his middle name; his real first name was William.*

Sonny—Nickname for names starting or ending with "Son"

Sorrell—French: With reddish brown hair
Sorel, Sorell

Spalding—English: Divided field

Spangler—French: Glittering one

Spark—English: Flash of light
Sparky

Speed—English: Wealth, power, success
Speedy

Spencer—English: Administrator
Spence, Spense, Spenser

Spike—Latin: Ear of grain
*Spike Lee, born Shelton Jackson Lee, is a moviemaker who
attracts a lot of attention with his sometimes controversial
work.*

Spiro—Latin: To breathe

Squire—English: Attendant to nobility

Stacey—Latin: Firmly established
Stace, Stacy

Stan—Nickname for names starting with "Stan"
*Baseball Hall of Famer Stan "the Man" Musial played for
the St. Louis Cardinals (1941–63) and is one of the all-time
great hitters.*

Stancil—English: Upright bar, beam

Stanford—English: Stone river crossing

Stanhope—English: From the stony land

Stanislaus—Polish: Glorious position
Stanislao, Stanislas, Stanislav, Stanislaw, Stanislus

Stanley—English: Glory of the camp
Stanleigh, Stanly

Stanton—English: Town near the stony field
Stanten, Stantin

Stavros—Greek: Crowned

Steadman/Stedman—English: Occupant of farmstead

Stefan—See: Stephen

Stephen—Greek: Crown
Estaban, Estevan, Etienne, Stefan, Stefano, Stephan,
Stephanos, Stephanus, Stevan, Steve, Steven, Stevie,
Stevin, Stevy, Tiennot

Sterling/Stirling—English: Genuine, valued

Sterne—English: Austere
    Stearn, Stearne, Stern

Steve/Steven—See: Stephen

Stewart—English: Steward of the manor
    Stew, Steward, Stewie, Stewy, Stu, Stuart

Stinson—English: Son of stone

Stockton—English: Town near the tree trunk

Stoddard—English: Keeper of the horses

Stoke—English: Village

Storm—English: Storm
    *New York TV weatherman Frank Field named his son
    Storm. Now Storm Field is also a TV weatherman . . . how
    fitting!*

Strom—Greek: Bed, mattress

Stuart—See: Stewart

Sullivan—Latin: Uplifter
    Sullavan, Sullie, Sully

Sultan—Swahili: Ruler

Sumner—English: One who summons or calls

Sutherland—Norse: From the southern land

Sutton—English: From the southern town

Sven—Norse: Youth
    Svend, Swain, Swen, Swend

Sweeney—Gaelic: Little hero

Sylvester—Latin: From the forest
    Silvester, Silvestre, Silvestro, Sly
    *Bet Sylvester Stallone is the only actor in Hollywood who
    chose to use Sylvester (his middle name) instead of Michael
    (his real first name). And it works for him!*

T

Tab—See: Tabor

Tabor—Persian: Drummer; Hungarian: Encampment; Gaelic:
    Wellspring
    Tab, Tabbie, Tabby, Taber

Tad—See: Thaddeus

Taffy—Welsh: Beloved one
    This beloved name is the Welsh version of David.

Taggart—Gaelic: Son of the church official
   Tag
Tait/Tate—Norse, Swedish: Cheerful one
Tal—Hebrew: Rain (Also, a nickname for names starting with "Tal")
   Tallie, Tally
Talbott—French: One given rewards from war gains
   Tal, Talbot, Tallie, Tally
Tallis—Persian: Learned, wise
   Tal, Tallie, Tally
   A tallis is a white, fringed prayer shawl with blue or black bands and is worn by Jewish men during prayer.
Talmadge—English: Lake midway between two towns
   Tal, Tallie, Tally
Talman—Aramaic: Oppress, injure
   Tal, Tallie, Tally, Talmon
Tanner—English: Leatherworker
   Tan, Tann, Tannie, Tanny
Taro—Japanese: Firstborn male, big boy
   Taro is a tropical plant with an edible rootstock.
Tarrant—Welsh: Thunder
   Tarr, Tarrent, Tarrie, Tarry
Tauno—Finnish: World ruler
Tavish—Gaelic: Twin
Taylor—English: Tailor
   Tailer, Talor, Tayler
Teague—Irish: Poet
   Teige
Ted/Teddie/Teddy—Nicknames for names starting with "Ed" or "Ted"
   Edward Moore Kennedy, the ninth and last child of Joseph and Rose Kennedy, is probably the most famous Ted/Teddy since Teddy Roosevelt. The current runner-up is "the King of Cable," Robert Edward Turner III, better known as Ted Turner and sometimes called "the Mouth from the South."
Telford—Latin: Shallow stream
Templeton—English: From the town of the temple
   Temple
Terence—Latin: Tender, good, gracious
   Terrel, Terrence, Terrie, Terrill, Terris, Terry, Terryal
Terry—See: Terence

Everyone knows Milt Caniff's famous comic strip "Terry and the Pirates." But do you know Terry's whole name? It's Terry Lee.

Teva—Hebrew: Nature
Tev, Tevie, Tevy, Tevya

Thaddeus—Greek: Gift of God; Hebrew: Praising God
Tad, Tadd, Taddeo, Thaddaus, Thaddeo, Thaddy, Thadeus

Thatcher—English: Roof mender
Thacher, Thatch, Thax, Thaxter

Theobald—German: Prince of the people
Ted, Teddy, Teobald, Thebaud, Thebault, Theo, Thibaud, Thibaut, Tibald, Tibalt, Tibold

Theodore—Greek: Gift of God
Feodor, Feodore, Ted, Teddie, Teddy, Tellie, Telly, Teodor, Teodoro, Theo, Theodor, Theodorus, Theodosios, Tudo.
Theodore Roosevelt was the first president to ride in an automobile, fly in an airplane, and go in a submarine. Pulitizer Prize–winning author and illustrator Theodor Seuss Geisel was known to millions of children as Dr. Seuss.

Theodoric—German: Ruler of the people
Tedric, Teodorico, Theodric, Thierry

Thomas—Aramaic: Twin
Tam, Tamas, Tammeas, Tammen, Tammie, Tammy, Tavis, Tavish, Thom, Thoma, Thomaz, Thumas, Tom, Tomas, Tomaso, Tome, Tomkin, Tomlin, Tommie, Tommy
Now this name is popular! There's Thomas Jefferson, Thomas à Becket, Thomas Aquinas, Thomas Wolfe, Thomas Alva Edison, and former House Majority Leader Thomas Philip O'Neill, Jr. (better known as Tip O'Neill), to name just a few.

Thor—Norse: Thunder
Thorin, Thorley, Thorr, Tor, Tore, Torin
Norwegian explorer Thor Heyerdahl sailed a balsa-wood raft forty-three hundred miles from Peru to Polynesia and then wrote about his experience in the best-seller Kon-Tiki, which was translated into sixty-four languages.

Thormond—English: Thor's protection
Thormund, Thurmond, Thurmund

Thorndike—English: From the thorny meadow
Thorn, Thorndyke, Thornie, Thorny

Thorpe—English: From the village

Thurman/Thurmon—English: Servant of Thor

Thurstan/Thurston—Norse: Thor's stone

If you catch a rerun of the 1960s TV hit "Gilligan's Island," you'll see Thurston Howell III, the millionaire castaway played by Jim Backus.

Tim/Timmie/Timmy—Nicknames for names starting with "Tim"

Timon/Tymon—Greek: Reward

Timothy—Greek: Honoring God

Timur—Hebrew: Stately

Titus—Greek: Great size and power
Titan, Tito, Titos

Tobias—Hebrew: God is good
Tobe, Tobia, Tobiah, Tobie, Tobin, Tobit, Toby

Toby—See: Tobias

Todd—Latin: Fox
Tod, Toddie, Toddy

Toler—English: Tax collector
Toller, Tollie, Tolly

Tom/Tommy—See: Thomas
Have you ever thought about how many successful contemporary actors use the name Tom? Tom Selleck, Tom Cruise, Tom Hulce, Tom Berenger, Tom Hanks. Who did we leave out?

Tony—See: Anthony
This nickname is a popular show-biz name: Tony Danza, Tony Randall, Tony Curtis, Tony Bennett, and more.

Torrance/Torrence—Irish: From the place of little hills
Tor, Torrey, Torrie, Torry, Tory

Tracey/Tracy—Latin: Courageous
Tracy Tupman is the well-fed, well-groomed young man in Charles Dickens's Pickwick Papers.

Travis—Latin: From the crossroads
Traver, Travers

Trent—Latin: From the swift stream
Trenten, Trentin, Trenton

Trevor—Celtic: Prudent

Trini—Latin: Trinity, triad, three

Tristram—Latin: Sorrowful, mournful
Tris, Tristam, Tristan

Troy—Irish: Son of a foot soldier

Troy Donahue was a popular actor in the 1960s. In 1974, he played a character in The Godfather, Part II *named Merle Johnson, which, strangely enough, is Troy's real name.*

Truman—English: Faithful man
Writer Truman Capote was originally Truman Streckfus Persons. His mother divorced Truman's father and remarried Joseph Capote, who legally adopted the young boy.

Tucker—English: One who cleans and thickens cloth

Tully—Irish: To live with the peace of God

Turner—Latin: Lathe worker

Twain—English: Separated into two parts

Tyler—English: Tile and brick maker

Tynan—Gaelic: Dark haired, dark complected

Tyrone—Greek: Sovereign
Tyrone Power was the oh-so-handsome romantic lead in films of the late 1930s and 1940s. Tyrone was also the name of Arte Johnson's strange little-old-man character on TV's "Laugh-In."

Tyrus—Latin: One from Tyre (a port in Lebanon)

Tyson—French: Firebird

U

Udell—English: From the valley of the yew trees
Udale, Udall

Ulrick—German: Strong and powerful ruler; Danish: Wolf
Ulric, Ulrich, Ulu

Ulysses—Latin: Wrathful
Ulises
The eighteenth president of the United States was born Hiram Ulysses Grant. At West Point, his name was changed to Ulysses Simpson Grant so that his initials no longer spelled HUG. But he then had to put up with the new nickname of "Useless."

Umberto—Italian: Color of the earth
The name Umberto Eco belongs to the novelist who wrote the best-seller The Name of the Rose.

Uno—Latin: The one

Upton—English: From the upper town
American novelist Upton Sinclair was the voice of social protest during the first half of the twentieth century.

Uranus—Greek: Heavenly
Urban/Urbane—Latin: Courteous, from town
Urbain, Urbano, Urbanus, Urvan
Uriah—Hebrew: God is my light
Uri, Urie, Uriel
Ursel—Latin: Bear
Ursa, Urshell
Uziel—Hebrew: My strength
Uzi, Uzziah, Uzziel

V

Vachel—French: One who raises cows
American poet Vachel Lindsay was called "the Tramp Poet" because of the time he had spent as a hobo trading poems for food.
Vada—Latin: Shallow place
Vail—English: From the valley
Vale, Valle
Valdemar/Waldemar—German: Powerful, mighty
Valentine—Latin: Strong, powerful
Val, Valentin, Valentino, Valerian, Valerio, Valerius, Valery, Vallie, Vally
Van—Dutch: From, of (usually used with another name)
Vane, Vanne
Vance—English: Very high places
Vardon—French: Green knoll
Varden, Verden, Verdon
Varian—Latin: Clever
Vasilis/Vassily—See: Basil
Vaughan/Vaughn—Celtic: Small
Vere—Latin: Faithful, true
Verlin—Latin: Flourishing
Verion, Verle, Verlon
Vernon—Latin: Springlike
Vern, Verne
Popular and classical music composer Vladimir Dukelsky wrote songs such as "April in Paris" and "I Can't Get Started with You" under the name "Vernon Duke" and used his real name for the symphonies, concertos, sonatas, and ballets he composed.

Verrill—French: True one
  Verall, Verill, Verrall, Verrell, Verroll
Victor—Latin: Conqueror
  Vic, Vick, Vickers, Victoir, Victorien, Victorin, Viktor,
  Vitorio, Vittorio
  *The great Danish pianist-comedian Victor Borge was born
  Borge Rosenbaum.*
  *Vic was the name of General George Armstrong Custer's
  horse.*
Vidor—Hungarian: Cheerful
Vincent—Latin: Conquering
  Vin, Vince, Vincente, Vincenz, Vincenzio, Vincenzo, Vini-
  cent, Vinicio, Vinnie, Vinny
  *Vincent van Gogh lived in poverty, but exactly one hundred
  years after his death, his* Portrait of Dr. Gachet *sold at auc-
  tion for $82.5 million.*
Vinson—Latin: Son of Vincent
Virgil—Latin: Staff bearer
  Verge, Vergil, Vergit, Virge, Virgie, Virgilio
  In the film In the Heat of the Night, *Virgil Tibbs is played by
  Sidney Poitier.*
Vitas—Latin: Life
  Vida, Vidal, Vite, Vito
  *"Asymmetric," "Five Point," "Eye-Eye," and "Greek God-
  dess" are some of the hairstyles that helped make Vidal Sas-
  soon one of the world's wealthiest hairdressers.*
Vito—See: Vitas
Vladimir—Slavic: Powerful prince
  Vladamir, Vladmir
  *Vladimir Horowitz was one of classical music's greatest
  pianists.*
Volley—Latin: To fly
  Vollon
Volney—German: Spirit of the people
Von—German: From, of (usually used with another name)

W

Wade—English: One who moves forward
Wadsworth—English: Estate with a wading pool
Wagner—Dutch: Wagon driver

Waggoner, Wagoner

Wainwright—English: Wagon maker

Wain, Waine, Wayne

Walden—English: From the forest valley

Waldo—English: Ruler

Waldron

Where's Martin Handford? He's laughing all the way to the bank for creating those "Where's Waldo?" books.

Walker—English: One who thickens cloth

Wallace—English: Welshman

Walach, Wallach, Wallie, Wally, Walman, Walsh, Welch, Welsh

Wallie/Wally—Nicknames for names starting with "Wal"

Wally Cleaver, played by Tony Dow, was the Beaver's teenage brother in TV's "Leave It to Beaver" (1957–63).

Walt—See: Walter

The great, innovative animator and producer Walt Disney was born Walter Elias Disney. He won a record seventeen Oscars from 1931 through 1969 (some of them awarded posthumously).

Walter—German: Powerful warrior

Gauthier, Gualter, Gualterio, Gualtiero, Wallie, Wally, Walt, Walther

Walter (Leland) Cronkite, Jr., has turned up on polls as the most trusted man in the country. His colleagues nicknamed him "Uncle Walter."

Walton—English: From the walled town

Ward—English: Guardian

Warde, Warden, Worden

Warner—German: Protective warrior

Werner, Wernher

Warner LeRoy, the successful New York restaurateur (Tavern on the Green), is the son of film producer/director Mervyn LeRoy and Doris Warner, the daughter of one of film's famous Warner Brothers. This is a good example of a child being given the mother's maiden name as a first name.

Warren—German: Defender

Ware, Waring, Waringer

Warren Beatty! Need we say more?

Warwick—English: Village hero

Warick, Warrick

Washington—English: From the washing place

Watson—English: Son of the warrior

Waverly—German: From the rippling water

Wayland—German: From the land by the highway
Way, Waylan, Waylen, Waylin, Waylon
Waylon (Arnold) Jennings, known for his special country-rock style, wrote the theme for the TV series "The Dukes of Hazzard."

Wayne—See: Wainwright
As Nevada's highest-grossing entertainer to date, Wayne Newton is to Las Vegas what Mickey Mouse is to Disneyland.

Webster—English: Weaver
Webb, Weber
The TV sitcom "Webster" (1983–87) starred Emmanuel Lewis in the title role.

Welby—Scandinavian: From the farm by the spring

Weldon—English: Willow trees on the hill

Wells—English: From the spring

Wenceslaus—Slavic: Crown of glory
Wenceslas, Wenzel

Wendel/Wendell—German: Wanderer

Werner—See: Warner

Wes—Nickname for names starting with "Wes"

Wesley—English: From the west meadow
Wes, Westleigh, Westley

Westbrooke—English: From the west brook
Wes, West, Westbrook

Westcott—English: From the west cottage

Weston—English: From the west town

Wheeler—English: Wheel maker

Whit—Nickname for names starting with "Whit"

Whitcomb/Whitcombe—English: Small valley

Whitelaw—English: From the small hill

Whitfield—English: Tiny field

Whitney—English: Small parcel of land near water

Whittaker—English: Small area of land

Wilbert/Wilburt—English: Bright willow

Wilbur—See: Gilbert
Wilbur Wright and his brother Orville were American avia-

tion pioneers who flew high in a heavier-than-air craft (1903) that they invented and constructed.

Wilder—English: Person from the wilderness

Wiley/Wylie—English: From the willow meadow

Wilfred—English: Hope for peace
Wilfried, Willfrid

Will/Willie/Willy—Nicknames for names starting with "Wil"

Willard/Willerd—German: Courageous; English: Yard full of willows

William—German: Resolute protector
Bill, Billie, Billy, Guglieimo, Guillaume, Guillermo, Uilleam, Uilliam, Wil, Wilek, Wilhelm, Wilkie, Will, Willan, Willem, Willet, Willie, Willis, Willy, Wilmar, Wilmer, Wilmot
The name William is a solid name that, according to birth records, was in the top ten from the end of the nineteenth century through the 1960s. Here are just a few Williams and forms of William to give you an idea of the name's popularity throughout the years: William Shakespeare, William Butler Yeats, William Howard Taft, William Henry Harrison, William McKinley, William Penn, William Randolph Hearst, William Faulkner, William Devane, William Hurt, Willem Dafoe, Willie Mays, Willy Wonka, Willy Loman, Will Rogers, and Wil Shriner.

Wilson—German: Son of William

Wilton—English: Town near the well
Wilt
Born Wilton Norman Chamberlain, 7'1" "Wilt the Stilt" was responsible for rewriting a lot of pro basketball's records (he scored one hundred points in a single game), and supposedly made Casanova seem like a sissy.

Win/Winnie/Winny—Nicknames for names starting or ending with "Win"
And what about the name Winnie? Pooh!

Windell—English: Tree from which baskets are woven
Win, Windlan, Windy

Windsor—German: From the river bend

Winfield—English: Productive field

Winfred/Winfrid—English: Friend of peace

Wingate—English: Divine protector

Winslow/Winslowe—English: Victory hill

Winston—English: Town of victory
Sir Winston (Leonard Spencer) Churchill, prime minister of the United Kingdom, was born two months prematurely. That gave him two more months to smoke the more than 300,000 cigars that it is thought he smoked during his ninety-one years.

Winthrop—English: Victory at the crossroads

Wolf/Wolfe—English: Wolf
Wolff, Woolf, Woulfe

Wolfgang—German: Advancing wolf
Wolfgang Puck has made a name for himself as the owner and chef of Spago, the Los Angeles celebrity-hangout restaurant.

Wolfram—German: Wolf-raven

Woodley—English: From the woody meadow

Woodrow—English: From the hedge by the forest

Woody—Nickname for names starting or ending with "Wood"
The story goes that Woody Allen, whose real name was Allen Stewart Konigsberg, changed his first name to Woody because of his desire to be a great clarinetist like his musical idol, Woody Herman.

Worth—English: Valuable homestead

Wray—English: Accuser

Wren—Welsh: Chief or ruler
Wrennie, Wrenny

Wright—English: Artisan, worker

Wyatt—French: Guide
Wiatt, Wyatte
Wyatt (Berry Stapp) Earp was an American frontier law officer in Tombstone, Arizona.

Wycliff/Wycliffe—German: Village near the cliff
Wyche, Wyck

Wyman/Wayman—English: Warrior

Wynn—English: White, fair

Wynono—Native American: Firstborn son

X

Xavier—Arabic: Splendid, bright
Javier, Xever

As a young violinist, bandleader Xavier Cugat toured the country with opera great Enrico Caruso. They had something in common: They were both caricaturists.

Xenos—Greek: Stranger
Xeno, Zeno, Zenos

Xenophon—Greek: Strange voices
Xenophon was a Greek general and writer way back when. When? About 400 B.C.

Xerxes—Persian: Ruler; Greek: Pertaining to Caesar
Jerez, Xeres, Xerus
Xerxes was the king of Persia who invaded Greece in or about 400 B.C.

Ximens—See: Simon

Xylon—Greek: From the forest

Y

Yaakov—Hebrew: God is gracious
Yaacob, Yaacov, Yachov, Yacov, Yago, Yakob, Yakov
Comedian Yakov Smirnov is the Russian émigré who explained, "In America, you can always find a party. In Russia, the party always finds you."

Yagel/Yagil—Hebrew: To rejoice

Yale—German: One who pays or produces

Yancy—French: Englishman
Yan, Yance, Yank, Yankee, Yantsey

Yaphet—See: Japhet
Actor Yaphet Kotto is best known for his parts in Alien *and* Live and Let Die.

Yardley—English: From the enclosed meadow

Yates—English: Keeper of the gates

Yavin—Hebrew: He will understand

Yehoram—Hebrew: God will exalt

Yehuda/Yehudah—See: Judah

Yehudi—See: Judah

Yigael—Hebrew: God will redeem
Yagel, Yigal

Yitzhak—Hebrew: Laughter
Itzak, Izaak, Yitzak
Yitzhak is a popular name for Israeli leaders. There's Yitzhak Shamir and Yitzhak Rabin.

Yogi—Sanskrit: Person who practices yoga
Baseball Hall of Famer Yogi Berra was born Lawrence Peter Berra.

Yona/Yonah—Native American: Bear; Hebrew: Dove

York—Celtic: From the farm of the yew trees
Yorick, Yorke

Yul/Yule—English: Jolly (as referring to the Christmas season)
There are many stories about Yul Brynner's real name and nationality. Most accounts say he was born Taidje Kahn, either on the Siberian island of Sakhalin or in Outer Mongolia, and that his mother was either a Russian or a Romany gypsy.

Yuma—Native American: Son of a chief

Yvan—See: John

Yves—See: Ivar/Iver
Yves Montand was born Ivo Montand Livi. He was an Italian Jew. (And you thought he was French!) What about Yves Saint Laurent? His real name is Henri Donat Mathieu, and he was born in Oran, Algeria.

Z

Zabdiel—Hebrew: God is my gift
Zabdi, Zavdi, Zavdiel

Zachary—Hebrew: The Lord has remembered
Zac, Zacarias, Zaccaria, Zach, Zachariah, Zacharias, Zacharie, Zack, Zak, Zakarias, Zechariah, Zecharias, Zeke
When the twelfth president of the U.S., Zachary Taylor, was a general in the Mexican War, he was nicknamed "Old Rough and Ready" because of his sloppy dress, tobacco chewing, and cussing.

Zale/Zales—English: To sell

Zalman/Zalmen/Zalmon—See: Solomon

Zane—See: John
Pearl Zane Grey was called Pearl until he graduated from the University of Pennsylvania School of Dentistry and opened his practice. Then he was Dr. P. Zane Grey. When he gave up his practice, he dropped the "P" and went on to write fifty-four novels, including Riders of the Purple Sage.

Zared—Hebrew: Ambush

Zebulon/Zebulun—Hebrew: To exalt, to honor
  Zeb, Zubin
Zedekiah—Hebrew: Justice of the Lord
  Zed
Zeeman—Dutch: Sailor, seaman
Zeke—See: Ezekiel, Zachary
Zelig—Yiddish: Blessed, holy
Zeus—Greek: Living
  Zeus was the presiding god of the Greek pantheon, ruler of the heavens and father of other gods and mortal heroes.
Zeviel—Hebrew: Gazelle of the Lord
  Zev, Zevi, Zevy, Zvi
Zion—Hebrew: A sign, excellent
Ziv—Hebrew: Full of life
  Ziven, Zivon
Zoltan—See: Sultan
  Dr. Zoltan Ovary, a gynecologist, is listed in a local telephone book. We kid you not.
Zubin—See: Zebulon/Zebulun
  When Indian-born Zubin Mehta was appointed musical director of the Los Angeles Symphony, Californians started calling him Zubie Baby, and it stuck. Zubie Baby went on to become the conductor of the New York Philharmonic.
Zuriel—Hebrew: God is my foundation

Favorite Names of Girls

_____

_____

_____

_____

_____

_____

_____

_____

_____

_____

_____

_____

_____

_____

_____

_____

_____

_____

Favorite Names of Boys

_____

_____

_____

_____

_____

_____

_____

_____

_____

_____

_____

_____

_____

_____

_____

_____

_____

_____

_____

_____

Index

Also by
Joan Wilen and Lydia Wilen

Chicken Soup & Other Folk Remedies

More Chicken Soup & Other Folk Remedies

Chock-full of age-old wisdom, common-sense advice, and up-to-date nutrition, these books contain time-tested strategies and easy-to-prepare recipes for treating all kinds of ailments.

Published by Fawcett Books.
Available in your local bookstore.

More than sugar and spice . . .

The Little Girl Book

**Everything You Need to Know
to Raise a Girl Today**

by David Laskin and Kathleen O'Neill

Illuminating, informative, and thoroughly practical, this book guides parents step-by-step through every period of their daughter's development from birth through the early school years.

Published by Ballantine Books.
Available at your local bookstore.

Yes, boys are different . . .

The Little Boy Book

A Guide to the First Eight Years

by Sheila Moore and Roon Frost

The authors, both parents of boys and one an early childhood educator, draw on four years of research, and numerous studies and interviews, to tell you everything you need to know about the world of boys.

Published by Ballantine Books.
Available in your local bookstore.